Bloom's Major Literary Characters:

Hamlet

*Bloom's Major Literary Characters*

King Arthur

George F. Babbitt

Elizabeth Bennet

Leopold Bloom

Sir John Falstaff

Jay Gatsby

Hamlet

Raskolnikov and Svidrigailov

*Bloom's Major Literary Characters*

# *Hamlet*

*Edited and with an introduction by*
## Harold Bloom
Sterling Professor of the Humanities
Yale University

**CHELSEA HOUSE**
PUBLISHERS
A Haights Cross Communications Company

Philadelphia

Library of Congress Cataloging-in-Publication Data applied for.

Hamlet / edited and with an introduction by Harold Bloom.
        p. cm. — (Bloom's Major Literary Characters)
    Includes bibliographical references and index.
    ISBN 0-7910-7669-5 — ISBN 0-7910-7981-3 (pbk.)
  1. Shakespeare, William, 1564–1616. Hamlet. 2. Hamlet (Lengendary
character) I. Bloom, Harold. II. Major literary characters
    PR2807.H26237
    822.3'3—dc22

                                                            2003019983


Contributing editor: Janyce Marson

Cover design by  Keith Trego

Cover: © Historical Picture Archive/CORBIS

Layout by EJB Publishing Services


Chelsea House Publishers
1974 Sproul Road, Suite 400
Broomall, PA 19008-0914

www.chelseahouse.com

# Contents

HAROLD BLOOM

# The Analysis of Character

"Character," according to our dictionaries, still has as a primary meaning a graphic symbol, such as a letter of the alphabet. This meaning reflects the word's apparent origin in the ancient Greek character, a sharp stylus. *Charactēr* also meant the mark of the stylus' incisions. Recent fashions in literary criticism have reduced "character" in literature to a matter of marks upon a page. But our word "character" also has a very different meaning, matching that of the ancient Greek *ēthos*, "habitual way of life." Shall we say then that literary character is an imitation of human character, or is it just a grouping of marks? The issue is between a critic like Dr. Samuel Johnson, for whom words were as much like people as like things, and a critic like the late Roland Barthes, who told us that "the fact can only exist linguistically, as a term of discourse." Who is closer to our experience of reading literature, Johnson or Barthes? What difference does it make, if we side with one critic rather than the other?

Barthes is famous, like Foucault and other recent French theorists, for having added to Nietzsche's proclamation of the death of God a subsidiary demise, that of the literary author. If there are no authors, then there are no fictional personages, presumably because literature does not refer to a world outside language. Words indeed necessarily refer to other words in the first place, but the impact of words ultimately is drawn from a universe of fact. Stories, poems, and plays are recognizable as such because they are human utterances within traditions of utterances, and traditions, by achieving authority, become a kind of fact, or at least the sense of a fact. Our sense that literary characters, within the context of a fictive cosmos, indeed are fictional

vii

personages is also a kind of fact. The meaning and value of every character in a successful work of literary representation depend upon our ideas of persons in the factual reality of our lives.

Literary character is always an invention, and inventions generally are indebted to prior inventions. Shakespeare is the inventor of literary character as we know it; he reformed the universal human expectations for the verbal imitation of personality, and the reformation appears now to be permanent and uncannily inevitable. Remarkable as the Bible and Homer are at representing personages, their characters are relatively unchanging. They age within their stories, but their habitual modes of being do not develop. Jacob and Achilles unfold before us, but without metamorphoses. Lear and Macbeth, Hamlet and Othello severely modify themselves not only by their actions, but by their utterances, and most of all through *overhearing themselves*, whether they speak to themselves or to others. Pondering what they themselves have said, they will to change, and actually do change, sometimes extravagantly yet always persuasively. Or else they suffer change, without willing it, but in reaction not so much to their language as to their relation to that language.

I do not think it useful to say that Shakespeare successfully imitated elements in our characters. Rather, it could be argued that he compelled aspects of character to appear that previously were concealed, or not available to representation. This is not to say that Shakespeare is God, but to remind us that language is not God either. The mimesis of character in Shakespeare's dramas now seems to us normative, and indeed became the accepted mode almost immediately, as Ben Jonson shrewdly and somewhat grudgingly implied. And yet, Shakespearean representation has surprisingly little in common with the imitation of reality in Jonson or in Christopher Marlowe. The origins of Shakespeare's originality in the portrayal of men and women are to be found in the *Canterbury Tales* of Geoffrey Chaucer, insofar as they can be located anywhere before Shakespeare himself, Chaucer's savage and superb Pardoner overhears his own tale-telling, as well as his mocking rehearsal of his own spiel, and through this overhearing he is emboldened to forget himself, and enthusiastically urges all his fellow-pilgrims to come forward to be fleeced by him. His self-awareness, and apocalyptically rancid sense of spiritual fall, are preludes to the even grander abysses of the perverted will in Iago and in Edmund. What might be called the character trait of a negative charisma may be Chaucer's invention, but came to its perfection in Shakespearean mimesis.

The analysis of character is as much Shakespeare's invention as the representation of character is, since Iago and Edmund are adepts at analyzing both themselves and their victims. Hamlet, whose overwhelming charisma has many negative components, is certainly the most comprehensive of all literary characters, and so necessarily prophesies the labyrinthine complexities of the will in Iago and Edmund. Charisma, according to Max Weber, its first codifier, is primarily a natural endowment, and implies a primordial and idiosyncratic power over nature, and so finally over death. Hamlet's uncanniness is at its most suggestive in the scene of his long dying, where the audience, through the mediation of Horatio, itself is compelled to meditate upon suicide, if only because outliving the prince of Denmark scarcely seems an option.

Shakespearean representation has usurped not only our sense of literary character, but our sense of ourselves as characters, with Hamlet playing the part of the largest of these usurpations. Insofar as we have an idea of human disinterestedness, we tend to derive it from the Hamlet of Act V, whose quietism has about it a ghostly authority. Oscar Wilde, in his profound and profoundly witty dialogue, "The Decay of Lying," expressed a permanent insight when he insisted that art shaped every era, far more than any age formed art. Life imitates art, we imitate Shakespeare, because without Shakespeare we would perish for lack of images. Wilde's grandest audacity demystifies Shakespearean mimesis with a Shakespearean vivaciousness: "This unfortunate aphorism about art holding the mirror up to Nature is deliberately said by Hamlet in order to convince the bystanders of his absolute insanity in all art-matters." Of *Hamlet*'s influence upon the ages Wilde remarked that: "The world has grown sad because a puppet was once melancholy." "Puppet" is Wilde's own deconstruction, a brilliant reminder that Shakespeare's artistry of illusion has so mastered reality as to have changed reality, evidently forever.

The analysis of character, as a critical pursuit, seems to me as much a Shakespearean invention as literary character was, since much of what we know about how to analyze character necessarily follows Shakespearean procedures. His hero-villains, from Richard III through Iago, Edmund, and Macbeth, are shrewd and endless questers into their own self-motivations. If we could bear to see Hamlet, in his unwearied negations, as another hero-villain, then we would judge him the supreme analyst of the darker recalcitrances in the selfhood. Freud followed the pre-Socratic Empedocles, in arguing that character is fate, a frightening doctrine that maintains the fear that there are no accidents, that overdetermination rules us all of our lives. Hamlet assumes the same, yet adds to this argument the terrible passivity he manifests in Act V. Throughout Shakespeare's tragedies, the most interesting personages seem doom-eager, reminding us again that a Shakespearean reading of Freud would be more illuminating than a Freudian exegesis of

Shakespeare. We learn more when we discover Hamlet in the Freudian Death Drive, than when we read *Beyond the Pleasure Principle* into *Hamlet*.

In Shakespearean comedy, character achieves its true literary apotheosis, which is the representation of the inner freedom that can be created by great wit alone. Rosalind and Falstaff, perhaps alone among Shakespeare's personages, match Hamlet in wit, though hardly in the metaphysics of consciousness. Whether in the comic or the modern mode, Shakespeare has set the standard of measurement in the balance between character and passion.

In Shakespeare the self is more dramatized than theatricalized, which is why a Shakespearean reading of Freud works out so well. Character-formation after the passing of the Oedipal stage takes the place of fetishistic fragmentings of the self. Critics who now call literary character into question, and who proclaim also the death of the author, invariably also regard all notions, literary and human, of a stable character as being mere reductions of deeper pre-Oedipal desires. It becomes clear that the fortunes of literary character rise and fall with the prestige of normative conceptions of the ego. Shakespeare's Iago, who wars against being, may be the first deconstructionist of the self, with his proclamation of "I am not what I am." This constitutes the necessary prologue to any view that would regard a fixed ego as a virtual abnormality. But deconstructions of the self are no more modern than Modernism is. Like literary modernism, the decentered ego came out of the Hellenistic culture of ancient Alexandria. The Gnostic heretics believed that the psyche, like the body, was a fallen entity, mechanically fashioned by the Demiurge or false creator. They held however that each of us possessed also a spark or pneuma, which was a fragment of the original Abyss or true, alien God. The soul or psyche within every one of us was thus at war with the self or pneuma, and only that sparklike self could be saved.

Shakespeare, following after Chaucer in this respect, was the first and remains still the greatest master of representing character both as a stable soul and a wavering self. There is a substance that endures in Shakespeare's figures, and there is also a quicksilver rendition of the unsettling sparks. Racine and Tolstoy, Balzac and Dickens, follow in Shakespeare's wake by giving us some sense of pre-Oedipal sparks or drives, and considerably more sense of post-Oedipal character and personality, stabilizations or sublimations of the fetish-seeking drives. Critics like Leo Bersani and René Girard argue eloquently against our taking this mimesis as the only proper work of literature. I would suggest that strong fictions of the self, from the Bible through Samuel Beckett, necessarily participate in both modes, the sublimation of desire, and the persistence of a primordial desire. The mystery of Hamlet or of Lear is intimately invested in the tangled mixture of the two modes of representation.

Psychic mobility is proposed by Bersani as the ideal to which deconstructions of the literary self may yet guide us. The ideal has its pathos, but the realities of literary representation seem to me very different, perhaps destructively so. When a novelist like D. H. Lawrence sought to reduce his characters to Eros and the Death Drive, he still had to persuade us of his authority at mimesis by lavishing upon the figures of *The Rainbow* and *Women in Love* all of the vivid stigmata of normative personality. Birkin and Ursula may represent antithetical and uncanny drives, but they develop and change as characters pondering their own pronouncements and reactions to self and others. The cost of a non-Shakespearean representation is enormous. Pynchon, in *The Crying of Lot 49* and *Gravity's Rainbow*, evades the burden of the normative by resorting to something like Christopher Marlowe's art of caricature in *The Jew of Malta*. Marlowe's Barabas is a marvelous rhetorician, yet he is a cartoon alongside the troublingly equivocal Shylock. Pynchon's personages are deliberate cartoons also, as flat as comic strips. Marlowe's achievement, and Pynchon's, are beyond dispute, yet they are like the prelude and the postlude to Shakespearean reality. They do not wish to engage with our hunger for the empirical world and so they enter the problematic cosmos of literary fantasy.

No writer, not even Shakespeare or Proust, alters the available stock that we agree to call reality, but Shakespeare, more than any other, does show us how much of reality we could encounter if only we retained adequate desire. The strong literary representation of character is already an analysis of character, and is part of the healing work of a literary culture, which implicitly seeks to cure violence through a normative mimesis of ego, *as if it were stable*, whether in actuality it is or is not. I do not believe that this is a social quest taken on by literary culture, but rather that we confront here the aesthetic essence of what makes a culture *literary*, rather than metaphysical or ethical or religious. A culture becomes literary when its conceptual modes have failed it, which means when religion, philosophy, and science have begun to lose their authority. If they cannot heal violence, then literature attempts to do so, which may be only a turning inside out of the critical arguments of Girard and Bersani.

I conclude by offering a particular instance or special case as a paradigm for the healing enterprise that is at once the representation and the analysis of literary character. Let us call it the aesthetics of being outraged, or rather of successfully representing the state of being outraged. W. C. Fields was one modern master of such representation, and Nathanael West was another, as was Faulkner before him. Here also the greatest master remains Shakespeare, whose Macbeth, himself a bloody outrage, yet retains our imaginative sympathy precisely because he grows increasingly outraged as he experiences the equivocation of the fiend that lies like truth. The double-natured promises and the prophecies of the weird sisters finally induce in Macbeth an apocalyptic version of the stage actor's anxiety at missing cues, the horror of a phantasmagoric stage fright of missing one's time, of always reacting too late. Macbeth, a veritable monster of solipsistic inwardness but no intellectual, counters his dilemma by fresh murders, that prolong him in time yet provoke him only to a perpetually freshened sense of being outraged, as all his expectations become still worse confounded. We are moved by Macbeth, however estrangedly, because his terrible inwardness is a paradigm for our own solipsism, but also because none of us can resist a strong and successful representation of the human in a state of being outraged.

The ultimate outrage is the necessity of dying, an outrage concealed in a multitude of masks, including the tyrannical ambitions of Macbeth. I suspect that our outrage at being outraged is the most difficult of all our affects for us to represent to ourselves, which is why we are so inclined to imaginative sympathy for a character who strongly conveys that affect to us. The Shrike of West's *Miss Lonelyhearts* or Faulkner's Joe Christmas of *Light in August* are crucial modern instances, but such figures can be located in many other works, since the ability to represent this extreme emotion is one of the tests that strong writers are driven to set for themselves.

However a reader seeks to reduce literary character to a question of marks on a page, she will come at last to the impasse constituted by the thought of death, her death, and before that to all the stations of being outraged that memorialize her own drive towards death. In reading, she quests for evidences that are strong representations, whether of her desire or her despair. Such questings constitute the necessary basis for the analysis of literary character, an enterprise that always will survive every vagary of critical fashion.

# Editor's Note

After my Series Introduction, which is a defense of the persuasive reality of literary character, my Introduction to this volume compares Hamlet's personality with that of the Biblical King David, believed by Christians to be an ancestor of Jesus.

The great English Romantic critic William Hazlitt strikingly affirms that: "It is we who are Hamlet," after which A.C. Bradley, a superb exegete of Shakespearean tragedy, emphasizes the man of action rather than the melancholy Dane.

My personal favorite among Shakespeare's critics in the Twentieth Century, Harold C. Goddard, sees Hamlet as a poet and metaphysician, while Richard A. Lanham studies the Prince as self-dramatizer.

William Empson, a major poet-critic, rightly suggests that if we resist Hamlet, it is because we cannot abide humankind, after which the Canadian Northrop Frye, our Magus of the North, reminds all of us that, without Hamlet, the Romantic movement and tormented sages like Nietzsche and Kierkegaard could not have existed.

The French poet Yves Bonnefoy meditates upon "readiness" and "ripeness" in *Hamlet* and *King Lear*, while Julia Lupton brings together Hamlet and the "the stage Machiavel," shrewdly observing that the actual Machiavelli defined politics as a mode of theatre.

Hamlet is wisely seen by Bert O. States as an egoist but not at all a solipsist, after which Anthony Low learnedly observes that nowhere in Hamlet does anyone pray for the dead, or even mention Purgatory.

In this volume's final essay John Lee usefully shows Hamlet's strong distrust both of rhetoric and of selfhood.

HAROLD BLOOM

# Introduction

Hamlet is the most persuasive representative we have of intellectual skepticism, with the single exception of Montaigne's self-portrayal, which would appear to have had considerable effect upon Shakespeare the dramatist. Montaigne's skepticism was so beautifully sustained that he very nearly could persuade us to share his conviction that Plato essentially was a skeptic. Hamlet's skepticism, though powerful and protracted, dominates the prince rather less than Montaigne's preoccupies the greatest of all essayists. In the mimesis of a consciousness, Hamlet exceeds Montaigne's image of himself as man thinking. Even Plato's Socrates does not provide us with so powerful and influential an instance of cognition in all its processes as does Hamlet.

Yet Hamlet is as much a man of action as he is an intellectual. His intellectuality indeed is an anomaly; by rights he should resemble Fortinbras more than he does those equally formidable wits, Rosalind and Falstaff, or those brilliant skeptics gone rancid, Iago and Edmund. We tend not to situate Hamlet between Rosalind and Edmund, since good and evil hardly seem fit antinomies to enfold the Western hero of consciousness, the role that Hamlet has fulfilled since he first was enacted. Harry Levin eloquently warns against sentimentalizing Hamlet's tragedy, against "the obscurantist conclusion that thought is Hamlet's tragedy; Hamlet is the man who thinks too much; ineffectual because he is intellectual; his nemesis is failure of nerve, a nervous prostration." Surely Levin is accurate; Hamlet thinks not too much but too well, and so is a more-than-Nietzsche, well in advance of

1

Nietzsche. Hamlet abandons art, and perishes of the truth, even becomes the truth in the act of perishing. His tragedy is not the tragedy of thought, but the Nietzschean tragedy of truth.

The character of Hamlet is the largest literary instance of what Max Weber meant by *charisma*, the power of a single individual over nature, and so at last over death. What matters most about Hamlet is the universality of his appeal; the only rival representation of a secular personality would appear to be that of King David in 2 Samuel, and David is both of vast historical consequence, and perhaps not wholly secular, so that Hamlet's uniqueness is not much diminished. David, after all, has the eternal blessing of Yahweh, while Hamlet's aura is self-generated, and therefore more mysterious. No other figure in secular literature induces love in so universal an audience, and no one else seems to need or want that love so little. It may be that negative elements in Hamlet's charisma are the largest single component in our general psychological sense that it is easier to love than to accept love. Hamlet is the subject and object of his own quest, an intolerable truth that helps render him into so destructive an angel, so dangerous an aesthetic pleasure that he can survive only as a story able to be told by Horatio, who loves Hamlet precisely as the audience does, because we are Horatio. Remove Horatio from the play, and we would have no way into the play, whether now or later.

What are we to make of Horatio as a literary character? He is the character as playgoer and reader, passive yet passionately receptive, and necessarily the most important figure in the tragedy except for Hamlet himself. Why? Because, without Horatio, Hamlet is forbiddingly beyond us. The prince is an agonist who engages supernal powers, even while he attempts to see his uncle Claudius as his almighty opposite. Hamlet's contention is with forces within his own labyrinthine nature, and so with the spirit of evil in heavenly places. Like wrestling Jacob, Hamlet confronts a nameless one among the Elohim, a stranger god who is his own Angel of Death. Does Hamlet win a new name? Without Horatio, the question would be unanswerable, but the presence of Horatio at the close allows us to see that the new name is the old one, but cleansed from the image of the dead father. Horatio is the witness who testifies to the apotheosis of the dead son, whose transfiguration has moved him, and us, from the aesthetics of being outraged to the purified aesthetic dignity of a final disinterestedness, beyond ritual sacrifice, and beyond the romances of the family and of society.

Why does Horatio attempt suicide, when he realizes that Hamlet is dying? I blink at this moment, which strikes me as the most negative of all the many negative moments in the play:

HAMLET                              Horatio, I am dead,
Thou livest. Report me and my cause aright
To the unsatisfied.
HORATIO:                           Never believe it,
I am more an antique Roman than a Dane.
Here's yet some liquor left.

Are we to associate Horatio with Eros, Antony's follower who kills himself to "escape the sorrow / Of Anthony's death," or with other heroic sacrificers to a shame culture? The court and kingdom of the wretched Claudius constitute something much closer to a guilt culture, and Horatio, despite his assertion of identity, hardly has wandered in from one of Shakespeare's Roman tragedies. Horatio's desire to die with Hamlet is a contamination from the audience that Shakespeare creates as a crucial element in *The Tragedy of Hamlet, Prince of Denmark*. Even as Iago writes a play with Othello and Desdemona as characters, or as Edmund writes with Gloucester and Edgar, so Shakespeare writes with Horatio and ourselves. Freud's Death Drive beyond the Pleasure Principle is a hyperbolical trope that we barely recognize as a trope, and similarly, we have difficulty seeing that Horatio's suicidal impulse is a metaphor for the little death that we die in conjunction with the apocalyptic end of a charismatic leader. Horatio truly resembles not the self-slain Eros of *Antony and Cleopatra* but the self-castrating Walt Whitman who gives up his tally of the sprig of lilac in his extraordinary elegy for Lincoln, the best of all American poems ever. The most extraordinary of Hamlet's universal aspects is his relationship to death. Whitman's Lincoln dies the exemplary death of the martyred father, the death of God, but Hamlet dies the death of the hero, by which I do not mean the death so much of the hero of tragedy but of the hero of Scripture, the death of Jonathan slain upon the high places. The death of Hamlet is upon the highest of all high places, the place of a final disinterestedness, which is otherwise inaccessible to us.

Can we not name that highest of high places as Hamlet's place, a new kind of stance, one that he himself does not assume until he returns in Act V from his abortive voyage to England? Strangely purged of mourning and melancholia for the dead father, Hamlet seems also beyond incestuous jealousy and a revenger's fury. In his heart there is a kind of fighting, and a sense of foreboding, not of death but of the inadequacies of life: "Thou wouldst not think how ill all's here about my heart." Speaking to Horatio, and so to us, Hamlet announces a new sense that there are no accidents, or need not be:

If it be now, 'tis not to come; if it be not to come, it will be now;
if it be not now, yet it will come. The readiness is all. Since no
man, of aught he leaves, knows aught, what is't to leave betimes?
Let be.

"It" has to be the moment of dying, and "the readiness is all" might be
regarded as Hamlet's motto throughout Act V. "To be or not to be" is
answered now by "let be," which is a sort of heroic quietism, and clearly is
the prince's final advice to the audience. There is an ultimate skepticism in
Hamlet's assurance that none of us knows anything of what we will leave
behind us when we die, and yet this skepticism does not dominate the prince
as he dies:

> You that look pale and tremble at this chance,
> That are but mutes or audience to this act,
> Had I but time—as this fell sergeant, Death,
> Is strict in his arrest—O, I could tell you—
> But let it be.

What he could tell us might concern a knowledge that indeed he has
achieved, which I think is a knowledge of his relationship to us, and
necessarily to our surrogate, Horatio. Hamlet's extraordinary earlier praise of
Horatio (Act III, Scene 2, lines 54–74) may seem excessive or even
hyperbolical, but not when we consider it as being in what Emerson called
the optative mood, particularly in regard to the audience, or to the ideal of
an audience:

>           ... for thou hast been
> As one in suff'ring all that suffers nothing,
> A man that Fortune's buffets and rewards
> Hast ta'en with equal thanks; and blest are those
> Whose blood and judgment are so well co-meddled,
> That they are not a pipe for Fortune's finger
> To sound what stop she please. Give me that man
> That is not passions' slave, and I will wear him
> In my heart's core, ay, in my heart of heart,
> As I do thee.

Hamlet himself is hardly one who, in suffering all, suffers nothing, but
then Hamlet is the hero, beyond Horatio and ourselves, and perhaps, at the
close, so far beyond that he transcends the limits of the human. Horatio is

the man that the wily Claudius would not be able to use, partly because Horatio, like the audience, loves Hamlet, but partly also because Horatio stands apart from passion, from self-interest, from life. We are Horatio because he too is a spectator at Elsinore, yet a spectator who has taken sides, once and for all. Hamlet does not need Horatio's love, or ours, though he has it anyway. He needs Horatio to survive to tell his story, and us to receive his story, but he does not need our passion.

To discuss Hamlet as a literary character is to enter a labyrinth of speculation, past and present, that is bewildering in its diversity and in its self-contradictions. The personalities of Hamlet are a manifold, a veritable picnic of selves. Excess is the mark of Hamlet as it is of Falstaff, but the Falstaffian gusto, despite all its complexities, does not compare either to Hamlet's vitalism or to Hamlet's negative exuberance. To be the foremost single representation in all of Western literature, you ought to be the hero of an epic or at least a chronicle, but not the protagonist of a revenge tragedy. A consciousness as vast as Hamlet's ought to have been assigned a Faustian quest, or a journey to God, or a national project of renewal. All Hamlet has to do (if indeed he ought to do it) is chop down Claudius. Avenging the father does not require a Hamlet; a Fortinbras would be more than sufficient. What it was that could have inspired Shakespeare to this amazing disproportion between personage and enterprise seems to me fit subject for wonder.

The wonder is not that Hamlet should be too large for Elsinore, but that he may be too comprehensive for tragedy, just as Nietzsche may be too aesthetic for philosophy. We can envision Hamlet debating Freud, or Nietzsche; hardly a role for Lear or Othello, Yet we do not think of Hamlet as running away from the play, the way that Falstaff takes on a mimetic force that dwarfs the action of *Henry the Fourth, Part One*. Rather, Hamlet transforms his drama from within, so that as its center he becomes also a circumference that will not cease expanding. Long as the play is, we sense that Shakespeare legitimately could have made it much longer, by allowing Hamlet even more meditations upon the perplexities of being human. Indeed it is hardly possible to exclude any matter whatsoever as being irrelevant to a literary work centering upon Hamlet. We welcome Hamlet's opinions upon everything, just as we search the writings of Nietzsche or of Freud to see what they say upon jealousy or mourning or art or authority or whatsoever. Hamlet, a mere literary character, seems the only literary character who has and is an authorial presence, who could as well be a Montaigne, or a Proust, or a Freud. How Shakespeare renders such an illusion persuasive has been illuminated by a rich tradition of criticism. Why he should have ventured so drastic and original an illusion remains a burden for critics to come.

Doubtless it is wrong to see Hamlet as a Shakespearean self-portrait, but though wrong it seems inevitable, and has a sanction in Joyce's witty interpretation, when Stephen expounds his theory of *Hamlet* in *Ulysses*. What is clear is that Shakespeare has lavished intelligence upon Hamlet, who is not so much the most intelligent personage ever to be represented in language, as he is a new kind of intelligence, one without faith either in itself or in language. Hamlet is the precursor of Schopenhauer and Wittgenstein, as well as of Nietzsche and Freud. The prince understands that each of us is her own worst enemy, unable to distinguish desire from playacting, and liable to create disaster out of her equivocal doom-eagerness, a drive against death that courts death. The diseases of consciousness, one by one, seem invented by Hamlet as defenses that contaminate and are contaminated by the drive. Hamlet invents Freud in the sense that Freud is always in Hamlet's wake, condemned to map Hamlet's mind as the only route to a general map of the mind.

The consequence is that *Hamlet* is a Shakespearean reading of Freud that makes redundant any Freudian reading of Shakespeare. Hamlet is the theologian of the unconscious, anticipating Wordsworth as well as Freud. In the same way, Hamlet precedes Kafka and Beckett, by systematically evading every interpretation that might confine him to some reductive scheme that too easily transcends the realities of suffering. Hamlet, as an intelligence, is perpetually ahead of all later literature, which cannot deconstruct his dilemmas any more forcefully or overtly than he himself has done. Shakespeare makes all theorists of interpretation into so many instances of poor Rosencrantz and Guildenstern, who would pluck out the heart of the mystery yet cannot play upon Hamlet, call him what instrument they will. Historicizing Hamlet, whether in old modes or new, ends in reducing the exegete to an antiquarian, unable to separate past values from impending immediacies. There is a politics to Hamlet's spirit, but it is not our politics, though it remains our spirit.

The sickness of the spirit, in Hamlet as in our lives, is perhaps the most perplexing issue of the tragedy. Feigning derangement, Hamlet also becomes deranged, and then returns, apparently self-purged of his alienations from reality. We never do learn the precise nature of his illness, except that it ensued from the trauma brought on by the murder of the father and the mother's fast remarriage. But for a moral intelligence that extraordinary, the squalors of the family romance, or even the king's murder, do not seem the necessary origins of the falling away from selfhood. Imaginative revulsion seems the source of madness in Shakespeare, whether in *Hamlet, Timon of*

*Athens*, or *Macbeth* Hamlet was as much a new kind of man as the King David of 2 Samuel had been: a figure who seemed to realize all of human possibility, an ultimate charismatic whose aura promised almost a triumph over nature. The biblical David has a superb pragmatic intelligence, but his changes are natural, or else presided over by the favor of God's blessing. Hamlet changes in the Shakespearean way, by overhearing himself, whether he speaks to himself or to others. His study of himself is absolute, and founded upon a pondering of his own words. Divinity lies principally within himself, and manifests itself in his fate, as in the fates of all connected with him. His character is his *daimon*, and overdetermines every event.

Literary character, like authorial presence, always returns, whatever the tides of critical fashion. Hamlet's particular union of representational force and linguistic authority has much to do with his universal appeal, and makes it likely also that a return to the study of personality in literature must find one of its centers in this most radiant of all fictional consciousnesses.

# WILLIAM HAZLITT

# *Hamlet*

Hamlet is a name; his speeches and sayings but the idle coinage of the poet's brain. What then, are they not real? They are as real as our own thoughts. Their reality is in the reader's mind. It is we who are Hamlet. This play has a prophetic truth, which is above that of history. Whoever has become thoughtful and melancholy through his own mishaps or those of others; whoever has borne about with him the clouded brow of reflection, and thought himself 'too much i' th' sun'; whoever has seen the golden lamp of day dimmed by envious mists rising in his own breast, and could find in the world before him only a dull blank with nothing left remarkable in it; whoever has known 'the pangs of despised love, the insolence of office, or the spurns which patient merit of the unworthy takes'; he who has felt his mind sink within him, and sadness cling to his heart like a malady, who has had his hopes blighted and his youth staggered by the apparitions of strange things; who cannot be well at ease, while he sees evil hovering near him like a spectre; whose powers of action have been eaten up by thought, he to whom the universe seems infinite, and himself nothing; whose bitterness of soul makes him careless of consequences, and who goes to a play as his best resource to shove off, to a second remove, the evils of life by a mock representation of them—this is the true Hamlet. We have been so used to this tragedy that we hardly know how to criticise it any more than we should

From *The Collected Works of William Hazlitt*, ed. A.R. Waller and Arnold Glover. © 1902 by McClure, Phillips & Co.

know how to describe our own faces. But we must make such observations as we can. It is the one of Shakespear's plays that we think of the oftenest, because it abounds most in striking reflections on human life, and because the distresses of Hamlet are transferred, by the turn of his mind, to the general account of humanity. Whatever happens to him we apply to ourselves, because he applies it so himself as a means of general reasoning. He is a great moraliser; and what makes him worth attending to is, that he moralises on his own feelings and experience. He is not a common-place pedant. If *Lear* is distinguished by the greatest depth of passion, HAMLET is the most remarkable for the ingenuity, originality, and unstudied development of character. Shakespear had more magnanimity than any other poet, and he has shewn more of it in this play than in any other. There is no attempt to force an interest: every thing is left for time and circumstances to unfold. The attention is excited without effort, the incidents succeed each other as matters of course, the characters think and speak and act just as they might do, if left entirely to themselves. There is no set purpose, no straining at a point. The observations are suggested by the passing scene—the gusts of passion come and go like sounds of music borne on the wind. The whole play is an exact transcript of what might be supposed to have taken place at the court of Denmark, at the remote period of time fixed upon, before the modern refinements in morals and manners were heard of. It would have been interesting enough to have been admitted as a bystander in such a scene, at such a time, to have heard and witnessed something of what was going on. But here we are more than spectators. We have not only 'the outward pageants and the signs of grief'; but 'we have that within which passes skew.' We read the thoughts of the heart, we catch the passions living as they rise. Other dramatic writers give us very fine versions and paraphrases of nature; but Shakespear, together with his own comments, gives us the original text, that we may judge for ourselves. This is a very great advantage.

The character of Hamlet stands quite by itself. It is not a character marked by strength of will or even of passion, but by refinement of thought and sentiment. Hamlet is as little of the hero as a man can well be: but he is a young and princely novice, full of high enthusiasm and quick sensibility—the sport of circumstances, questioning with fortune and refining on his own feelings, and forced from the natural bias of his disposition by the strangeness of his situation. He seems incapable of deliberate action, and is only hurried into extremities on the spur of the occasion, when he has no time to reflect, as in the scene where he kills Polonius, and again, where he alters the letters which Rosencraus and Guildenstern are taking with them to England, purporting his death. At other times, when he is most bound to act, he remains puzzled, undecided, and sceptical, dallies with his purposes, till the occasion is lost, and finds out some pretence to relapse into indolence and thoughtfulness again. For this reason he refuses to kill the King when he is at his prayers, and by a refinement in malice, which is in truth only an excuse for his own want of resolution, defers his revenge to a more fatal opportunity, when he shall be engaged in some act 'that has no relish of salvation in it.'

'He kneels and prays,
And now I'll do't, and so he goes to heaven,
And so am I reveng'd: *that would be scann'd*.
He kill'd my father, and for that,
I, his sole son, send him to heaven.
Why this is reward, not revenge.
Up sword and know thou a more horrid time,
When he is drunk, asleep, or in a rage.'

He is the prince of philosophical speculators; and because he cannot have his revenge perfect, according to the most refined idea his wish can form, he declines it altogether. So he scruples to trust the suggestions of the ghost, contrives the scene of the play to have surer proof of his uncle's guilt, and then rests satisfied with this confirmation of his suspicions, and the success of his experiment, instead of acting upon it. Yet he is sensible of his own weakness, taxes himself with it, and tries to reason himself out of it.

'How all occasions do inform against me,
And spur my dull revenge! What is a man,
If his chief good and market of his time
Be but to sleep and feed? A beast; no more.
Sure he that made us with such large discourse,
Looking before and after, gave us not
That capability and god-like reason
To rust in us unus'd. Now whether it be
Bestial oblivion, or some craven scruple
Of thinking too precisely on th' event,—
A thought which quarter'd, hath but one part wisdom,
And ever three parts coward; I do not know
Why yet I live to say, this thing's to do;
Sith I have cause, and will, and strength, and means
To do it. Examples gross as earth exhort me
Witness this army of such mass and charge,
Led by a delicate and tender prince,

Whose spirit with divine ambition puff'd,
Makes mouths at the invisible event,
Exposing what is mortal and unsure
To all that fortune, death, and danger dare,
Even for an egg-shell. 'Tis not to be great
Never to stir without great argument;
But greatly to find quarrel in a straw,
When honour's at the stake. How stand I then,
That have a father kill'd, a mother stain'd,
Excitements of my reason and my blood,
And let all sleep, while to my shame I see
The imminent death of twenty thousand men,
That for a fantasy and trick of fame,
Go to their graves like beds, fight for a plot
Whereon the numbers cannot try the cause,
Which is not tomb enough and continent
To hide the slain?—O, from this time forth,
My thoughts be bloody or be nothing worth.'

Still he does nothing; and this very speculation on his own infirmity only affords him another occasion for indulging it. It is not from any want of attachment to his father or of abhorrence of his murder that Hamlet is thus dilatory, but it is more to his taste to indulge his imagination in reflecting upon the enormity of the crime and refining on his schemes of vengeance, than to put them into immediate practice. His ruling passion is to think, not to act: and any vague pretext that flatters this propensity instantly diverts him from his previous purposes.

The moral perfection of this character has been called in question, we think, by those who did not understand it. It is more interesting than according to rules; amiable, though not faultless. The ethical delineations of that 'noble and liberal casuist' (as Shakespear has been well called) do not exhibit the drab-coloured quakerism of morality. His plays are not copied either from The Whole Duty of Man, or from The Academy of Compliments! We confess we are a little shocked at the want of refinement in those who are shocked at the want of refinement in Hamlet. The neglect of punctilious exactness in his behaviour either partakes of the 'licence of the time,' or else belongs to the very excess of intellectual refinement in the character, which makes the common rules of life, as well as his own purposes, sit loose upon him. He may be said to be amenable only to the tribunal of his own thoughts, and is too much taken up with the airy world of contemplation to lay as much stress as he ought on the practical consequences of things. His habitual principles of action are unhinged and out of joint with the time. His conduct to Ophelia is quite natural in his circumstances. It is that of assumed severity only. It is the effect of disappointed hope, of bitter regrets, of affection suspended, not obliterated, by the distractions of the scene around him! Amidst the natural and preternatural horrors of his situation, he might be excused in delicacy from carrying on a regular courtship. When 'his father's spirit was in arms,' it was not a time for the son to make love in. He could neither marry Ophelia, nor wound her mind by explaining the cause of his alienation, which he durst hardly trust himself to think of. It would have taken him years to have come to a direct explanation on the point. In the harassed state of his mind, he could not have done much otherwise than he did. His conduct does not contradict what he says when he sees her funeral,

> 'I loved Ophelia: forty thousand brothers
> Could not with all their quantity of love
> Make up my sum.'

Nothing can be more affecting or beautiful than the Queen's apostrophe to Ophelia on throwing the flowers into the grave.

> ——'Sweets to the sweet, farewell.
> I hop'd thou should'st have been my Hamlet's wife:
> I thought thy bride-bed to have deck'd, sweet maid,
> And not have strew'd thy grave.'

Shakespear was thoroughly a master of the mixed motives of human character, and he here shews us the Queen, who was so criminal in some respects, not without sensibility and affection in other relations of life.— Ophelia is a character almost too exquisitely touching to be dwelt upon. Oh rose of May, oh flower too soon faded! Her love, her madness, her death, are described with the truest touches of tenderness and pathos. It is a character which nobody but Shakespear could have drawn in the way that he has done, and to the conception of which there is not even the smallest approach, except in some of the old romantic ballads.[1] Her brother, Laertes, is a character we do not like so well: he is too hot and choleric, and somewhat rhodomontade. Polonius is a perfect character in its kind; nor is there any foundation for the objections which have been made to the consistency of this part. It is said that he acts very foolishly and talks very sensibly. There is no inconsistency in that. Again, that he talks wisely at one time and foolishly at another; that his advice to Laertes is very excellent, and his advice to the

King and Queen on the subject of Hamlet's madness very ridiculous. But he gives the one as a father, and is sincere in it; he gives the other as a mere courtier, a busy-body, and is accordingly officious, garrulous, and impertinent. In short, Shakespear has been accused of inconsistency in this and other characters, only because he has kept up the distinction which there is in nature, between the understandings and the moral habits of men, between the absurdity of their ideas and the absurdity of their motives. Polonius is not a fool, but he makes himself so. His folly, whether in his actions or speeches, comes under the head of impropriety of intention.

We do not like to see our author's plays acted, and least of all, HAMLET. There is no play that suffers so much in being transferred to the stage. Hamlet himself seems hardly capable of being acted. Mr. Kemble unavoidably fails in this character from a want of ease and variety. The character of Hamlet is made up of undulating lines; it has the yielding flexibility of 'a wave o' th' sea.' Mr. Kemble plays it like a man in armour, with a determined inveteracy of purpose, in one undeviating straight line, which is as remote from the natural grace and refined susceptibility of the character, as the sharp angles and abrupt starts which Mr. Kean introduces into the part. Mr. Kean's Hamlet is as much too splenetic and rash as Mr. Kemble's is too deliberate and formal. His manner is too strong and pointed. He throws a severity, approaching to virulence, into the common observations and answers. There is nothing of this in Hamlet. He is, as it were, wrapped up in his reflections, and only *thinks aloud*. There should therefore be no attempt to impress what he says upon others by a studied exaggeration of emphasis or manner no *talking* at his hearers. There should be as much of the gentleman and scholar as possible infused into the part, and as little of the actor. A pensive air of sadness should sit reluctantly upon his brow, but no appearance of fixed and sullen gloom. He is full of weakness and melancholy, but there is no harshness in his nature. He is the most amiable of misanthropes.

### NOTE

1. In the account of her death, a friend has pointed out an instance of the poet's exact observation of nature:—

'There is a willow growing o'er a brook,
That shews its hoary leaves i' th' glassy stream.'

The inside of the leaves of the willow, next the water, is of a whitish colour, and the reflection would therefore be 'hoary.'

# A.C. BRADLEY

# *Hamlet*

Let us first ask ourselves what we can gather from the play, immediately or by inference, concerning Hamlet as he was just before his father's death. And I begin by observing that the text does not bear out the idea that he was one-sidedly reflective and indisposed to action. Nobody who knew him seems to have noticed this weakness. Nobody regards him as a mere scholar who has 'never formed a resolution or executed a deed.' In a court which certainly would not much admire such a person he is the observed of all observers. Though he has been disappointed of the throne everyone shows him respect; and he is the favourite of the people, who are not given to worship philosophers. Fortinbras, a sufficiently practical man, considered that he was likely, had he been put on, to have proved most royally. He has Hamlet borne by four captains 'like a soldier' to his grave; and Ophelia says that Hamlet *was* a soldier, If he was fond of acting, an aesthetic pursuit, he was equally fond of fencing, an athletic one: he practised it assiduously even in his worst days.[1] So far as we can conjecture from what we see of him in those bad days, he must normally have been charmingly frank, courteous and kindly to everyone, of whatever rank, whom he liked or respected, but by no means timid or deferential to others; indeed, one would gather that he was rather the reverse, and also that he was apt to be decided and even imperious if thwarted or interfered with. He must always have been fearless,—in the

From *Shakespearean Tragedy: Lectures on* Hamlet, Othello, King Lear, Macbeth 2 ed. © 1905 by MacMillan.

play he appears insensible to fear of any ordinary kind. And, finally, he must have been quick and impetuous in action; for it is downright impossible that the man we see rushing after the Ghost, killing Polonius, dealing with the King's commission on the ship, boarding the pirate, leaping into the grave, executing his final vengeance, could *ever* have been shrinking or slow in an emergency. Imagine Coleridge doing any of these things!

If we consider all this, how can we accept the notion that Hamlet's was a weak and one-sided character? 'Oh, but he spent ten or twelve years at a University!' Well, even if he did, it is possible to do that without becoming the victim of excessive thought. But the statement that he did rests upon a most insecure foundation.[2]

Where then are we to look for the seeds of danger?

(1) Trying to reconstruct from the Hamlet of the play, one would not judge that his temperament was melancholy in the present sense of the word; there seems nothing to show that; but one would judge that by temperament he was inclined to nervous instability, to rapid and perhaps extreme changes of feeling and mood, and that he was disposed to be, for the time, absorbed in the feeling or mood that possessed him, whether it were joyous or depressed. This temperament the Elizabethans would have called melancholic; and Hamlet seems to be an example of it, as Lear is of a temperament mixedly choleric and sanguine. And the doctrine of temperaments was so familiar in Shakespeare's time—as Burton, and earlier prose-writers, and many of the dramatists show—that Shakespeare may quite well have given this temperament to Hamlet consciously and deliberately. Of melancholy in its developed form, a habit, not a mere temperament, he often speaks. He more than once laughs at the passing and half-fictitious melancholy of youth and love; in Don John in *Much Ado* he had sketched the sour and surly melancholy of discontent; in Jaques a whimsical self-pleasing melancholy; in Antonio in the *Merchant of Venice* a quiet but deep melancholy, for which neither the victim nor his friends can assign any cause.[3] He gives to Hamlet a temperament which would not develop into melancholy unless under some exceptional strain, but which still involved a danger. In the play we see the danger realised, and find a melancholy quite unlike any that Shakespeare had as yet depicted, because the temperament of Hamlet is quite different.

(2) Next, we cannot be mistaken in attributing to the Hamlet of earlier days an exquisite sensibility, to which we may give the name 'moral,' if that word is taken in the wide meaning it ought to bear. This, though it suffers cruelly in later days, as we saw in criticising the sentimental view of Hamlet, never deserts him; it makes all his cynicism, grossness and hardness appear to us morbidities, and has an inexpressibly attractive and pathetic effect. He

had the soul of the youthful poet as Shelley and Tennyson have described it, an unbounded delight and faith in everything good and beautiful. We know this from himself. The world for him was *herrlich wie am ersten Tag*—'this goodly frame the earth, this most excellent canopy the air, this brave o'erhanging firmament, this majestical roof fretted with golden fire.' And not nature only: 'What a piece of work is a man! how noble in reason! how infinite in faculty! in form and moving how express and admirable! in action how like an angel! in apprehension how like a god!' This is no commonplace to Hamlet; it is the language of a heart thrilled with wonder and swelling into ecstasy.

Doubtless it was with the same eager enthusiasm he turned to those around him. Where else in Shakespeare is there anything like Hamlet's adoration of his father? The words melt into music whenever he speaks of him. And, if there are no signs of any such feeling towards his mother, though many signs of love, it is characteristic that he evidently never entertained a suspicion of anything unworthy in her,—characteristic, and significant of his tendency to see only what is good unless he is forced to see the reverse. For we find this tendency elsewhere, and find it going so far that we must call it a disposition to idealise, to see something better than what is there, or at least to ignore deficiencies. He says to Laertes, 'I loved you ever,' and he describes Laertes as a 'very noble youth,' which he was far from being. In his first greeting of Rosencrantz and Guildenstern, where his old self revives, we trace the same affectionateness and readiness to take men at their best. His love for Ophelia, too, which seems strange to some, is surely the most natural thing in the world. He saw her innocence, simplicity and sweetness, and it was like him to ask no more; and it is noticeable that Horatio, though entirely worthy of his friendship, is, like Ophelia, intellectually not remarkable. To the very end, however clouded, this generous disposition, this 'free and open nature,' this unsuspiciousness survive. They cost him his life; for the King knew them, and was sure that he was too 'generous and free from all contriving' to 'peruse the foils.' To the very end, his soul, however sick and tortured it may be, answers instantaneously when good and evil are presented to it, loving the one and hating the other. He is called a sceptic who has no firm belief in anything, but he is never sceptical about *them*.

And the negative side of his idealism, the aversion to evil, is perhaps even more developed in the hero of the tragedy than in the Hamlet of earlier days. It is intensely characteristic. Nothing, I believe, is to be found elsewhere in Shakespeare (unless in the rage of the disillusioned idealist Timon) of quite the same kind as Hamlet's disgust at his uncle's drunkenness, his loathing of his mother's sensuality, his astonishment and horror at her shallowness, his contempt for everything pretentious or false, his indifference to everything merely external. This last characteristic appears in his choice of the friend of his heart, and in a certain impatience of distinctions of rank or wealth. When Horatio calls his father 'a goodly king,' he answers, surely with an emphasis on 'man,'

> He was a man, take him for all in all,
> I shall not look upon his like again.

He will not listen to talk of Horatio being his 'servant.' When the others speak of their 'duty' to him, he answers, 'Your love, as mine to you.' He speaks to the actor precisely as he does to an honest courtier. He is not in the least a revolutionary, but still, in effect, a king and a beggar are all one to him. He cares for nothing but human worth, and his pitilessness towards Polonius and Osric and his 'school-fellows' is not wholly due to morbidity, but belongs in part to his original character.

Now, in Hamlet's moral sensibility there undoubtedly lay a danger. Any great shock that life might inflict on it would be felt with extreme intensity. Such a shock might even produce tragic results. And, in fact, *Hamlet* deserves the title 'tragedy of moral idealism' quite as much as the title 'tragedy of reflection.'

(3) With this temperament and this sensibility we find, lastly, in the Hamlet of earlier days, as of later, intellectual genius. It is chiefly this that makes him so different from all those about him, good and bad alike, and hardly less different from most of Shakespeare's other heroes. And this, though on the whole the most important trait in his nature, is also so obvious and so famous that I need not dwell on it at length. But against one prevalent misconception I must say a word of warning. Hamlet's intellectual power is not a specific gift, like a genius for music or mathematics or philosophy. It shows itself, fitfully, in the affairs of life as unusual quickness of perception, great agility in shifting the mental attitude, a striking rapidity and fertility in resource; so that, when his natural belief in others does not make him unwary, Hamlet easily sees through them and masters them, and no one can be much less like the typical helpless dreamer. It shows itself in conversation chiefly in the form of wit or humour; and, alike in conversation and in soliloquy, it shows itself in the form of imagination quite as much as in that of thought in the stricter sense. Further, where it takes the latter shape, as it very often does, it is not philosophic in the technical meaning of the word. There is really nothing in the play to show that Hamlet ever was 'a student of philosophies,' unless it be the famous lines which, comically enough, exhibit this supposed victim of philosophy as its critic

There are more things in heaven and earth, Horatio,
Than are dreamt of in your philosophy.[4]

His philosophy, if the word is to be used, was, like Shakespeare's own, the immediate product of the wondering and meditating mind; and such thoughts as that celebrated one, 'There is nothing either good or bad but thinking makes it so,' surely needed no special training to produce them. Or does Portia's remark, 'Nothing is good without respect,' *i.e.*, out of relation, prove that she had studied metaphysics?

Still Hamlet had speculative genius without being a philosopher, just as he had imaginative genius without being a poet. Doubtless in happier days he was a close and constant observer of men and manners, noting his results in those tables which he afterwards snatched from his breast to make in wild irony his last note of all, that one may smile and smile and be a villain. Again and again we remark that passion for generalisation which so occupied him, for instance, in reflections suggested by the King's drunkenness that he quite forgot what it was he was waiting to meet upon the battlements. Doubtless, too, he was always considering things, as Horatio thought, too curiously. There was a necessity in his soul driving him to penetrate below the surface and to question what others took for granted. That fixed habitual look which the world wears for most men did not exist for him. He was for ever unmaking his world and rebuilding it in thought, dissolving what to others were solid facts, and discovering what to others were old truths. There were no old truths for Hamlet. It is for Horatio a thing of course that there's a divinity that shapes our ends, but for Hamlet it is a discovery hardly won. And throughout this kingdom of the mind, where he felt that man, who in action is only like an angel, is in apprehension like a god, he moved (we must imagine) more than content, so that even in his dark days he declares he could be bounded in a nutshell and yet count himself a king of infinite space, were it not that he had bad dreams.

If now we ask whether any special danger lurked *here*, how shall we answer? We must answer, it seems to me, 'Some danger, no doubt, but, granted the ordinary chances of life, not much.' For, in the first place, that idea which so many critics quietly take for granted—the idea that the gift and the habit of meditative and speculative thought tend to produce irresolution in the affairs of life—would be found by no means easy to verify. Can you verify it, for example, in the lives of the philosophers, or again in the lives of men whom you have personally known to be addicted to such speculation? I cannot. Of course, individual peculiarities being set apart, absorption in any intellectual interest, together with withdrawal from affairs, may make a man slow and unskilful in affairs; and doubtless, individual peculiarities being again set apart, a mere student is likely to be more at a loss in a sudden and great practical emergency than a soldier or a lawyer. But in all this there is no difference between a physicist, a historian, and a philosopher; and again, slowness, want of skill, and even helplessness are something totally different from the peculiar kind of irresolution that Hamlet shows. The notion that speculative thinking specially tends to produce this is really a mere illusion.

In the second place, even if this notion were true, it has appeared that Hamlet did not live the life of a mere student, much less of a mere dreamer, and that his nature was by no means simply or even one-sidedly intellectual, but was healthily active. Hence, granted the ordinary chances of life, there would seem to be no great danger in his intellectual tendency and his habit of speculation; and I would go further and say that there was nothing in them, taken alone, to unfit him even for the extraordinary call that was made upon him. In fact, if the message of the Ghost had come to him within a week of his father's death, I see no reason to doubt that he would have acted on it as decisively as Othello himself, though probably after a longer and more anxious deliberation. And therefore the Schlegel-Coleridge view (apart from its descriptive value) seems to me fatally untrue, for it implies that Hamlet's procrastination was the normal response of an over-speculative nature confronted with a difficult practical problem.

On the other hand, under conditions of a peculiar kind, Hamlet's reflectiveness certainly might prove dangerous to him, and his genius might even (to exaggerate a little) become his doom. Suppose that violent shock to his moral being of which I spoke; and suppose that under this shock, any possible action being denied to him, he began to sink into melancholy; then, no doubt, his imaginative and generalising habit of mind might extend the effects of this shock through his whole being and mental world. And if, the state of melancholy being thus deepened and fixed, a sudden demand for difficult and decisive action in a matter connected with the melancholy arose, this state might well have for one of its symptoms an endless and futile mental dissection of the required deed. And, finally, the futility of this process, and the shame of his delay, would further weaken him and enslave him to his melancholy still more. Thus the speculative habit would be *one* indirect cause of the morbid state which hindered action; and it would also reappear in a degenerate form as one of the *symptoms* of this morbid state.

Now this is what actually happens in the play. Turn to the first words Hamlet utters when he is alone; turn, that is to say, to the place where the author is likely to indicate his meaning most plainly. What do you hear?

O, that this too too solid flesh would melt,
Thaw and resolve itself into a dew!
Or that the Everlasting had not fix'd
His canon 'gainst self-slaughter! O God! God!
How weary, stale, flat and unprofitable,
Seem to me all the uses of this world!
Fie on't! ah fie! 'tis an unweeded garden,
That grows to seed; things rank and gross in nature
Possess it merely.

Here are a sickness of life, and even a longing for death, so intense that nothing stands between Hamlet and suicide except religious awe. And what has caused them? The rest of the soliloquy so thrusts the answer upon us that it might seem impossible to miss it. It was not his father's death; that doubtless brought deep grief, but mere grief for some one loved and lost does not make a noble spirit loathe the world as a place full only of things rank and gross. It was not the vague suspicion that we know Hamlet felt. Still less was it the loss of the crown; for though the subserviency of the electors might well disgust him, there is not a reference to the subject in the soliloquy, nor any sign elsewhere that it greatly occupied his mind. It was the moral shock of the sudden ghastly disclosure of his mother's true nature, falling on him when his heart was aching with love, and his body doubtless was weakened by sorrow. And it is essential, however disagreeable, to realise the nature of this shock. It matters little here whether Hamlet's age was twenty or thirty: in either case his mother was a matron of mature years. All his life he had believed in her, we may be sure, as such a son would. He had seen her not merely devoted to his father, but hanging on him like a newly-wedded bride, hanging on him

As if increase of appetite had grown
By what it fed on.

He had seen her following his body 'like Niobe, all tears.' And then within a month—'O God! a beast would have mourned longer'—she married again, and married Hamlet's uncle, a man utterly contemptible and loathsome in his eyes; married him in what to Hamlet was incestuous wedlock;[5] married him not for any reason of state, nor even out of old family affection, but in such a way that her son was forced to see in her action not only an astounding shallowness of feeling but an eruption of coarse sensuality, 'rank and gross,'[6] speeding post-haste to its horrible delight. Is it possible to conceive an experience more desolating to a man such as we have seen Hamlet to be; and is its result anything but perfectly natural? It brings bewildered horror, then loathing, then despair of human nature. His whole mind is poisoned. He can never see Ophelia in the same light again: she is a woman, and his mother is a woman: if she mentions the word 'brief' to him, the answer drops from his lips like venom, 'as woman's love.' The last words of the soliloquy, which is wholly concerned with this subject, are,

> But break, my heart, for I must hold my tongue!

He can do nothing. He must lock in his heart, not any suspicion of his uncle that moves obscurely there, but that horror and loathing; and if his heart ever found relief, it was when those feelings, mingled with the love that never died out in him, poured themselves forth in a flood as he stood in his mother's chamber beside his father's marriage-bed.[7]

If we still wonder, and ask why the effect of this shock should be so tremendous, let us observe that now the conditions have arisen under which Hamlet's highest endowments, his moral sensibility and his genius, become his enemies. A nature morally blunter would have felt even so dreadful a revelation less keenly. A slower and more limited and positive mind might not have extended so widely through its world the disgust and disbelief that have entered it. But Hamlet has the imagination which, for evil as well as good, feels and sees all things in one. Thought is the element of his life, and his thought is infected. He cannot prevent himself from probing and lacerating the wound in his soul. One idea, full of peril, holds him fast, and he cries out in agony at it, but is impotent to free himself ('Must I remember?' 'Let me not think on't'). And when, with the fading of his passion, the vividness of this idea abates, it does so only to leave behind a boundless weariness and a sick longing for death.

And this is the time which his fate chooses. In this hour of uttermost weakness, this sinking of his whole being towards annihilation, there comes on him, bursting the bounds of the natural world with a shock of astonishment and terror, the revelation of his mother's adultery and his father's murder, and, with this, the demand on him, in the name of everything dearest and most sacred, to arise and act. And for a moment, though his brain reels and totters,[8] his soul leaps up in passion to answer this demand. But it comes too late. It does but strike home the last rivet in the melancholy which holds him bound.

The time is out of joint! O cursed spite
That ever I was born to set it right,—

so he mutters within an hour of the moment when he vowed to give his life
to the duty of revenge; and the rest of the story exhibits his vain efforts to
fulfil this duty, his unconscious self-excuses and unavailing self-reproaches,
and the tragic results of his delay.

4

'Melancholy,' I said, not dejection, nor yet insanity. That Hamlet was
not far from insanity is very probable. His adoption of the pretence of
madness may well have been due in part to fear of the reality; to an instinct
of self-preservation, a fore-feeling that the pretence would enable him to
give some utterance to the load that pressed on his heart and brain, and a fear
that he would be unable altogether to repress such utterance. And if the
pathologist calls his state melancholia, and even proceeds to determine its
species, I see nothing to object to in that; I am grateful to him for
emphasising the fact that Hamlet's melancholy was no mere common
depression of spirits; and I have no doubt that many readers of the play
would understand it better if they read an account of melancholia in a work
on mental diseases. If we like to use the word 'disease' loosely, Hamlet's
condition may truly be called diseased. No exertion of will could have
dispelled it. Even if he had been able at once to do the bidding of the Ghost
he would doubtless have still remained for some time under the cloud. It
would be absurdly unjust to call *Hamlet* a study of melancholy, but it contains
such a study.

But this melancholy is something very different from insanity, in
anything like the usual meaning of that word. No doubt it might develop
into insanity. The longing for death might become an irresistible impulse to
self-destruction; the disorder of feeling and will might extend to sense and
intellect; delusions might arise; and the man might become, as we say,
incapable and irresponsible. But Hamlet's melancholy is some way from this
condition. It is a totally different thing from the madness which he feigns;
and he never, when alone or in company with Horatio alone, exhibits the
signs of that madness. Nor is the dramatic use of this melancholy, again, open
to the objections which would justly be made to the portrayal of an insanity
which brought the hero to a tragic end. The man who suffers as Hamlet
suffers—and thousands go about their business suffering thus in greater or

less degree—is considered irresponsible neither by other people nor by himself: he is only too keenly conscious of his responsibility. He is therefore, so far, quite capable of being a tragic agent, which an insane person, at any rate according to Shakespeare's practice, is not.[9] And, finally, Hamlet's state is not one which a healthy mind is unable sufficiently to imagine. It is probably not further from average experience, nor more difficult to realise, than the great tragic passions of Othello, Antony or Macbeth.

Let me try to show now, briefly, how much this melancholy accounts for.

It accounts for the main fact, Hamlet's inaction. For the *immediate* cause of that is simply that his habitual feeling is one of disgust at life and everything in it, himself included,—a disgust which varies in intensity, rising at times into a longing for death, sinking often into weary apathy, but is never dispelled for more than brief intervals. Such a state of feeling is inevitably adverse to any kind of decided action; the body is inert, the mind indifferent or worse; its response is, 'it does not matter,' 'it is not worth while,' 'it is no good.' And the action required of Hamlet is very exceptional. It is violent, dangerous, difficult to accomplish perfectly, on one side repulsive to a man of honour and sensitive feeling, on another side involved in a certain mystery (here come in thus, in their subordinate place, various causes of inaction assigned by various theories). These obstacles would not suffice to prevent Hamlet from acting, if his state were normal; and against them there operate, even in his morbid state, healthy and positive feelings, love of his father, loathing of his uncle, desire of revenge, desire to do duty. But the retarding motives acquire an unnatural strength because they have an ally in something far stronger than themselves, the melancholic disgust and apathy; while the healthy motives, emerging with difficulty from the central mass of diseased feeling, rapidly sink back into it and 'lose the name of action.' We *see* them doing so; and sometimes the process is quite simple, no analytical reflection on the deed intervening between the outburst of passion and the relapse into melancholy.[10] But this melancholy is perfectly consistent also with that incessant dissection of the task assigned, of which the Schlegel-Coleridge theory makes so much. For those endless questions (as we may imagine them), 'Was I deceived by the Ghost? How am I to do the deed? When? Where? What will be the consequence of attempting it—success, my death, utter misunderstanding, mere mischief to the State? Can it be right to do it, or noble to kill a defenceless man? What is the good of doing it in such a world as this?'—all this, and whatever else passed in a sickening round through Hamlet's mind, was not the healthy and right deliberation of a man with such a task, but otiose thinking hardly deserving the name of thought, an unconscious weaving of pretexts for inaction, aimless tossings on a sick bed, symptoms of melancholy which only increased it by deepening self-contempt.

Again, (*a*) this state accounts for Hamlet's energy as well as for his lassitude, those quick decided actions of his being the outcome of a nature normally far from passive, now suddenly stimulated, and producing healthy impulses which work themselves out before they have time to subside. (*b*) It accounts for the evidently keen satisfaction which some of these actions give to him. He arranges the play-scene with lively interest, and exults in its success, not really because it brings him nearer to his goal, but partly because it has hurt his enemy and partly because it has demonstrated his own skill (III. ii. 286–304). He looks forward almost with glee to countermining the King's designs in sending him away (III. iv. 209), and looks back with obvious satisfaction, even with pride, to the address and vigour he displayed on the voyage (V. ii. 1–55). These were not *the* action on which his morbid self-feeling had centred; he feels in them his old force, and escapes in them from his disgust. (*c*) It accounts for the pleasure with which he meets old acquaintances, like his 'school-fellows' or the actors. The former observed (and we can observe) in him a 'kind of joy' at first, though it is followed by 'much forcing of his disposition' as he attempts to keep this joy and his courtesy alive in spite of the misery which so soon returns upon him and the suspicion he is forced to feel. (*d*) It accounts no less for the painful features of his character as seen in the play, his almost savage irritability on the one hand, and on the other his self-absorption, his callousness, his insensibility to the fates of those whom he despises, and to the feelings even of those whom he loves. These are frequent symptoms of such melancholy, and (*e*) they sometimes alternate, as they do in Hamlet, with bursts of transitory, almost hysterical, and quite fruitless emotion. It is to these last (of which a part of the soliloquy, 'O what a rogue,' gives a good example) that Hamlet alludes when, to the Ghost, he speaks of himself as 'lapsed in passion,' and it is doubtless partly his conscious weakness in regard to them that inspires his praise of Horatio as a man who is not 'passion's slave.'[11]

Finally, Hamlet's melancholy accounts for two things which seem to be explained by nothing else. The first of these is his apathy or 'lethargy.' We are bound to consider the evidence which the text supplies of this, though it is usual to ignore it. When. Hamlet mentions, as one possible cause of his inaction, his 'thinking too precisely on the event,' he mentions another, 'bestial oblivion'; and the thing against which he inveighs in the greater part of that soliloquy (IV. iv.) is not the excess or the misuse of reason (which for him here and always is god-like), but this *bestial* oblivion or '*dullness*,' this 'letting all *sleep*,' this allowing of heaven-sent reason to 'fust unused':

> What is a man,
> If his chief good and market of his time
> Be but to *sleep* and feed? a *beast*, no more.[12]

So, in the soliloquy in II. ii. he accuses himself of being 'a dull and muddy-mettled rascal,' who 'peaks [mopes] like John-a-dreams, unpregnant of his cause,' dully indifferent to his cause.[13] So, when the Ghost appears to him the second time, he accuses himself of being tardy and lapsed in *time*; and the Ghost speaks of his purpose being almost *blunted*, and bids him not to *forget* (cf. 'oblivion'). And so, what is emphasised in those undramatic but significant speeches of the player-king and of Claudius is the mere dying away of purpose or of love.[14] Surely what all this points to is not a condition of excessive but useless mental activity (indeed there is, in reality, curiously little about that in the text), but rather one of dull, apathetic, brooding gloom, in which Hamlet, so far from analysing his duty, is not thinking of it at all, but for the time literally *forgets* it. It seems to me we are driven to think of Hamlet *chiefly* thus during the long time which elapsed between the appearance of the Ghost and the events presented in the Second Act. The Ghost, in fact, had more reason than we suppose at first for leaving with Hamlet as his parting injunction the command, 'Remember me,' and for greeting him, on reappearing, with the command, 'Do not forget.'[15] These little things in Shakespeare are not accidents.

The second trait which is fully explained only by Hamlet's melancholy is his own inability to understand why he delays. This emerges in a marked degree when an occasion like the player's emotion or the sight of Fortinbras's army stings Hamlet into shame at his inaction. 'Why,' he asks himself in genuine bewilderment, 'do I linger? Can the cause be cowardice? Can it be sloth? Can it be thinking too precisely of the event? And does *that* again mean cowardice? What is it that makes me sit idle when I feel it is shameful to do so, and when I have *cause, and will, and strength, and means*, to act?' A man irresolute merely because he was considering a proposed action too minutely would not feel this bewilderment. A man might feel it whose conscience secretly condemned the act which his explicit consciousness approved; but we have seen that there is no sufficient evidence to justify us in conceiving Hamlet thus. These are the questions of a man stimulated for the moment to shake off the weight of his melancholy, and, because for the moment he is free from it, unable to understand the, paralysing pressure which it exerts at other times.

I have dwelt thus at length on Hamlet's melancholy because, from the psychological point of view, it is the centre of the tragedy, and to omit it from consideration or to underrate its intensity is to make Shakespeare's story unintelligible. But the psychological point of view is not equivalent to the tragic; and, having once given its due weight to the fact of Hamlet's melancholy, we may freely admit, or rather may be anxious to insist, that this pathological condition would excite but little, if any, tragic interest if it were not the condition of a nature distinguished by that speculative genius on which the Schlegel-Coleridge type of theory lays stress. Such theories misinterpret the connection between that genius and Hamlet's failure, but still it is this connection which gives to his story its peculiar fascination and makes it appear (if the phrase may be allowed) as the symbol of a tragic mystery inherent in human nature. Wherever this mystery touches us, wherever we are forced to feel the wonder and awe of man's godlike 'apprehension' and his 'thoughts that wander through eternity,' and at the same time are forced to see him powerless in his petty sphere of action, and powerless (it would appear) from the very divinity of his thought, we remember Hamlet. And this is the reason why, in the great ideal movement which began towards the close of the eighteenth century, this tragedy acquired a position unique among Shakespeare's dramas, and shared only by Goethe's *Faust*. It was not that *Hamlet* is Shakespeare's greatest tragedy or most perfect work of art; it was that *Hamlet* most brings home to us at once the sense of the soul's infinity, and the sense of the doom which not only circumscribes that infinity but appears to be its offspring.

## NOTES

1. He says so to Horatio, whom he has no motive for deceiving (V. ii: 218). His contrary statement (II. ii. 308) is made to Rosencrantz and Guildenstern.

2. See Note B.

3. The critics have laboured to find a cause, but it seems to me Shakespeare simply meant to portray a pathological condition; and a very touching picture he draws. Antonio's sadness, which he describes in the opening lines of the play, would never drive him to suicide, but it makes him indifferent to the issue of the trial, as all his speeches in the trial-scene show.

4. Of course 'your' does not mean Horatio's philosophy in particular. 'Your' is used as the Gravedigger uses it when he says that 'your water is a sore decayer of your ... dead body.'

5. This aspect of the matter leaves us comparatively unaffected, but Shakespeare evidently means it to be of importance. The Ghost speaks of it twice, and Hamlet thrice (once in his last furious words to the King). If, as we must suppose, the marriage was universally admitted to be incestuous, the corrupt acquiescence of the court and the electors to the crown would naturally have a strong effect on Hamlet's mind.

6. It is most significant that the metaphor of this soliloquy reappears in Hamlet's adjuration to his mother (III. iv. 150)

> Repent what's past; avoid what is to come;
> And do not spread the compost on the weeds
> To make them ranker.

7. If the reader will now look at the only speech of Hamlet's that precedes the soliloquy, and is more than one line in length—the speech beginning 'Seems, madam! nay, it *is*'—he will understand what, surely, when first we come to it, sounds very strange and almost boastful. It is not, in effect, about Hamlet himself at all; it is about his mother (I do not mean that it is intentionally and consciously so; and still less that she understood it so).

8. See Note D.

9. See p. 13.

10. *E.g.* in the transition, referred to above, from desire for vengeance into the wish never to have been born; in the soliloquy, 'O what a rogue'; in the scene at Ophelia's grave. The Schlegel-Coleridge theory does not account for the psychological movement in those passages.

11. Hamlet's violence at Ophelia's grave, though probably intentionally exaggerated, is another example of this want of self-control. The Queen's description of him (V. i. 307),

> This is mere madness;
> And thus awhile the fit will work on him;
> Anon, as patient as the female dove,
> When that her golden couplets are disclosed,
> His silence will sit drooping,

may be true to life, though it is evidently prompted by anxiety to excuse his violence on the ground of his insanity. On this passage see further Note G.

12. Throughout, I italicise to show the connection of ideas.

13. Cf. *Measure for Measure*, IV. iv. 23, 'This deed ... makes me unpregnant and dull to all proceedings.'

14. III. ii. 196 ff., IV. vii. 111 ff.: *e.g.*,

> Purpose is but the slave to memory,
> Of violent birth but poor validity.

15. So, before, he had said to him:

> And duller sbould'st thou be than the fat weed
> That roots itself in ease on Lethe wharf,
> Would'st thou not stir in this.

On Hamlet's soliloquy after the Ghost's disappearance see Note D.

HAROLD C. GODDARD

# Hamlet

When such a spacious mirror's set before him,
He needs must see himself.

## I

There is no mystery in a looking glass until someone looks into it. Then, though it remains the same glass, it presents a different face to each man who holds it in front of him. The same is true of a work of art. It has no proper existence as art until someone is reflected in it—and no two will ever be reflected in the same way. However much we all see in common in such a work, at the center we behold a fragment of our own soul and the greater the art the greater the fragment. *Hamlet* is possibly the most convincing example in existence of this truth. In a less "spacious mirror" it is often concealed or obscured. But "Hamlet wavered for all of us," as Emily Dickinson said, and everyone admits finding something of himself in the Prince of Denmark. *Hamlet* criticism seems destined, then, to go on being what it has always been: a sustained difference of opinion. It is quite as if *Hamlet* were itself a play within a play. *The Murder of Gonzago* was one thing to the Prince, another to the King, and others still to the Queen, Polonius, Ophelia, and the rest. So *Hamlet* is to us. The heart of its hero's mystery will never be plucked out. No theory of his character will ever satisfy all men, and even if

From *The Meaning of Shakespeare*. © 1951 by The University of Chicago.

one should convince one age, it would not the next. But that does not mean
that a deep man will not come closer to that mystery than a shallow man, or
a poetic age than a prosaic one—just as Hamlet saw more in "The Mousetrap" than Rosencrantz or Guildenstern could conceivably have seen. No
one but a dead man can escape projecting himself on the Prince of Denmark.
But some will project themselves on many, others on only a few, of the
innumerable facets of his personality. The former, compared with the latter,
will obtain a relatively objective view of the man. And this process will
continue to create what might be called the world's slowly growing portrait
of Hamlet. Over the years the cairn of *Hamlet* criticism is more than any
stone that has been thrown upon it.

## II

To nearly everyone both Hamlet himself and the play give the
impression of having some peculiarly intimate relation to their creator. What
that relation may originally have been we shall probably never know. But it
is hard to refrain from speculating. When we learn that Dostoevsky had a
son, Alyosha (Alexey), whom he loved dearly and who died before he was
three, and that the father began writing *The Brothers Karamazov* that same
year, the temptation is irresistible to believe that its hero, Alexey Karamazov,
is an imaginative reincarnation of the child, a portrayal of what the author
would have liked the boy to become. In this instance the father bestowed an
immortality that there is only a negligible chance the son would have
achieved if he had lived. Shakespeare's son Hamnet died at the age of eleven,
possibly not long before his father began to be attracted by the Hamlet story.
Was there any connection? We do not know. But the name, in its
interchangeable forms, must have had strong emotional associations for
Shakespeare. Hamnet and Judith Sadler, neighbors and friends of the
Shakespeares, were godparents to their twins, to whom they gave their
names. When Shakespeare was sixteen, a girl, Katherine Hamlett, was
drowned near Stratford under circumstances the poet may have remembered
when he told of Ophelia's death. Resemblances between Hamlet and the Earl
of Essex, who, in turn, figured significantly in Shakespeare's life, have
frequently been pointed out.

However all this may be, there is no doubt that Shakespeare endowed
Hamlet with the best he had acquired up to the time he conceived him. He
inherits the virtues of a score of his predecessors—and some of their
weaknesses. Yet he is no mere recapitulation of them. In him, rather, they
recombine to make a man as individual as he is universal. He has the passion
of Romeo ("Romeo is Hamlet in love," says Hazlitt), the dash and audacity

of Hotspur, the tenderness and genius for friendship of Antonio, the wit, wisdom, resourcefulness, and histrionic gift of Falstaff, the bravery of Faulconbridge, the boyish charm of the earlier Hal at his best, the poetic fancy of Richard II, the analogic power and meditative melancholy of Jaques, the idealism of Brutus, the simplicity and human sympathy of Henry VI, and, after the assumption of his antic disposition, the wiliness and talent for disguise of Henry IV and the cynicism and irony of Richard III—not to mention gifts and graces that stem more from certain of Shakespeare's heroines than from his heroes—for, like Rosalind, that inimitable boy-girl, Hamlet is an early draft of a new creature on the Platonic order, conceived in the *Upanishads*, who begins to synthesize the sexes. "He who understands the masculine and keeps to the feminine shall become the whole world's channel. Eternal virtue shall not depart from him and he shall return to the state of an infant." If Hamlet does not attain the consummation that Laotse thus describes, he at least gives promise of it. What wonder that actresses have played his role, or that among the theories about him one of the most inevitable, if most insane, is that he is a woman in disguise! Mad literally, the idea embodies a symbolic truth and helps explain why Hamlet has been pronounced both a hero and a dreamer, hard and soft, cruel and gentle, brutal and angelic, like a lion and like a dove. One by one these judgments are all wrong. Together they are all right—

These contraries such unity do hold,

a line which those who object to such paradoxes as "modernizing" should note is Shakespeare's, as is also the phrase "mighty opposites."

For what was such a man made? Plainly for the ultimate things: for wonder, for curiosity and the pursuit of truth, for love, for creation—but first of all for freedom, the condition of the other four. He was made, that is, for religion and philosophy,[1] for love and art, for liberty to "grow unto himself"—five forces that are the elemental enemies of Force.

And this man is called upon to kill. It is almost as if Jesus had been asked to play the role of Napoleon (as the temptation in the wilderness suggests that in some sense he was). If Jesus had been, ought he to have accepted it? The absurdity of the question prompts the recording of the strangest of all the strange facts in the history of *Hamlet*: the fact, namely, that nearly all readers, commentators, and critics are agreed in thinking that it was Hamlet's duty to kill, that he ought indeed to have killed much sooner than he did. His delay, they say, was a weakness and disaster, entailing, as it did, many unintended deaths, including his own. He should have obeyed much earlier the Ghost's injunction to avenge his father's murder. "Surely it is clear," says Bradley, giving expression to this idea for a multitude of others, "that, whatever we in the twentieth century may think about Hamlet's duty, we are meant in the play to assume that he *ought* to have obeyed the Ghost." "As for the morality of personal vengeance," says Hazelton Spencer, "however abhorrent the concept we must accept it in the play as Hamlet's sacred duty, just as we must accept the Ghost who urges it." "John-a-dreams tarried long," says Dover Wilson at the end of *What Happens in Hamlet*, "but this Hercules 'sweeps' to his revenge." And with plain approval he pronounces Hamlet's "task accomplished," his "duty now performed."

Now whatever we are "meant" to assume, there is no doubt that nearly every spectator and reader the first time he encounters the play does assume that Hamlet ought to kill the King—and nearly all continue in that opinion on further acquaintance in the face of the paradox just stated.

How can that be?

It can be for the same reason that we exult when Gratiano cries, "Now, infidel, I have thee on the hip," and we see Shylock get what he was about to give, for the same reason that we applaud when Romeo sends Tybalt to death, and are enthralled by Henry V's rant before Harfleur or his injunction to his soldiers to imitate the action of the tiger. It can be because we all have stored up within ourselves so many unrequited wrongs and injuries, forgotten and unforgotten, and beneath these such an inheritance of racial revenge, that we like nothing better than to rid ourselves of a little of the accumulation by projecting it, in a crowd of persons similarly disposed, on the defenseless puppets of the dramatic imagination. There is no mystery about it. Anyone can follow the effect along his own backbone.

But if we are all repositories of racial revenge, we are also repositories of the rarer tendencies that over the centuries have resisted revenge. Against the contagion of a theater audience these ethereal forces have practically no chance, for in the crowd we are bound to take the play as drama rather than as poetry. But in solitude and in silence these forces are sure to lead a certain number of sensitive readers to shudder at the thought of Hamlet shedding blood. Let them express their revulsion, however, and instantly there will be someone to remind them that, whatever may be true now, "in those days" blood revenge was an accepted part of the moral code. As if Shakespeare were a historian and not a poet!

"Those days" never existed. They never existed poetically, I mean. No doubt the code of the vendetta has prevailed in many ages in many lands and revenge has been a favorite theme of the poets from Homer down. History itself, as William James remarked, has been a bath of blood. Yet there is a sense in which the dictum "Thou shalt not kill" has remained just as absolute in the kingdom of the imagination as in the Mosaic law. Moralize bloodshed by custom, legalize it by the state, camouflage it by romance, and still to the finer side of human nature it is just bloodshed; and always where poetry has become purest and risen highest there has been some parting of Hector and Andromache, some lament of the Trojan women, to show that those very deeds of vengeance and martial glory that the poet himself is ostensibly glorifying have somehow failed to utter the last word. To utter that last word—or try to—is poetry's ultimate function, to defend man against his own brutality, against

> That monster, custom, who all sense doth eat,
> Of habits devil,

a much emended line-and-a-half of *Hamlet* that makes excellent sense exactly as it stands.

If Shakespeare was bent in this play on presenting the morality of a primitive time, why did he make the mistake of centering it around a man who in endowment is as far ahead of either the Elizabethan age or our own as the code of blood revenge is behind both? "The ultimate fact is," says J. M. Robertson, "that Shakespeare *could not* make a psychologically or otherwise consistent play out of a plot which retained a strictly barbaric action while the hero was transformed into a supersubtle Elizabethan." *Hamlet*, the conclusion is, is a failure because the materials Shakespeare inherited were too tough and intractable. Too tough and intractable for what? That they were too tough and intractable for a credible historical picture may be readily granted. But what of it? And since when was poetry supposed to defer to history? Two world wars in three decades ought to have taught us that our history has not gone deep enough. But poetry has. The greatest poetry has always depicted the world as a little citadel of nobility threatened by an immense barbarism, a flickering candle surrounded by infinite night. The "historical" impossibility of *Hamlet* is its poetical truth, and the paradox of its central figure is the universal psychology of man.

Yet, in the face of the correspondingly universal fascination that both the play and its hero have exercised, T. S. Eliot can write: "*Hamlet*, like the sonnets, is full of some stuff that the writer could not drag to light, contemplate, or manipulate into art. We must simply admit that here Shakespeare tackled a problem which proved too much for him. Why he attempted it at all is an insoluble enigma." In which case, why all this fuss over a play that failed? To reason as Eliot does is to indict the taste and intelligence of three centuries. If Hamlet is just a puzzle, why has the world not long since transferred its adulation to Fortinbras and Laertes? They, at any rate, are clear. If action and revenge were what was wanted, they understood them. The trouble is that by no stretch of the imagination can we think of Shakespeare preferring their morality to that of his hero. They are living answers to the contention that Hamlet ought to have done what either of them, in his situation, would have done instantly. For what other purpose indeed did Shakespeare put them in than to make that plain?

But Hamlet himself, it will be said, accepts the code of blood revenge. Why should we question what one we so admire embraces with such unquestioning eagerness? With such suspicious eagerness might be closer to the mark. But waiving that for the moment, let us see what is involved in the assumption that Shakespeare thought it was Hamlet's duty to kill the King.

It involves nothing less than the retraction of all the Histories, of *Romeo and Juliet* and *Julius Caesar*. Private injury, domestic feud, civil revolution, imperialistic conquest: one by one in these plays Shakespeare had demonstrated how bloodshed invoked in their name brings on the very thing it was intended to avert, how, like seeds that propagate their own kind, force begets force and vengeance vengeance. And now in *Hamlet* Shakespeare is supposed to say: "I was wrong. I take it all back. Blood should be shed to avenge blood." And more incredible yet, we must picture him a year or two later taking his new opinion back and being reconverted in turn to his original conviction in *Othello*, *Macbeth*, *King Lear*, and the rest. If you find a term in a mathematical series fitting perfectly between what has gone before and what follows, you naturally assume it is in its right place, as you do a piece that fits into the surrounding pieces in a jigsaw puzzle. Only on the assumption that Hamlet ought not to have killed the King can the play be fitted into what then becomes the unbroken progression of Shakespeare's spiritual development. The only other way out of the difficulty for those who do not themselves believe in blood revenge is to hold that Shakespeare in *Hamlet* is an archeologist or anthropologist interested in the customs of primitive society rather than a poet concerned with the eternal problems of man. (...)

## IV

In the notes Dostoevsky made when composing *The Brothers Karamazov* there is one especially remarkable revelation: the fact that in its earliest stages the hero, who was to become Alyosha, is identified with the hero of a previous novel, *The Idiot*, being even called the Idiot by name. It shows how akin to the dream the creative faculty is—one character splitting off from another. What was at first a vague differentiation ends as a distinct individual, but an individual always bearing traces of his origin, as traces of the parent can be found in the child and in the man.

Shakespeare is not Dostoevsky, and it is not likely that an early draft of *Hamlet* will ever be found in which the Prince's name is first set down as Brutus. Yet there is a bit of dialogue in the play as we have it that links the two almost as intimately as Alyosha is linked with Prince Myshkin. The passage is brief and apparently parenthetical. Shortly before the performance of *The Murder of Gonzago*, Hamlet suddenly addresses Polonius:

HAM.: My lord, you played once i' the university, you say?
POL.: That did I, my lord, and was accounted a good actor.
HAM.: What did you enact?
POL.: I did enact Julius Caesar: I was killed i' the Capitol;
Brutus killed me.
HAM.: It was a brute part of him to kill so capital a calf there.

It is interesting, to begin with, that Polonius was accounted a good actor in his youth. He has been playing a part ever since, until his mask has become a part of his face. The roles that men cast themselves for often reveal what they are and may prophesy what they will become. That Polonius acted Julius Caesar characterizes both men: Caesar, the synonym of imperialism, Polonius, the petty domestic despot—the very disparity of their kingdoms makes the comparison all the more illuminating.

But it is not just Caesar and Polonius. Brutus is mentioned too. And Brutus killed Caesar. In an hour or so Hamlet is to kill Polonius. If Polonius is Caesar, Hamlet is Brutus. This is the rehearsal of the deed. For to hate or scorn is to kill a little. "It was a brute part ... to kill so capital a calf there." The unconscious is an inveterate punster and in that "brute part" Hamlet passes judgment in advance on his own deed in his mother's chamber. Prophecy, rehearsal, judgment: was ever more packed into fewer words?[2] *Et tu*, Hamlet?

And it is not Brutus only who stands behind Hamlet. There is another behind him. And another behind *him*.

A third is like the former....
A fourth! start, eyes!
What! will the line stretch out to the crack of doom?
Another yet!

We need not follow it as far as did Macbeth to perceive that, as Hamlet listens to the spirit of his father, behind him are the ghosts of Brutus, Hal, and Romeo. "Beware, Hamlet," says Romeo, "my soul told me to embrace Juliet and with her all the Capulets. But my 'father' bade me kill Tybalt and carry on the hereditary quarrel. And I obeyed him." "Beware, Hamlet," says Hal, "my soul told me to hold fast to Falstaff's love of life. But, instead, I did what is expected of a king, rejected Falstaff, and following my dying father's advice, made war on France." "Beware, Hamlet," says Brutus, "Portia and my soul gave ample warning. But Cassius reminded me that there was once a Brutus who expelled a tyrant from Rome, and, in the name of 'our fathers,' tempted me to exceed him in virtue by killing one. And I did. Beware, Hamlet." Each of these men wanted to dedicate himself to life. Romeo wanted to love. Hal wanted to play. Brutus wanted to read philosophy. But in each case a commanding hand was placed on the man's shoulder that disputed the claim of life in the name of death. Romeo defied that command for a few hours, and then circumstances proved too strong for him. Hal evaded it for a while, and then capitulated utterly. Brutus tried to face the issue, with the result of civil war within himself. But death won. Brutus' suppressed compunctions, however, ejected themselves in the form of a ghost that, Delphically, was both Caesar and Brutus' own evil spirit, his reliance on force.

Hamlet is the next step. He is a man as much more spiritually gifted than Brutus as Brutus is than Hal. The story of Hamlet is the story of Hal over again, subtilized, amplified, with a different ending. The men themselves seem so unlike that the similarities of their situations and acts are obscured. Like Hal, Hamlet is a prince of charming quality who cares nothing at the outset for his royal prospects but is absorbed in playing and savoring life. Only with him it is playing in a higher sense: dramatic art, acting, and playwriting rather than roistering in taverns and perpetrating practical jokes. And, like all men genuinely devoted to art, he is deeply interested in philosophy and religion, drawing no sharp lines indeed between or among the three. Because he is himself an imaginative genius, he needs no Falstaff to spur him on. Hamlet is his own Falstaff.

Hamlet's father, like Hal's, was primarily concerned with war, and after death calls his son to a deed of violence, not to imperial conquest, as the elder Henry did, but to revenge. Like Hal, Hamlet accepts the injunction. But instead of initiating a change that gradually alters him into his father's likeness,the decision immediately shakes his being to its foundations. The "antic disposition" under which he hides his real design is an exaggerated counterpart of the "wildness" under which Hal had previously concealed his own political ambition—however much less selfish and better grounded Hamlet's deception was.

The far more shattering effect on Hamlet than on Hal or even on Brutus of the task he assumes shows how much more nearly balanced are the opposing forces in his case. Loyalty to his father and the desire to grow unto himself—thirst for revenge and thirst for creation—are in Hamlet almost in equilibrium, though of course he does not know it. Henry V was vaguely troubled by nocturnal stirrings of the spirit He saw no ghost. Brutus became the victim of insomnia. He stifled his conscience by action and saw no ghost until after the deed. Hamlet saw his before the deed—as Brutus would have if his soul had been stronger—and it made night hideous for him. No spirit but one from below would have produced that effect, and the fact that "this fellow in the cellarage" speaks from under the platform when he echoes Hamlet's "swear" is in keeping with Shakespeare's frequent use of the symbolism that associates what is physically low with what is morally wrong. Hamlet's delay, then, instead of giving ground for condemnation, does him credit. It shows his soul is still alive and will not submit to the demands of the father without a struggle. If two forces pulling a body in opposite directions are unequal, the body will move in response to the preponderant force. If the two are nearly equal, but alternately gain slight ascendancy, it will remain unmoved except for corresponding vibrations. In a tug of war between evenly matched teams the rope at first is almost motionless, but ultimately the strength of one side ebbs and then the rope moves suddenly and violently. So mysterious, and no more, is Hamlet's hesitation, followed, as it finally was, by lightning-like action. "Shakespeare, as everyone knows," says Dover Wilson, "never furnishes an explanation for Hamlet's inaction." "No one knows," says Professor Alden, "why Hamlet delays." And many others have said the same. Yet Shakespeare puts in the mouth of Claudius words that seem expressly inserted to explain the riddle. The King, caught in the same way between opposing forces—desire to keep the fruits of his sin and desire to pray—declares:

> And, like a man to double business bound,
> I stand in pause where I shall first begin,
> And both neglect.

That seems plain enough. But what is true of Claudius in this one scene is true of Hamlet during all the earlier part of the play. It is as if his soul were a body in space so delicately poised between the gravitation of the earth and, the gravitation, or we might say the levitation, of the sun that it "hesitates" whether to drop into the one or fly up to the other. It sometimes seems as if *Homo sapiens* were in just that situation.

People who think Shakespeare was just a playwright say Hamlet delayed that there might be a five-act play! Others, who calmly neglect much of the text, say he delayed because of external obstacles. Coleridge thinks it was because he thought too much. Bradley, because he was so melancholy.[3]

It would be nearer the truth to say he thought too much and was melancholy because he delayed. The more powerful an unconscious urge, the stronger and the more numerous the compensations and rationalizations with which consciousness attempts to fight it. Hence the excess of thought and feeling. Goethe, I would say, is far closer to the mark than Coleridge and Bradley in attributing Hamlet's hesitation to a feminine element in the man. But then he proceeds to spoil it all by implying that Hamlet is weak and effeminate: "a lovely, pure and most moral nature, without the strength of nerve that makes a hero, sinks beneath a burden which it cannot bear and must not cast away." The implication is that Hamlet ought to have killed the King at once; also that loveliness, purity, and moral insight are not sources of strength and heroism!

On the contrary, they are the very higher heroism that challenges a more primitive one in this play. Hamlet is the battlefield where the two meet. It is war in that psychological realm where all war begins. Hamlet is like Thermopylae, the battle that stands first among all battles in the human imagination because of its symbolic quality—a contest between the Persian hordes of the lower appetites and the little Greek band of heroic instincts.

They have the numbers, we, the heights.

At Thermopylae the Persians won. Yet we think of it as a Greek victory because it was the promise of Salamis and Plataea. So with Hamlet. Hamlet lost. But *Hamlet* is the promise of *Othello* and *King Lear*.

## V

Is it the death of Hamlet's father or the marriage of his mother that has plumed their soil into the depressed state in which we find him at the opening of the play? Obviously the two are too closely associated in his mind to permit their separation. One is the seed, the other is the soil, of all that follows.

Freud made the suggestion that the killing of the Elder Hamlet and the marriage of the murderer with Hamlet's mother were realizations of Hamlet's own repressed childish wishes. His condition when the action begins would be accounted for, then, by the workings of incestuous fantasy. And later, when he learns of the murder from the Ghost, the nephew cannot kill the uncle because he recognizes in him the image of his own desire. Dr. Ernest Jones has written an extended interpretation of the play founded on these ideas.[4]

"*The main theme of this story*," says Dr. Jones, summing up his thesis in italics, "*is a highly elaborated and disguised account of a boy's love for his mother and consequent jealousy of and hatred towards his father.*" Whatever truth there may be in this view, it is certainly superfluous to posit any such pathological love to account for Hamlet's state of mind when the play opens. His father has died under mysterious circumstances, so mysterious that when the Ghost reveals the murder Hamlet cries, "O my prophetic soul!" as if he had already suspected the guilt of his uncle, an exclamation that immediately reminds us of his earlier:

> I doubt some foul play: would the night were come!
> Till then sit still, my soul: foul deeds will rise,
> Though all the earth o'erwhelm them, to men's eyes.

Before Hamlet has had time to recover from the shock of his father's death, his mother, with unseemly haste, marries his uncle. Even without the stigma of incest which such a union then carried, the impact of this disaster on top of the other is enough to explain the disillusionment and near-suicidal mood of a youth as sensitive as Hamlet, a son as devoted to his mother. Stunned by the double blow, he is halted dead in his tracks. Blocked by the double obstruction, his life energy flows backward and floods his mind with images of disintegration and death. If it is not sustained too long, there is nothing morbid in such a reaction. Who would have had as rare a man as Hamlet take these thing's casually or callously, or even stoically—not to mention taking them pugnaciously as Laertes and Fortinbras took the deaths of their fathers? All we know of what Hamlet was before his father's murder suggests that any abnormality in the man was on the side of genius and the future rather than on that of degeneracy and the past. That prolongation of "infancy" which is the special mark and glory of human nature (as Shakespeare himself shows in *Venus and Adonis*) is at the opposite pole from that pathological reversion to infancy that is a sign of the Oedipus complex. How many a genius has owed to a love of his mother preservation from too early initiation into sexual experience. This may well have been the case with Hamlet. But that his attachment to his mother was neither too strong nor too prolonged is indicated, first, by his friendship with Horatio, and second, by his falling in love with Ophelia—a girl of very different temperament from his mother— apparently at just the right time. If Hamlet had been a victim of the Oedipus complex, and the play a highly elaborated and disguised account of a boy's love for his mother, such a transference of his affections would have been unthinkable.

But the trouble with the psychoanalytic interpretation of *Hamlet* lies not so much in what it includes as in what it omits. What would we think of a study of *Romeo and Juliet* that traced everything in the play to the hereditary quarrel between the two houses? Every statement in such an analysis might be correct *as far as it went*, yet it would be destined in advance to miss the secret of the play because it would leave out the love of Romeo and Juliet as an autonomous and creative flame. The same is true of an analysis of *Hamlet* that makes an even more extreme sacrifice of the present and future to the past, that traces everything to the hero's infantile fantasies and has nothing to say of his imagination. The players and the play within the play figure scarcely at all in Jones's interpretation of the drama. But they are the heart of the whole matter. As well write a biography of Shakespeare and leave out his interest in dramatic art! It is like trying to explain the earth without taking the sun into account.

Here is the greatest character in all literature—or so at least many have called him. Here is the Shakespearean character who most resembles Shakespeare, the only one, as Bradley has observed, whom we can conceive of as the author of Shakespeare's plays. But to Freudian analysis all that is apparently nothing. And when it has done its probing work what is revealed? Not a genius who made an effort to transcend the morality of his time with thoughts beyond the reaches of his soul, but a mind reduced to its most infantile impulses, a body pushed about by the most primitive biological drives.

That these drives are present deep down in Hamlet as they are in all of us need not be denied. That Hamlet was ultimately overthrown by his instincts may not only be granted but should be insisted on. But the fact of interest is that he was conquered only after a protracted struggle. About this the Freudians have practically nothing to say. Jones does indeed speak of Hamlet's "desperate struggle" against Fate. But when we search his essay for an account of that struggle it turns out to be nothing but the struggle of a trapped animal. Hamlet's dramatic battle, which is a symbolic embodiment of the perennial attempt of life, in the face of the forces that would drag it backward, to ascend to a higher level, the Freudian interpretation reduces to nothing but the picture of a man foredoomed to destruction. If this be so, *Hamlet* may indeed be a supreme treatise on pathology. But it is no longer drama, let alone poetry.

Lucifer is the archetype of all tragic heroes. He fell. The fascination of his fate lies not in the fact that he fell, but in the fact that he who fell was the light-bearer—that his light, before he fell, was transformed into pride. What he did in hell is significant only because he was once an inhabitant of heaven. So with all tragic heroes. So with Hamlet. He too was a light-bearer ("in action how like an angel! in apprehension how like a god!"). His mind was focused on philosophy, on religion, and on art—regions into which something that stands above and is wiser than physical life has long been trying to channel the blind urgencies of selfish will and sex. Is it not immeasurably more in keeping with the character of such a man to attribute his aversion to sensuality and blood to these loftier aspirations of his soul than to primordial and atavistic instincts—to believe that he drew back from the killing of his uncle because he did not want to degrade himself to his level by becoming a murderer than to think he hesitated because he saw in him an image of his own incestuous fantasies?

It has been argued that if repugnance to the act of killing had been the ground of Hamlet's hesitation he would have been conscious of the reason for his delay.[5] But this is to forget the atmospheric pressure to which his mind was subjected. New moralities do not spring into existence in the face of entrenched custom in full-fledged conscious and conceptual form. They begin in dumb feelings around the heart ("thou wouldst not think how ill all's here about my heart") and in momentary gleams of the imagination. What person of any sensitiveness looking back on his childhood cannot remember some occasion when he conformed to the morality of the crowd against the un-understood protests of what only long after he recognized was his own higher nature—or when possibly he did *not* conform, but instead of taking pride in what was an act of courage lashed himself inwardly for what he supposed was abject cowardice? Hamlet was like that. If he was indeed trying to repudiate the morals of his herd, it is absurd to suppose that he opposed to them a clear-cut moral theory of his own. What he opposed to them was a combined imaginative courage and unconscious compassion that embrace the strongest and the tenderest elements of his nature.

To the Freudians, Hamlet's hesitation comes from a literal jealousy of his father and a literal love of his mother. He wants to kill his uncle because he recognizes him as a rival for the possession of his mother. But he also does not want to kill him, because he recognizes in him an image, of his own desire. Hence he hesitates. But one can argue just as cogently that Hamlet wants to kill his uncle because he has murdered the father whom Hamlet as a youth has idealized and loved. But also he does not want to kill him, because he would thereby be converting himself into an image of the father whose life was dedicated to violence and whom he therefore, unconsciously hates—and at the same time into an image of his murderer-uncle. Hence he hesitates. Logically the one argument is as good as the other. But poetically and pragmatically there is simply no comparison between them, so much more creative and enlightening is the second. When the facts of a dream make it susceptible of either of two interpretations, how foolish the dreamer would be not to believe the one that makes for the richer unfolding of his own life. Our choice between two interpretations of a work of art, provided they are equally faithful to the text, should be similarly determined.

How much more illuminating to translate all this about Hamlet's "love" and "hatred," about his "father" and "mother," from crudely sexual into symbolic terms, thus giving the future as well as the past a share in their meaning: Hamlet's "mother" is then on one side his creativeness (for whoever gives birth to new life, as the artist does, is a mother) and on the other side his sensuality. The one he loves; the other he loathes. We see him in the play fluctuating between the two. And he responds in a similarly ambivalent way to his two "fathers." One, his sun and the source of his inspiration, is the product of that idealization of the older generation by the younger which ensures the continuity and, in so far as it is justified, the uplifting of life. This father Hamlet worships. The other is a type of that authority and violence that the racial father always represents and that his own father as renowned warrior (pirate in the original version) specifically' incarnates. This father, however unconsciously, Hamlet abhors.

A full half of this picture the Freudian interpretation calmly omits. To it the dice are perpetually loaded on the side of the past. To it the flower is nothing but a differentiated root, and the tragic mysteries of Hamlet nothing but his infantile fantasies in disguise. What a "nothing but"! Echoing it, we may well say that a psychology that is contented with it is "nothing but" the last variation of that ancient and mildewed view that would make the universe itself "nothing but" a vortex of atoms. "Look you, this brave o'erhanging firmament, this majestical roof fretted with golden fire, why, it appears no other thing to me but a foul and pestilent congregation of vapours." There is Hamlet himself in a "nothing but" mood! But it is nothing but a fragment of Hamlet! It is Hamlet at his most abject, the Hamlet who went on down into Macbeth with his ultimate belief that life is nothing but a tale told by an idiot, full of sound and fury, signifying nothing. So is the Freudian interpretation of *Hamlet Hamlet* at its most abject. It is a reduction of the tremendous battle between spirit and the instincts, wherein the drama of life consists, to the spectacle of the mere writhings of a predestined victim.

If there is any truth in all this, it is as if Hamlet, of all characters in literature, were specifically created *not* to be understood by the Freudian psychology. For the things closest to Hamlet's heart are precisely the ones that Freud dismisses as mere by-products of the evolutionary process. Art, Freud declares, "does not seek to be anything else but an illusion." Philosophy is an interest of only a small number of "the thin upper stratum of intellectuals." Religion is nothing but an attempt to replace reality by a wish-world: "the truth of religion may be altogether disregarded." So are Laotse and Jesus, Plato and Aristotle, Homer and Dante, Michelangelo and Rembrandt, Bach and Beethoven wiped off the slate, as it were, in a single stroke. Talk about substituting a wish-world for reality! If Hamlet could have heard, would he not have exclaimed

> There are more things in heaven and earth, dear Sigmund,
> Than are dreamt of in your psychology.

"Shakespeare is a great psychologist," said Goethe, "and whatever can be known of the heart of man may be found in his plays." Yet the Freudians would have it that this great psychologist was unaware of the main meaning of what not a few consider his greatest play, that he projected that meaning on his material because of some hidden analogy in it to a situation in his own life. If this be so, we shall be compelled to ask whether Shakespeare himself was not mad. If this be so, we shall be put to it to explain Coriolanus—one of the most searching and obviously conscious accounts in all literature of a son under the unduly prolonged influence of his mother. And Coriolanus is not the only play that makes us wonder whether Shakespeare, though he had never heard of the super-ego and the id, may not have known as much in his own way about the deeper strata of the human mind as Freud himself. It is the familiar confusion of terminology with knowledge—a confusion that makes each age think it has discovered the truth for the first time because it has a new nomenclature in which to dress it. The unconsciousness of ignorance must be discriminated from the unconsciousness of genius, the unconsciousness of deficient mind, of which there is not a trace in Shakespeare, from the unconsciousness of superabundant imagination in which he abounds. It was in that latter unconsciousness indeed that Thoreau found the heart of the "Shakespeare miracle." If Shakespeare did not know what he was doing in *Hamlet*, we would at least like to know what he thought he was doing, and, even more, what his imagination *was* doing. ( ... )

## VIII

> From the moment when Hamlet cries:
> The time is out of joint; O cursed spite,
> That ever I was born to set it right!

he becomes an example, unequalled in modern literature until Dostoevsky, of the Divided Man. "God and the Devil are fighting there, and the battlefield is the heart of man." That sentence of Dmitri Karamazov's expresses it, and because the infernal and celestial powers that are contending for the possession of Hamlet are so nearly in balance, the torture is prolonged and exquisite. He alternates between phases of anguished thought and feverish activity. Hence, as the one mood or the other is stressed, the opposing theories of his character. Hamlet is like a drunken man and you cannot determine where he is going from his direction at any one moment. He lurches now to the right, now to the left. He staggers from passion to apathy, from daring to despair. To select his melancholy as the key to his conduct, as Bradley does, is to offer the drunkard's fall as an explanation of his drunkenness. It is taking the effect for the cause, or fooling one's self, as Polonius did, with a word:

> Your noble son is mad:
> Mad call I it; for, to define true madness,
> What is't but to be nothing else but mad?
> But let that go.

Shakespeare is content with no such solution. To him melancholy is a symptom. He insists on getting under it to the cause that makes his melancholy characters melancholy.

Shakespeare dissects the cases of two such men, Richard II and Antonio, at length, two others, Jaques and Orsino, more briefly, and gives us a glimpse into the melancholy stage of still another, Brutus. Melancholy, he concludes in all these instances, is a sign that a man is living or trying to live a miscast, partial, or obstructed life—is functioning far under his capacity or against the grain of his nature. Richard II was a poetic soul attempting to enact a royal role. Antonio was a man made for better things who dedicated his life to trade. In *As You Like It* and *Twelfth Night* the record is not so complete, but it is sufficient. Jaques was a philosophic nature that had wasted itself in sensuality, Orsino an artistically gifted person who led an idle life. Brutus stifled his melancholy in action. He was a rare man who reverted to what any common ruffian can do—stab with a knife. There is no resisting so many instances.

Does the same diagnosis fit Hamlet? Obviously it does.

If these others were exceptional, Hamlet was as much one man among millions as Shakespeare was. He had precisely Shakespeare's interest in acting, playmaking, and drama. What if Shakespeare had turned from writing *Hamlets* and *King Lears* to go to war like Essex, or, like Hamlet, to run his rapier through an old man behind a curtain! What if Beethoven had fought with Napoleon instead of composing the *Eroica*! That, *mutatis mutandis*, is what Hamlet did. He did not know it. But his soul supplied plenty of evidence to that effect, if only he had had the power to read it.

We all hate in others the faults of which we are unaware in ourselves. And men of high endowment who are not doing what nature made them for exhibit this tendency in conspicuous degree.

He that is giddy thinks the world turns round.

In that line Shakespeare caught in a striking image this propensity of the mind to project its unconscious contents. As early as *The Rape of Lucrece* he had written:

Men's faults do seldom to themselves appear;
Their own transgressions partially they smother:
This guilt would seem death-worthy in thy brother,

and in the 121st sonnet:

No, I am that I am, and they that level
At my abuses reckon up their own:
I may be straight, though they themselves be bevel;
By their rank thoughts my deeds must not be shown.

Plainly Shakespeare had not merely observed this psychological effect in isolated instances. He understood it as a principle.

Now the moment we put Hamlet to this test we perceive that those around him become looking glasses in which, unknown to himself, his secret is reflected. (And this is particularly fitting in a work through which the symbol of the looking glass runs like a leitmotiv and whose central scene consists in the holding-up of a dramatic mirror in the form of a play within the play.)

To begin with, because Hamlet is trying to force himself to obey orders from his father to do something that his soul abhors, he hates with equal detestation those who issue orders and those who obey them, particularly fathers and children. This is plainly a main reason why Shakespeare allots to Polonius and his family so important a part in the play. Each of them seems expressly created to act as a mirror of some aspect of Hamlet. Polonius is a domestic tyrant wreaking on his son and his daughter revenge for his own spoiled life. His wife is dead, and except for one unrevealing allusion by her son, we are told nothing about her. Yet there she is! How she lived and what she died of we can readily imagine. As for Laertes, governments that want pugnacity in the younger generation should study his upbringing and act accordingly. But Ophelia is different. She is one more inexplicable daughter of her father (there are so many in Shakespeare). She is a mere child, just awakening into womanhood, and she unquestionably gives a true account of Hamlet's honorable "tenders of affection" to her. But Polonius fancies that Hamlet must be what he himself was at the same age ("I do know") and in the scene in which we are first introduced to Ophelia we see first Laertes, aping his father, and then Polonius himself, pouring poison in her ear. Both brother and father fasten on her like insects on an opening rosebud.

Who plucks the bud before one leaf put forth?

It is like an echo of *Venus and Adonis* with the sexes reversed, the first step on the journey of which Ophelia's madness and death are the last. "Do not believe his vows." "I shall obey, my lord."

Who can doubt—what juxtapositions Shakespeare achieves!—that this scene was written to be placed just before the one between Hamlet and the Ghost? There another father pours poison of another kind into the ear of a son as innocent in his way as Polonius' daughter was in hers. The temptation this time is not to sensuality under the name of purity but to violence under the name of honor. It is Romeo's temptation as contrasted with Juliet's. The parallel is startling.

We tend to hate anyone we obey against the grain of our nature. "I'll shoot you!" says the small boy to his father, giving vent to his instincts. But after childhood, when anyone we love exacts obedience, unless we can forgive we suppress the hatred and to that extent become divided within. ("Who does not desire to kill his father?" says Ivan Karamazov.) Hamlet knows that he loved his father when he was alive. He does not know how he abhors that father when, dead, he orders him to kill. But any despotism is a kind of killing, and so he projects his abhorrence on another father who exacts obedience. How otherwise can we account for Hamlet's treatment of Polonius? After all, he was the father of the girl Hamlet loved. Stupidity and morality, it may be said, are always fair game for intelligence and virtue. And when Hamlet begins to suspect the father's part in the daughter's infidelity, it is easy to see how he could come to hate him. But even this does not explain the rattlesnake-like venom with which he strikes the old man at every opportunity. As in the case of Antonio's loathing of Shylock, only buried forces that Hamlet does not comprehend can account for it. Hamlet thinks he is pillorying Polonius, when, really, his insults are directed at the Ghost and himself, just as, later, he kills Polonius with the sword he thinks he is thrusting at the King. Scorn is a diluted form of murder.

Take one example. Hamlet has urged Guildenstern to play upon a pipe. Guildenstern has begged off: "I have not the skill." Whereupon Hamlet rebukes him for trying to make *him* a pipe to be played on. Polonius enters, and Hamlet proceeds to show how easily this yes-man can be played on by getting him to admit, in quick succession, that the same cloud resembles now a camel, now a weasel, and now a whale. Since the cloud doubtless resembled none of the three in any marked degree, what Hamlet pretended to see in it was the result of free association on his part. But free association is a basic method of modern analytical psychology for bringing to the surface the contents of the unconscious mind. A camel, a weasel, and a whale! A camel—the beast that bears burdens. A weasel—an animal noted for its combined wiliness and ferocity and for the fact that it can capture and kill snakes (remember the royal serpent!). A whale—a mammal that returned to a lower element and so still has to come to the surface of it occasionally for air, not a land creature, to be sure, nor yet quite a sea creature. What an astonishing essay on Hamlet in three words! (It is things like these that tempt one at moments to think that Shakespeare was omniscient.) This Prince piped on Polonius by his gibing experiment. What or who was piping upon him?

But Hamlet reads his own experience into Ophelia as well as into Polonius. Only in this case he knows what he is doing—up to a certain point. As unconsciously he sees the image of his father in the father, so consciously he sees the image of his mother in the daughter. That mother was false to his father. That daughter, he suspects, is false to him—if not in just the same sense. "Frailty, thy name is woman!" But Ophelia is not even a frail woman. She is still a child who obeys her father. She and Hamlet are two children who dare not trust the instinct to disobey. But this analogy he does not catch. And so, while he heaps conscious scorn on her for being like his mother, the unconscious scorn he heaps on her for being like himself is far more bitter. Read in this light, the nunnery scene is a revelation—not of Ophelia's but of Hamlet's soul. "I have heard of your paintings too, well enough; God hath given you one face, and you make yourselves another." There in a sentence is Hamlet's perfect indictment of himself for betraying the God within him (a reason why a main theme of this scene is prostitution). For who has made himself another face than the one God gave him if not this man who has put on an antic disposition to hide his revenge? His fierce onslaught on woman in general in this scene is motivated by his perfidy to the feminine element in his own nature. "Your everlasting attacks on female logic, lying, weakness and so on—doesn't it all look like a desire at all costs to force woman down into the mud that she may be on the same level as your attitude toward her?" The quotation is from Chekhov's *An Anonymous Story*, but it fits the nunnery scene as if it had been written about it.

Now all this only re-enforces what of course goes without saying: that Hamlet's treatment of Ophelia is profoundly affected by his attitude toward his mother. But for Gertrude's infidelity all might have been well—in spite of Polonius. Because of that infidelity, Hamlet's ideal of woman totters. And when Ophelia fails him, it falls. Deprived of its object, unless it can immediately find another, a love that believes itself deluded tends to revert to lust or violence, or both. Hamlet was no fickle lover to find another Ophelia overnight. And so he sinks into his instinctive nature. It is only in this generic sense that Hamlet loves his "mother" abnormally, a "loves" that might more accurately be written "loathes." His self-loathing is conspicuous not only in the nunnery scene, but in his conduct toward Ophelia at the play, and in the scene in his mother's closet. His "Get thee to a nunnery!" is a cry to his own polluted soul to purify itself, or, if "nunnery" be taken in its jocose Elizabethan sense, his notice to that soul that it is lost. His words to Ophelia at the play grate on the ear as do no others in his entire role. That Hamlet should descend to the level of Laertes is bad enough. But he goes below it. Here he actually pushes Ophelia toward the abyss of madness and the grave. It is from his coarsest utterance to her that Shakespeare has him pass instantaneously to his command to the murderer (Lucianus) to "begin." From sensuality to blood. And it is from Ophelia's side, when the play is broken up, that he goes to his mother's closet to brand her for an act that

> takes off the rose
> From the fair forehead of an innocent love
> And sets a blister there,

a perfect description of what he himself has just done, and enough in itself to show that his excoriations of his mother in this scene are unconscious denunciations of himself. (Of that more in its place.) What soil all this is for the seed of violence! Shakespeare seems to have agreed with Dostoevsky that "a cruel sensuality" is close to the fountainhead of all human evil whatsoever. It is "the expense of spirit in a waste of shame" of the 129th sonnet, that scorching poem that packs into fourteen lines all the poet had had to say on the subject in *Venus and Adonis* and *The Rape of Lucrece*:[6]

> perjur'd, murderous, bloody, full of blame,
> Savage, extreme, rude, cruel, not to trust.

The adjectives fit war or murder. Actually they are applied to lust. The union of cruelty and sensuality is one marriage to which the partners seem to have remained faithful down the ages.

Even at the risk of supererogation, one further example of Hamlet's tendency to project himself must be added. Of all the glasses that catch his image in the play none, oddly, is more revealing than that held up by Rosencrantz and Guildenstern. They are the Tweedledee and Tweedledee of the genteel world and their very nonentity makes them perfect reflecting surfaces. It is their function to be nothing except what they give back from

the world around them. They are conformists. They follow the prevailing
mode. They contaminate their friendship for Hamlet by obeying the King
when he invites them to be spies. But what is Hamlet himself doing but
obeying another king and following another mode in accepting the code of
blood revenge? Moral customs may be quite as corrupting as worldly
fashions, and it may be as fatal to surrender one's will to a royal ghost as to a
flesh-and-blood sovereign. This unperceived analogy is unquestionably the
ground of Hamlet's devastating contempt for these harmless fashion plates.
He scorns Guildenstern for attempting to play on him as on a pipe at the
very moment when unseen forces are playing upon him. And he is even more
savage with Rosencrantz:

| HAM.: | Besides, to be demanded of a sponge! what replication should be made by the son of a king? |
| ROS.: | Take you me for a sponge, my lord? |
| HAM.: | Ay, sir, that soaks up the king's countenance, his rewards, his authorities. But such officers do the king best service in the end: he keeps them, like an ape, in the corner of his jaw; first mouthed, to be last swallowed: when he needs what you have gleaned, it is but squeezing you, and, sponge, you shall be dry again. |
| ROS.: | I understand you not, my lord. |
| HAM.: | I am glad of it: a knavish speech sleeps in a foolish ear. |

But Hamlet's own ear is asleep. Rosencrantz may indeed have soaked up
orders to spy from a living king. But how is that worse than soaking up orders
to kill from a dead one?

All this is repeated *forte* in another key and in another octave near the
end of the play in the scene with Osric. That cockatoo of fashion and
conformity carries the same theme to the edge, but never quite over the
edge, of caricature.

## NOTES

1. Hamlet himself condemns this word as inadequate to the idea of the pursuit of
truth in his

"There are more things in heaven and earth, Horatio,
Than are dreamt of in your philosophy,"

"your philosophy" meaning, of course, not Horatio's, but philosophy in general.
2. A person interested in psychological symbols might find in "calf" an unconscious

allusion to Ophelia, at whose feet Hamlet is to lie down a moment later and whom he really kills in killing Polonius—just as Raskolnikov in *Crime and Punishment* kills the childlike Lizaveta in killing the Old Money Lender. Unlikely as this will sound to those who have never paid attention to the associative and prophetic ways of the unconscious mind, Shakespeare proves again and again that he is capable, exactly as dreams are, of just such psychological supersubtleties. Ophelia is life sacrificed before it has reached maturity.

3. I yield to no one in admiration of Bradley's *Shakespearean Tragedy* and indebtedness to it, but how little Bradley believes in his own theory of Hamlet is shown by the net of illogicality in which he entangles himself, a net that reminds one of the similar toils in which Henry V and Brutus get caught. On page 122 he says: "The action required of Hamlet is very exceptional. It is violent, dangerous, difficult to accomplish perfectly, on one side repulsive to a man of honour and sensitive feeling.... These obstacles would not suffice to prevent Hamlet from acting, if his state were normal; and against them there operate, even in his morbid state, healthy and positive feelings, love of his father, loathing of his uncle, desire of revenge, desire to do his duty." Revenge, then, and loathing, are healthy and positive feelings; also, they are on one side repulsive to a man of honor and sensitive feeling! Nothing can be made of such an argument (A. C. Bradley, *Shakespearean Tragedy* [2d ed.; Macmillan, 1929]).

4. I had not read Dr. Jones's essay when I wrote the present chapter. Apart from its intrinsic interest, the fact that the Rank-Olivier cinema production of the play has spread this conception far and wide justifies inserting a section on the subject at this point. The discussion will then be resumed as originally written.

5. Ivan Karamazov is an example of a man of high intellectual power who thought he believed in just what he really didn't believe in.

6. The detail that Tarquin was a king's son seems to have made an indelible impression on the young Shakespeare's imagination.

RICHARD A. LANHAM

# *Superposed Plays:* Hamlet

Shakespeare uses a variation on the sonnets strategy in *Hamlet*. He writes two plays in one. Laertes plays the revenge-tragedy hero straight. He does, true enough, veer toward self-parody, as when he complains that crying for Ophelia has interfered with his rants: "I have a speech o' fire, that fain would blaze / But that this folly drowns it" (4.7.189–90).[1] But he knows his generic duty and does it. No sooner has his "good old man" (Polonius's role in the straight, "serious" play) been polished off than he comes screaming with a rabble army. He delivers predictably and suitably stupid lines like "O thou vile king, / Give me my father" (4.5.115–16). And the Queen can scarcely manage a "Calmly, good Laertes" before he begins again: "That drop of blood that's calm proclaims me bastard, / Cries cuckold to my father, brands the harlot / Even here between the chaste unsmirched brows / Of my true mother" (4.5.117–20). And just before the King begins to calm him, to the villainous contentation of both: "How came he dead? I'll not be juggled with. / To hell allegiance, vows to the blackest devil, / Conscience and grace to the profoundest pit!" (4.5.130–32). He plays a straight, hard-charging revenge-hero.

Against him, Ophelia reenacts a delightfully tear-jerking madwoman stage prop. The King mouths kingly platitudes well enough ("There's such

From *The Motives of Eloquence: Literary Rhetoric in the Renaissance.* ©1976 by Richard A. Lanham.

divinity doth hedge a king ..." [4.5.123]), comes up with a suitably stagey, two-phase fail-safe plot, and urges the hero on ("Revenge should have no bounds"). And the whole comes suitably laced with moralizing guff. So the King plays a Polonius-of-the-leading-questions: "Laertes, was your father dear to you?" Laertes, with unusual common sense, returns, "Why ask you this?" And then the King is off for a dozen Polonian lines on love's alteration by time: "Not that I think you did not love your father, / But that I know love is begun by time ..." 4.7.109–10). Only then can he get back to, as he phrases it, "the quick o' th' ulcer." And the Queen plays out a careful scene on the brookside where Ophelia drowned. And wrestling in Ophelia's grave, Hamlet, annoyed at being upstaged by Laertes, protests, "I'll rant as well as thou." And, as superb finale, Laertes, at the fencing match, stands there prating about honor with the poisoned rapier in his hand. The poisoner-poisoned motif releases the Christian forgiveness that forgives us, too, for enjoying all that blood. *Hamlet* offers, then, a story frankly calculated to make the audience as well as the compositor run out of exclamation points.

Hamlet obligingly confesses himself Laertes' foil. "In mine ignorance / Your skill shall, like a star i'th'darkest night, / Stick fiery off indeed" (5.2.244–46). It is the other way about, of course. Laertes foils for Hamlet. Shakespeare is up to his old chiasmatic business, writing a play about the kind of play he is writing. The main play overlaps as well as glossing the play criticized—again, a strategy of superposition. Polonius plays a muddling old proverb-monger, and a connoisseur of language, in the Hamlet play, as well as good old man in the Laertes play. Ophelia, though sentimental from the start, is both more naive and more duplicitous in the Hamlet play; and so with the King and Queen, too, both are more complex figures. Shakespeare endeavors especially to wire the two plots in parallel: two avenging sons and two dead fathers; brother's murder and "this brother's wager"; both Hamlet and Laertes in love with Ophelia; both dishonest before the duel (Hamlet pretending more madness than he displays when he kills Polonius), and so on.

Now there is no doubt about how to read the Laertes play: straight revenge tragedy, to be taken—as I've tried to imply in my summary—without solemnity. We are to enjoy the rants as rants. When we get tears instead of a rant, as with the Laertes instance cited earlier, an apology for our disappointment does not come amiss. We are not to be caught up in Laertes' vigorous feeling any more than in Ophelia's bawdy punning. We savor it. We don't believe the fake King when he maunders on about Divine Right, the divinity that doth hedge a king. We don't "believe" anybody. It is not that kind of play. For explanation, neither the ketchup nor the verbal violence need go further than enjoyment. The more outrageous the stage effects, the more ghastly the brutality, the more grotesque the physical mutilation, the better such a play becomes. Shakespeare had done this kind of thing already and knew what he was about. Such a vehicle packed them in. Just so, when part-sales were falling, would Dickens kill a baby.

The real doubt comes when we ask, "What poetic do we bring to the Hamlet play?" As several of its students have pointed out, it is a wordy play. Eloquence haunts it. Horatio starts the wordiness by supplying a footnote from ancient Rome in the first scene, by improving the occasion with informative reflection. Everybody laughs at Polonius for his moralizing glosses but Hamlet is just as bad. Worse. Gertrude asks him, in the second scene, why he grieves to excess and he gives us a disquisition on seeming and reality in grief. The King follows with his bravura piece on grief. Everybody moralizes the pageant. The Hamlet play abounds with triggers for straight revenge-tragedy response. The whole "mystery" of Hamlet's hesitant revenge boils down to wondering why he doesn't go ahead and play his traditional part, complete with the elegant rants we know he can deliver.

The rhetorical attitude is triggered not only by obvious stylistic excess, as we have seen, or by *de trop* moralizing, but by talking about language, by surface reference to surface. This surface reference occurs at every level of the Hamlet play in *Hamlet*, as well as, of course, throughout the Laertes play. Polonius plays a main part here. His tedious prolixity ensures that we notice everyone else's tedious prolixity. And his relish of language, his speech for its own sake, makes us suspect the same appetite in others and in ourselves. The Queen's rejoinder to the marvelous "brevity is the soul of wit" speech in 2.2 could be addressed to almost anybody in the play, including the gravedigger: "More matter, with less art."

Everyone is manipulating everyone else with speechifying and then admitting he has done so. Every grand rhetorical occasion seems no sooner blown than blasted. Polonius offers the famous Gielgud encore about being true to oneself and then sends off Reynaldo to spy and tell fetching lies. The King plays king to angry Laertes then confesses to Gertrude that he has been doing just this. Ophelia is staked out to play innocent maiden so Hamlet can be drawn out and observed. *Hic et ubique.* Is she a stage contrivance or a character? What kind of audience are we to be? Everyone is an actor, Hamlet and his madness most of all. The play is full of minor invitations to attend the surface, the theme of speaking. Even the ghost has to remind himself to be brief—before continuing for thirty-odd lines (1.5). Theatrical gestures are not simply used all the time but described, as in Hamlet's inky cloak and windy suspiration for grief, or the costuming and gesture of the distracted lover, as the innocent Ophelia describes Hamlet's visit:

My lord, as I was sewing in my closet,
Lord Hamlet, with his doublet all unbraced,
No hat upon his head, his stockings fouled,
Ungartered, and down-gyved to his ankle,
Pale as his shirt, his knees knocking each other,
And with a look so piteous in purport
As if he had been loosed out of hell
To speak of horrors—he comes before me.

. . . . . . . . . . . . . . . . . . . . . . . .

He took me by the wrist and held me hard.
Then goes he to the length of all his arm,
And with his other hand thus o'er his brow
He falls to such perusal of my face
As 'a would draw it. Long stayed he so.
At last, a little shaking of mine arm
And thrice his head thus waving up and down,
He raised a sigh so piteous and profound
As it did seem to shatter all his bulk
And end his being. That done, he lets me go,
And with his head over his shoulder turned
He seemed to find his way without his eyes,
For out o'doors he went without their helps
And to the last bended their light on me.

[2.1.77–84, 87–100]

This might have come from an actor's manual. Do we take it as such, respond as professional actors?

The Hamlet play turns in on itself most obviously when the players visit. Dramatic self-consciousness retrogresses a step further as the tragedians of the city talk about themselves doing what they are just now doing in a play depicting them doing just what…. The debate is about rightful succession, of course, like both the Laertes and the Hamlet plays. "What, are they children? Who maintains 'em? How are they escorted? Will they pursue the quality no longer than they can sing? Will they not say afterwards, if they should grow themselves to common players (as it is most like, if their means are no better), their writers do them wrong to make them exclaim against their own succession?" (2.2.338–44). Who are the children in the "real" plays? Hamlet had invoked a typical cast a few lines earlier (314 ff.) such as *Hamlet* itself uses and stressed that "he that plays the king shall be welcome." Hamlet will use the play, that is, *as a weapon*, the propaganda side of rhetorical poetic, to complement the Polonius-pleasure side. But before that, there is a rehearsal, for effect, to see whether the players are good enough to play the play within the play. Here, even more clearly than in the Laertes play, we confront the connoisseur's attitude toward language. Polonius supplies a chorus that for once fits: "Fore God, my lord, well spoken, with good accent and good discretion" (2.2.454–55). This to Hamlet, a good actor, as Polonius was in his youth. They proceed in this vein, nibbling the words; "That's good. 'Mobled queen' is good."

The main question pressing is not, How does the feedback work?, What relation is there, for example, between rugged Pyrrhus and Hamlet, or Laertes? Or what relation with the King, who also topples a kingdom? And why is Hamlet so keen to reach Hecuba? The main question is, How does all this connoisseurship affect the "serious" part of *Hamlet*? *Hamlet* is one of the great tragedies. It has generated more comment than any other written document in English literature, one would guess, reverent, serious comment on it as a serious play. Yet finally can we take *any* of its rhetoric seriously? If so, how much and when? The play is full of the usual release mechanisms for the rhetorical poetic. And, at the end, the Laertes play is there as stylistic control, to mock us if we have made the naive response. But what is the sophisticated response?

Hamlet focuses the issue, and the play, the plays, when he finally gets to Hecuba. He who has been so eager for a passionate speech is yet surprised when it comes and when it seizes the player:

> O, what a rogue and peasant slave am I!
> Is it not monstrous that this player here,
> But in a fiction, in a dream of passion,
> Could force his soul so to his own conceit
> That from her working all his visage wanned,
> Tears in his eyes, distraction in his aspect,
> A broken voice, and his whole function suiting
> With forms to his conceit? And all for nothing,
> For Hecuba!
> What's Hecuba to him, or he to Hecuba,
> That he should weep for her? What would he do
> Had he the motive and the cue for passion
> That I have?
>
> [2.2.534–46]

Hamlet makes the point that dances before us in every scene. Dramatic, rhetorical motive is stronger than "real," serious motive. Situation prompts feeling in this play, rather than the other way round. Feelings are not real until played. Drama, ceremony, is always needed to authenticate experience. On the battlements Hamlet with ghostly reinforcement—makes his friends not simply swear but make a big scene of it. Laertes keeps asking for *more ceremonies* for Ophelia's burial and is upset by his father's hugger-mugger interment. Hamlet plays and then breaks off ("Something too much of this") a stoic friendship scene with Horatio in 3.2. The stronger, the more genuine the feeling, the greater the need to display it.

The answer, then, to "What would he do ...?" is, presumably, "Kill the King!"? Not at all. "He would drown the stage with tears I And cleave the general ear with horrid speech" (2.2.546–47). He would rant even better. And this Hamlet him-self, by way of illustration, goes on to do:

> Yet I,
> A dull and muddy-mettled rascal, peak
> Like John-a-dreams, unpregnant of my cause,
> And can say nothing. No, not for a king,
> Upon whose property and most dear life
> A damned defeat was made. Am I a coward?
> Who calls me villain? breaks my pate across?
> Plucks off my beard and blows it in my face?
> Tweaks me by the nose? gives me the lie i'th'throat
> As deep as to the lungs? Who does me this?
> Ha, 'swounds, I should take it, for it cannot be
> But I am pigeon-livered and lack gall
> To make oppression bitter, or ere this
> I should ha' fatted all the region kites
> With this slave's offal. Bloody, bawdy villain!
> Remorseless, treacherous, lecherous, kindless villain!
> O, vengeance!
>
> > [2.2.551–67]

Hamlet is here having a fine time dining off his own fury, relishing his sublime passion. He gets a bit confused, to be sure: saying nothing is not his problem. If somebody did call him villain or pluck his beard it would be better, for his grievance would then find some dramatic equivalent, would become real enough to act upon. But he enjoys himself thoroughly. He also sees himself clearly, or at least clearly enough to voice our opinion of his behavior: "Why, what an ass am I! This is most brave, / That I, the son of a dear father murdered, / Prompted to my revenge by heaven and hell, / Must like a whore unpack my heart with words" (2.2.568–71).

Hamlet is one of the most appealing characters the mind of man has ever created but he really is a bit of an ass, and not only here but all through the play. He remains incorrigibly dramatic. Do we like him because he speaks to our love of dramatic imposture? Because his solution, once he has seen his own posturing as such, is not immediate action but more playing? "I'll have these players / Play something like the murder of my father / Before mine uncle" (2.2.580–82). Playing is where we will find reality, find the truth. The play works, of course, tells Hamlet again what he already knows, has had a spirit come specially from purgatory to tell him. But that is not the point. Or rather, that is the point insofar as this is a serious play. The rhetorical purpose is to sustain reality until yet another dramatic contrivance—ship, grave scene, duel—can sustain it yet further.

We saw in the sonnets how a passage can invoke opaque attitudes by logical incongruity. Something of the sort happens in the scene after this speech, the "To be or not to be" centerpiece. Plays flourish within plays here, too, of course. The King and Polonius dangle Ophelia as bait and watch. Hamlet sees this. He may even be, as W. A. Bebbington suggested,[2] reading the "To be or not to be" speech from a book, using it, literally, as a stage prop to bemuse the spyers-on, convince them of his now-become-suicidal madness. No one in his right mind will fault the poetry. But it is irrelevant to anything that precedes. It fools Ophelia—no difficult matter—but it should not fool us. The question is whether Hamlet will act directly or through drama? Not at all. Instead, is he going to end it in the river? I put it thus familiarly to penetrate the serious numinosity surrounding this passage. Hamlet anatomizes grievance for all time. But does *he* suffer these grievances? He has a complaint indeed against the King and one against Ophelia. Why not do something about them instead of meditating on suicide? If the book is a stage prop, or the speech a trap for the hidden listeners, of course, the question of relevancy doesn't arise. The speech works beautifully. But we do not usually consider it a rhetorical trick. It is the most serious speech in the canon. But is it? It tells us nothing about Hamlet except what we already know—he is a good actor. Its relevance, in fact, may lurk just here. The real question by this point in the play is exactly this one: is Hamlet or not? Or does he just act? What kind of self does he possess?

The whole play, we know, seeks authenticity, reality behind the arras, things as they are. Hamlet, we are to assume, embodies the only true self, the central self amidst a cast of wicked phonies. The play, seen this way, provided a natural delight for both the Victorians and the existentialists; their sentimentalism about the central self ran the same way. Yet the question really is whether Hamlet is *to be*, to act rather than reenact. Much has been written on the Melancholy-Man-in-the-Renaissance and how his problems apply to Hamlet. Much more has been written on Hamlet's paralysis. Yet, how irrelevant all this commentary is to the real problem, not *what* Hamlet's motive is but *what kind of* motive. Why can't he act? Angels and ministers of grace, he does nothing else. Polonius, Rosencrantz and Guildenstern, Laertes, Claudius, all go to it. But Hamlet never breaks through to "reality." His motives and his behavior remain dramatic from first to last. So, in spite of all those bodies at the end, commentators wonder if *Hamlet* amounts to a tragedy and, if so, what kind. Hamlet lacks the serious, central self tragedy requires. We are compelled to stand back, hold off our identification, and hence to locate the play within rhetorical coordinates, a tragicomedy about the two kinds of self and the two kinds of motive.

We see this theme in that $Q_2$ scene (4.4) where Fortinbras and his army parade, with seeming irrelevance—at least to many directors, who cut it— across the stage. They parade so that Hamlet can reflect upon them. The theme is motive. The scene begins as a straightforward lesson in the vanity of human wishes. They go, the Captain tells Hamlet, "to gain a little patch of ground / That hath in it no profit but the name" (4.4.18–19). Hamlet seems to get the point, "the question of this straw," the absurd artificiality of human motive, and especially of aristocratic war, war for pleasure, for the pure glory of it. But then out jumps another non sequitur soliloquy:

> How all occasions do inform against me
> And spur my dull revenge! What is a man,
> If his chief good and market of his time
> Be but to sleep and feed? A beast, no more.
> Sure he that made us with such large discourse,
> Looking before and after, gave us not
> That capability and godlike reason
> To fust in us unused. Now, whether it be
> Bestial oblivion, or some craven scruple
> Of thinking too precisely on th' event—
> A thought which, quartered, hath but one part wisdom
> And ever three parts coward—I do not know
> Why yet I live to say, "This thing's to do,"
> Sith I have cause, and will, and strength, and means
> To do't.
>
> [4.4.32–46]

What has reason to do with revenge? His question—why, with all his compelling reasons, doesn't he go on—is again well taken. Shakespeare has carefully given him the realest reasons a revenge hero ever had—father murdered, mother whored, kingdom usurped, his innocent maiden corrupted in her imagination. The answer to Hamlet's question marches about on the stage before him. As usual, he does not fully understand the problem. It is the Player King's tears all over again. Fortinbras's motivation is sublimely artificial, entirely dramatic. Honor. It has no profit in it but the name. Hamlet cannot act because he cannot find a way to dramatize his revenge. Chances he has, but, as when he surprises Claudius praying, they are not dramatic. Claudius is alone. To fall upon him and kill him would not be revenge, as he says, not because Claudius will die shriven but because he will not see it coming, because nobody is watching.

So, when Hamlet continues his soliloquy, he draws a moral precisely opposite to the expected one. Again, logical discontinuity triggers stylistic attitude:

> Examples gross as earth exhort me.
> Witness this army of such mass and charge,
> Led by a delicate and tender prince,
> Whose spirit, with divine ambition puffed,
> Makes mouths at the invisible event,
> Exposing what is mortal and unsure
> To all that fortune, death, and danger dare,
> Even for an eggshell. Rightly to be great
> Is not to stir without great argument,
> But greatly to find quarrel in a straw
> When honor's at the stake. How stand I then,
> That have a father killed, a mother stained,
> Excitements of my reason and my blood,
> And let all sleep, while to my shame I see
> The imminent death of twenty thousand men
> That for a fantasy and trick of fame
> Go to their graves like beds, fight for a plot
> Whereon the numbers cannot try the cause,
> Which is not tomb enough and continent
> To hide the slain? O, from this time forth,
> My thoughts be bloody, or be nothing worth!
>
> [4.4.46–66]

He sees but does not see. In some way, Fortinbras represents where he wants to go, what he wants to be, how he wants to behave. But he doesn't see how, nor altogether do we. If ever an allegorical puppet was dragged across a stage it is Fortinbras. Yet he haunts the play. His divine ambition begins the action of the play; he gets that offstage introduction Shakespeare is so fond of; he marches to Norway to make a point about motive; and he marches back at the end, inherits Denmark. Yet he stays cardboard. It is not real motive he represents but martial honor much rather.

Shakespeare sought to give *Hamlet* a pronounced military coloration from first to last. The play begins on guard; the ghost wears armor; Denmark is a most warlike state. Military honor is the accepted motive in a Denmark Fortinbras rightly inherits. Honor will cure what is rotten in Denmark, restore its proper values. Hamlet cannot set the times right because he cannot find in martial honor a full and sufficient motive for human life. Hamlet, says Fortinbras, would have done well had he been king, but we may be permitted to doubt it. He thinks too much. Yet honor and the soldier's life provide the model motive for *Hamlet*. All his working life, Shakespeare was fascinated and perplexed by how deeply the military motive satisfied man. It constituted a sublime secular commitment which, like the religious commitment, gave all away to get all back. Hamlet's self-consciousness keeps him from it, yes, but even more his search for real purpose. Chivalric war—all war, perhaps—is manufactured purpose. Hamlet can talk about clutching it to his bosom but he cannot do it, for there is nothing *inevitable* about it.

Military honor is finally a role, much like Laertes' role as revenge hero. Both roles are satisfying, both integrate and direct the personality. But once you realize that you are playing the role for just these reasons, using it as a self-serving device, its attraction fades. As its inevitability diminishes, so does its reality. War and revenge both prove finally so rewarding because they provide, by all the killing, the irrefutable reality needed to bolster the role, restore its inevitability. Thus Shakespeare chose them, a revenge plot superposed on a Fortinbras—honor plot, for his play about motive. They provided a model for the kind of motive men find most satisfying; they combine maximum dramatic satisfaction with the irrefutable reality only bloody death can supply. In the Elizabethan absurdity as in our own, men kill others and themselves because that is the only real thing left to do. It is a rare paradox and Shakespeare builds his play upon it.

But even death is not dependable. We can learn to make sport of it, enjoy it. So the gravedigger puns on his craft. So, too, I suppose, Fortinbras laconically remarks at the end of the play: "Such a sight as this / Becomes the field, but here shows much amiss." Death's reality can vanish too. All our purposes end up, like the skull Hamlet meditates on, a stage prop. It is not accidental that the language which closes the play is theatrical. Hamlet even in death does not escape the dramatic self. When the bodies are "high on a stage ... placed to the view" Horatio will "speak to th' yet unknowing world," will authenticate the proceeding with a rhetorical occasion. Hamlet's body, Fortinbras commands, is to be borne "like a soldier to the stage, / For he was likely, had he been put on, I To have proved most royal."

Nor is it accidental that Hamlet kills Polonius. The act is his real attempt at revenge, Polonius his real enemy. Polonius embodies the dramatic self-consciousness which stands between Hamlet and the roles—Avenger and King—he was born to play. But Polonius pervades the whole of Hamlet's world and lurks within Hamlet himself. Only death can free Hamlet. Perhaps this is why he faces it with nonchalance. Much has been said about Hamlet's stoicism, but how unstoical the play really is! Honest feeling demands a dramatic equivalent to make it real just as artifice does. Stoicism demands a preexistent reality, a central self beyond drama, which the play denies. Stoicism is death and indeed, in *Hamlet*, the second follows hard upon the avowal of the first. We have no choice but to play.

And so Hamlet chooses his foil and plays. I have been arguing that the play invokes rhetorical coordinates as well as serious ones. It makes sense, if this is so, that it should end with a sublime game and the triumph of chance. Hamlet never solves his problem, nor does chance solve it for him, nor does the play solve it for us. No satisfactory model for motive, no movement from game to sublime, is suggested. Hamlet can finally kill the King because the King thoughtfully supplies a dramatic occasion appropriate to the deed. And Hamlet can kill Laertes because dramatic motive has destroyed naive purpose. And vice versa. But Hamlet cannot get rid of his dramatic self, his dramatic motives. The duel allegorizes the quarrel between kinds of motive which the play has just dramatized. And the duel, like the play, is a zero-sum game. Interest for both sides adds up to zero. The play leaves us, finally, where it leaves Hamlet. We have savored the violence and the gorgeous poetry and been made aware that we do. We have been made to reflect on play as well as purpose. We have not been shown how to move from one to the other. Nor that it *cannot* be done. We are left, like those in the play, dependent on death and chance to show us how to put our two motives, our two selves, together.

Shakespeare as a mature playwright is not supposed to be an opaque stylist. The great unity of his mature tragedies is a style we look through, not at. The gamesman with words fades out with the nondramatic poems and early infatuations like *Love's Labor's Lost*. *Hamlet* shows, by itself, how wrong this view of Shakespeare's development is. The play depends upon an alternation of opaque and transparent styles for its meaning. The alternation almost is the meaning. *Hamlet* is a play about motive, about style, and thus perhaps, of the mature plays, an exception? I don't think so. Where Shakespeare is most sublime he is also most rhetorical and both poetics are likely to be present in force. To illustrate such a thesis would constitute an agreeable task. The lines it would follow are clear enough. They would yield explanation of the double plot more basic than the comic/serious one. They would render the comic/tragic division altogether less important than it now seems.

In play after play the same stylistic strategy illustrates the same juxtaposition of motive, of play and purpose. Richard cannot learn the difference. Hal must. Lear can play the king but he has never *been* a king. *Antony and Cleopatra* juxtaposes not only public and private life but two poetics and two selves. The double plot becomes, over and over, a serious plot-poetic and a play plot-poetic. The fatal innocence of Shakespeare's characters turns out, over and over, to be innocence about the real nature of their motivation. All through the *Henriad* political rhetoric must be *seen* as rhetoric. Egypt is meant to be *seen* as more wordy and more metaphorical than Rome. *Romeo and Juliet* depends on our seeing the Petrarchan rhetoric as such, else we will mistake the kind of play it is, a play where death authenticates game. Lear on the heath, that centerpiece of Shakespearean sublimity, alters his outlines considerably within rhetorical coordinates. Shakespearean tragedy may come to seem, as in *Hamlet*, a juxtaposition of the two motives with a hole in the middle, with no way to connect them. The comedies collapse them. And the problem plays and romances try to make a path between the two, see them in dynamic interchange. The two things that obsessed Shakespeare were style and motive, and his career can be charted coherently from beginning to end in terms of their interrelation. In this he typifies the stylistic strategy of the Renaissance as a whole. The real question of motive lay beyond good and evil. It was the principal task of the self-conscious rhetorical style to point this moral. Human flesh is sullied with self-consciousness, with theatricality, and these will be the ground for whatever authentic morality any of us can muster.

## NOTES

1. Ed. Willard Farnham.
2. "Soliloquy?," *Times Literary Supplement*, 20 March 1969, p. 289.

WILLIAM EMPSON

# *Hamlet*

One feels that the mysteries of Hamlet are likely to be more or less exhausted, and I have no great novelty to offer here, but it has struck me, in the course of trying to present him in lectures, that the enormous panorama of theory and explanation falls into a reasonable proportion if viewed, so to speak, from Pisgah, from the moment of discovery by Shakespeare. To do that should also have a relation with the impressions of a fresh mind, meeting the basic legend of the play at any date. I was led to it from trying to answer some remarks of Hugh Kingsmill, in *The Return of William Shakespeare*, who said that Hamlet is a ridiculously theatrical and therefore unreal figure, almost solely concerned with scoring off other people, which the dialogue lets him do much too easily, and attractive to actors only because "they have more humiliations than other men to avenge". A number of critics seem to have felt like this, though few have said it so plainly; the feeling tends to make one indifferent to the play, and over-rides any "solution of its problems", but when followed up it leads to more interesting country. I think it allows of a reconsideration of the origins, along which one might even take fresh troops into the jungle warfare over the text.

The experts mostly agree that Kyd wrote a play on Hamlet about 1587, very like his surviving *Spanish Tragedy* except that it was about a son avenging a father instead of a father avenging a son. In any case there was some early

---

From *Essays on Shakespeare*, ed. David B. Pirie. © 1986 by William Empson.

play on Hamlet. The only record of a performance of it is in 1594, under conditions which make it likely to have become the property of Shakespeare's Company; jokes about it survive from 1589, 1596, and 1601, the later two regarding it as a standard out-of-date object. A keen sense of changing fashion has to be envisaged; when Shakespeare's Company were seduced into performing *Richard II* for the Essex rebels they said they would have to be paid because it was too old to draw an audience, and it wasn't half as old as effect is still meant to be frightening; it is like Zoo in *Back to Methuselah*, who says "This kind of thing is got up to impress you, not to impress me"; and it is very outfacing for persons in the audience who come expecting to make that kind of joke themselves.

Following this plan, there are of course satirical misquotations of the Revenge classics, as in "Pox! leave thy damnable faces and begin. Come— 'the croaking raven doth bellow for revenge'" (probably more of them than we realise, because we miss the contrast with the old *Hamlet*); but there also has to be a positive dramatisation of the idea, which is given in Hamlet's scenes with the Players. Critics have wondered how it could be endurable for Shakespeare to make the actor of Hamlet upbraid for their cravings for theatricality not merely his fellow actors but part of his audience (the term "groundlings" must have appeared an insult and comes nowhere else); but surely this carries on the central joke, and wouldn't make the author prominent. I agree that the Player's speech and so forth was a parody of the ranting style of the Admiral's Company (and when Hamlet praised it his actor had to slip in and out of real life, without turning the joke too much against the Prince); but even so the situation is that the Chamberlain's Company are shown discussing how to put on a modern-style Revenge Play, which the audience knows to be a problem for them. The "mirror" was being held close to the face. As to the talk about the War of the Theatres, people were curious to know what the Globe would say, and heard its leading actor speak for the Company; they were violently prevented from keeping their minds on "buried Denmark". What is technically so clever is to turn this calculated collapse of dramatic illusion into an illustration of the central theme. The first problem was how to get the audience to attend to the story again, solved completely by "O what a rogue" and so on, which moves from the shame of theatrical behaviour and the paradoxes of sincerity (Hamlet first blames himself for not feeling as much as the actors do and then for over-acting about it, feeling too much) into an immediate scheme to expose the king. Yet even here one might feel, as Dover Wilson said (with his odd power of making a deep remark without seeing its implications), that "the two speeches are for all the world like a theme given out by the First Violin and then repeated by the Soloist"—Hamlet has only proved he is a better actor, and indeed "rogue" might make him say this, by recalling that actors were legally rogues and vagabonds. We next see Hamlet in the "To be or not to be" soliloquy, and he has completely forgotten his passionate and apparently decisive self-criticism—but this time the collapse of interest in the story comes from the Prince, not merely from the audience; then when Ophelia enters he swings away from being completely disinterested into being more disgracefully theatrical than anywhere else (enjoying working up a fuss about a very excessive suspicion, and thus betraying himself to listeners he knows are present); next he lectures the Players with grotesque hauteur about the art of acting, saying that they must always keep cool (this is where the word "groundlings" comes); then, quite unexpectedly, he fawns upon Horatio as a man who is not "passion's slave", unlike himself, and we advance upon the Play-within-the-Play. The metaphor of the pipe which Fortune can blow upon as she pleases, which he used to Horatio, is made a symbol by bringing a recorder into bodily prominence during his moment of triumph after the Play scene, and he now boasts to the courtiers that he is a mystery, therefore they cannot play on him-we are meant to feel that there are real merits in the condition, but he has already told us he despises himself for it. Incidentally he has just told Horatio that he deserves a fellowship in a "cry" of players (another searching joke phrase not used elsewhere) but Horatio only thinks "half of one". The recovery from the point where the story seemed most completely thrown away has been turned into an exposition of the character of the hero and the central dramatic theme. No doubt this has been fully recognized, but I do not think it has been viewed as a frank treatment of the central task, that of making the old play seem real by making the hero life-like.

Dover Wilson rightly points out the obsessive excitability of Hamlet, as when in each of the scenes scolding one of the ladies he comes back twice onto the stage, each time more unreasonable, as if he can't make himself stop. "But it is no mere theatrical trick or device", he goes on, "it is meant to be part of the nature of the man"; and meanwhile psychologists have elaborated the view that he is a standard "manic-depressive" type, in whom long periods of sullen gloom, often with actual forgetfulness, are followed by short periods of exhausting excitement, usually with violence of language. By all means, but the nature of the man grows out of the original *donnée*; his nature had (first of all) to be such that it would make the old story "life-like". And the effect in the theatre, surely, is at least prior to any belief about his nature, though it may lead you on to one; what you start from is the *astonishment* of Hamlet's incessant changes of mood, which also let the one actor combine in himself elements which the Elizabethan theatre usually separates (e.g. simply tragedy and comedy). Every one of the soliloquies, it has been pointed out, contains a shock for the audience, apart from what it says, in what it doesn't say: the first in having no reference to usurpation; the second ("rogue and slave") no reference to Ophelia, though his feelings about her have been made a prominent question; the third ("To be or not to be") no reference to his plot or his self-criticism or even his own walk of life—he is considering entirely in general whether life is worth living, and it is startling for him to say no traveller returns from death, however complete the "explanation" that he is assuming the Ghost was a devil; the fourth ("Now might I do it pat") no reference to his obviously great personal danger now that the King knows the secret; the fifth ("How all occasions do inform") no reference to the fact that he can't kill the King now, or rather a baffling assumption that he still can; and one might add his complete forgetting of his previous self-criticisms when he comes to his last words. It is this power to astonish, I think, which keeps one in doubt whether he is particularly theatrical or particularly "life-like"; a basic part of the effect, which would be clear to the first audiences.

However, the theme of a major play by Shakespeare is usually repeated by several characters in different forms, and Hamlet is not the only theatrical one here. Everybody is "acting a part" except Horatio, as far as that goes; and Laertes is very theatrical, as Hamlet rightly insists over the body of Ophelia ("I'll rant as well as thou"). One might reflect that both of them trample on her, both literally and figuratively, just because of their common trait. And yet Laertes is presented as opposite to Hamlet in not being subject to delay about avenging his father or to scruples about his methods; the tragic flaw in Hamlet must be something deeper or more specific. We need therefore to consider what his "theatricality" may be, and indeed the reader may feel I am making too much play with a term that Elizabethans did not use; but I think it makes us start in the right place. The Elizabethans, though both more formal and more boisterous than most people nowadays, were well able to see the need for sincerity; and it is agreed that Shakespeare had been reading Montaigne about how quickly one's moods can change, so that to appear consistent requires "acting", a line of thought which is still current. But to understand how it was applied here one needs to keep one's mind on the immediate situation in the theatre. The *plot* of a Revenge Play seemed theatrical because it kept the audience waiting without obvious reason in the characters; then a theatrical *character* (in such a play) appears as one who gets undeserved effects, "cheap" because not justified by the plot as a whole. However, "theatrical behaviour" is never only "mean" in the sense of losing the ultimate aim for a petty advantage, because it must also "give itself away"—the idea "greedy to impress an audience" is required. Now the basic legend about Hamlet was that he did exactly this and yet was somehow right for it; he successfully kept a secret by displaying he had got one. The idea is already prominent in Saxo Grammaticus, where it is presented as wholly successful (the eventual bad end of Hamlet had a different cause). Many scholars recently have argued that Shakespeare looked up his sources more than we have supposed, and I imagine the text of Saxo could be borrowed for him when he was given the assignment, if he wanted a rapid check on the French version; "the Saxon who could write Latin" in 1200 would be an evidently impressive source of primitive legend. The differences from the French are not important, but if Shakespeare did look up Saxo he would get an even firmer reassurance that his natural bent was the right one; the brief pungent Latin sentences about Hamlet are almost a definition of Shakespeare's clown, and Dover Wilson is right in saying that Shakespeare presented Hamlet as a kind of generalisation of that idea ("they fool me to the top of my bent" he remarks with appalling truth). Here we reach the bedrock of Hamlet, unchanged by the local dramas of reinterpretation; even Dr Johnson remarks that his assumed madness, though entertaining, does not seem to help his plot.

Kyd would probably give him powerful single-line jokes when answering other characters; the extreme and sordid pretence of madness implied by Saxo would not be used. I think that Shakespeare's opening words for Hamlet, "A little more than kin and less than kind", are simply repeated from Kyd; a dramatic moment for the first-night audience, because they wanted to know whether the new Hamlet would be different. His next words are a passionate assertion that he is not the theatrical Hamlet—"I know not seems." Now this technique from Kyd, though trivial beside the final Hamlet, would present the inherent paradox of the legend very firmly: why are these jokes supposed to give a kind of magical success to a character who had obviously better keep his mouth shut? All Elizabethans, including Elizabeth, had met the need to keep one's mouth shut at times; the paradox might well seem sharper to them than it does to us. Shakespeare took care to laugh at this as early as possible in his version of the play. The idea that it is silly to drop hints as Hamlet does is expressed by Hamlet himself, not only with force but with winning intimacy, when he tells the other observers of the Ghost that they must keep silence completely, and not say "We could an if we would. There be an if they might" and so on, which is precisely what he does himself for the rest of the play. No doubt he needs a monopoly of this technique. But the first effect in the theatre was another case of "closing the hole by making it big"; if you can make the audience laugh *with* Hamlet about his method early, they aren't going to laugh *at* him for it afterwards. Instead they can wonder why he is or pretends to be mad, just as the other characters wonder; and wonder why he delays, just as he himself wonders. No other device could raise so sharply the question of "what is theatrical behaviour?" because here we cannot even be sure what Hamlet is aiming at. We can never decide flatly that his method is wrong, because the more it appears unwise the more it appears courageous; and at any rate we know that he sees all round it. There seem to be two main assumptions, that he is trying to frighten his enemies into exposing themselves, and that he is not so frightened himself as to hide his emotions though he hides their cause. I fancy Shakespeare could rely on some of his audience to add the apparently modern theory that the relief of self-expression saved Hamlet from going finally mad, because it fits well enough onto their beliefs about the disease "melancholy". But in any case the basic legend is a dream glorification of both having your cake and eating it, keeping your secret for years, till you kill, and yet perpetually enjoying boasts about it. Here we are among the roots of the race of man; rather a smelly bit perhaps, but a bit that appeals at once to any child. It would be absurd to *blame* Shakespeare for accentuating this traditional theme till it became enormous.

The view that Hamlet "is Shakespeare", or at least more like him than his other characters, I hope falls into shape now. It has a basic truth, because he was drawing on his experience as actor and playwright; these professions often do puzzle their practitioners about what is theatrical and what is not, as their friends and audiences can easily recognise; but he was only using what the theme required. To have to give posterity, let alone the immediate audiences, a picture of himself would have struck him as laying a farcical extra burden on an already difficult assignment. I think he did feel he was giving a good hand to actors in general, though with decent obscurity, when he worked up so much praise for Hamlet at the end, but you are meant to be dragged round to this final admiration for Hamlet, not to feel it all through. To suppose he "is Shakespeare" has excited in some critics a reasonable distaste for both parties, because a man who models himself on Hamlet in common life (as has been done) tends to appear a mean-minded neurotic; whereas if you take the *plot* seriously Hamlet is at least assumed to have special reasons for his behaviour.

We should now be able to reconsider the view which Stoll has done real service by following up: Hamlet's reasons are so good that he not only never delays at all but was never supposed to; the self-accusations of the revenger are always prominent in Revenge Plays, even classical Greek ones, being merely a necessary part of the machine—to make the audience continue waiting with attention. Any problem we may invent about Shakespeare's Hamlet, on this view, we could also have invented about Kyd's, but it wouldn't have occurred to us to want to. In making the old play "life-like" Shakespeare merely altered the style, not the story; except that it was probably he who (by way of adding "body") gave Hamlet very much better reasons for delay than any previous revenger, so that it is peculiarly absurd of us to pick him out and puzzle over his delay. I do not at all want to weaken this line of argument; I think Shakespeare did, intentionally, pile up all the excuses for delay he could imagine, while at the same time making Hamlet bewail and denounce his delay far more strongly than ever revenger had done before. It is the force and intimacy of the self-reproaches of Hamlet, of course, which ordinary opinion has rightly given first place; that is why these legal arguments that he didn't delay appear farcical. But the two lines of argument are only two halves of the same thing. Those members of the audience who simply wanted to see a Revenge Play again, without any hooting at it from smarter persons, deserved to be satisfied; and anyhow, for all parties, the suspicion that Hamlet was a coward or merely fatuous had to be avoided. The ambiguity was an essential part of the intention, because the more you tried to translate the balance of impulses in the old drama into a realistic story (especially if you make Hamlet older which you want to if he is to understand what he is doing) the more peculiar this story had to be made. The old structure was still kept firm, but its foundations had to be strengthened to carry so much extra weight. At the same time, a simpler view could be taken; whatever the stage characters may say, the real situation in the theatre is still that the audience knows the revenge won't come till the end. Their own foreknowledge is what they had laughed at, rather than any lack of motive in the puppets, and however much the motives of the Revenger for delay were increased he could still very properly blame himself for keeping the audience waiting. One could therefore sit through the new *Hamlet* (as for that matter the eighteenth century did) without feeling too startled by his self-reproaches. But of course the idea that "bringing the style up to date" did not involve any change of content seems to me absurd, whether held by Shakespeare's committee or by Stoll; for one thing, it made the old theatrical convention appear bafflingly indistinguishable from a current political danger. The whole story was brought into a new air, so that one felt there was much more "in it".

This effect, I think, requires a sudden feeling of novelty rather than a gradual evolution, but it is still possible that Shakespeare wrote an earlier draft than our present text. To discuss two lost plays at once, by Kyd and Shakespeare, is perhaps rather tiresome, but one cannot imagine the first audiences without forming some picture of the development of the play, of what struck them as new. Dover Wilson, to whom so much gratitude is due for his series of books on *Hamlet*, takes a rather absurd position here. He never edits a straightforward Shakespeare text without finding evidence for two or three layers of revision, and considering them important for a full understanding of the play; only in *Hamlet*, where there is positive evidence for them, and a long-recognised ground for curiosity about them, does he assume they can be ignored. He rightly insists that an editor needs to see the problems of a text as a whole before even choosing between two variant readings, and he sometimes actually asserts in passing that Shakespeare wrote earlier drafts of *Hamlet*; and yet his basis for preferring Q2 to F is a picture of Shakespeare handing in *one* manuscript (recorded by Q2) from which the Company at once wrote out *one* acting version (recorded by F), making drastic cuts and also verbal changes which they refused to reconsider. He says he is not concerned with "sixteenth century versions of Hamlet", a device of rhetoric that suggests a gradual evolution, too hard to trace. I am not clear which century 1600 is in (there was a surprising amount of quarrelling over the point in both 1900 and 1800), but even writing done in 1599 would not be remote from 1601. I postulate one main treatment of the play by Shakespeare, first acted in 1600, and then one quite minor revision of it by Shakespeare, first acted in 1601, written to feed and gratify the interest and discussion which his great surprise had excited the year before. To believe in this amount of revision does not make much difference, whereas a gradual evolution would, but it clears up some puzzling bits of evidence and I think makes the audiences more intelligible.

Dover Wilson's two volumes on *The Manuscripts of Shakespeare's Hamlet* are magnificently detailed and obviously right most of the time. I am only questioning this part of his conclusions: "we may venture to suspect that (always assuming Shakespeare to have been in London) *Hamlet* was not merely a turning-point in his career dramatically, but also marks some kind of crisis in his relations with his company". The idea that Shakespeare wasn't in London, I take it, is inserted to allow for the theory that he was in Scotland drafting his first version of *Macbeth*, which need not delay us. The cuts for time in the Folio seem to be his main argument, because he ends his leading volume (*Manuscripts*, p. 174) by saying that Shakespeare discovered his mistake if he imagined that the Company would act such a long play in full. "If" here is a delicacy only, because the purpose of the argument is to answer critics who had called our full-length *Hamlet* "a monstrosity, the creation of scholarly compromise" between rival shorter versions. I agree with Dover Wilson that Shakespeare did envisage a use for this whole text. But Dover Wilson had just been giving an impressive section (pp. 166–70) to prove that some of the Folio cuts are so skilful that Shakespeare must have done them himself—perhaps unwillingly, but at least he was not being ignored. Another part of the argument for a quarrel is that the producer "did not trouble to consult the author when he could not decipher a word or understand a passage", but this section argues that Shakespeare did make a few corrections in the Prompt Copy, when a mistake happened to he near the bits he had looked up to make his cuts. Surely this makes the author look culpably careless over details rather than in a huff because he hadn't been consulted over details. Another argument uses errors which are unchanged in the Quartos and Folio to suggest that the Company repeated the same bits of petty nonsense blindly for twenty years. But Dover Wilson also argues that the Prompt Copy used for the Folio was "brought up to date" in later years, at least on such points as the weapons fashionable for duelling; the same might apply to some slang terms which were already out of date when the Folio was published, though he labours to restore them now from the Quarto. I think he presumes an excessive desire to save paper in this quite wealthy company; they are not likely to have kept the same manuscript Prompt Copy of their most popular play in constant use for twenty years. There would have to be a copying staff, in any case, to give the actors their parts to learn from. The baffling question is how the Folio *Hamlet* with its mass of different kinds of error could ever occur; and the theory of Dover Wilson is that it was badly printed from a copy of the Company's (irremovable) Prompt Copy made by a Company employee who was careless chiefly because he knew what was currently acted, so that his mind echoed phrases in the wrong place. Surely I may put one more storey onto this card castle. Hemming and Condell, I suggest, set this man to copy the *original* Prompt Copy, which so far from being in current use had become a kind of museum piece; they tried to get a basic text for the printer, and only failed to realise that it isn't enough in these matters to issue an order. The basic object to be copied had neither the later corrections nor the extra passages which had been reserved for special occasions, and the interest of the man who copied it is that he could scribble down both old and new errors or variants without feeling he was obviously wrong. It seems improbable that the Globe actors, though likely to introduce corrections, would patiently repeat bits of unrewarding nonsense for twenty years; my little invention saves us from believing that, without forcing me to deny that Dover Wilson's theory has produced some good emendations.

We cannot expect to recover a correct text merely from an excess of error in the printed versions of it; and in no other Shakespeare play are they so confused. But surely this fact itself must have some meaning. I suggest that, while Shakespeare's *Hamlet* was the rage, that is, roughly till James became King without civil war, it was varied a good deal on the night according to the reactions of the immediate audience. This would be likely to make the surviving texts pretty hard to print from; also it relieves us from thinking of Shakespeare as frustrated by the Company's cuts in his first great tragedy. Surely any man, after a quarrel of this sort, would take some interest in "at least" getting the printed version right. No doubt there was a snobbery about print to which he was sensitive, and also the text belonged to the Company; but neither question would impinge here. The Company must have wanted a presentable text for the Second Quarto, designed to outface the First, and even the most anxious snob can correct proofs without attracting attention. Indeed there was at least one reprint of it during his lifetime, in which the printer can be observed trying to correct mistakes, obviously without help from the author (for example over the line which Dover Wilson well corrects into "Or of the most select, are generous chief in that", *chief* meaning "chiefly"). You might think he fell into despair over the incompetence of the printers, but they could do other jobs well enough, and were visibly trying to do better here. The only plausible view is that he refused to help them because he wouldn't be bothered, and I do not believe he could have felt this if he had been annoyed by the way *Hamlet* had been mangled at the Globe. I think he must have felt tolerably glutted by the performances.

Critics have long felt that the First Quarto probably contains evidence for a previous draft by Shakespeare which is hard to disentangle. This theory has been blown upon in recent years by E. K. Chambers and Dover Wilson, who regard Q1 as a perversion of the standard Globe performance; but I think the point of view I am recommending helps to strengthen it. One must admit, on Dover Wilson's side, that a text published in 1603 cannot be trusted to be unaffected by changes in the performance supposedly made in 1601; the idea that this was a travelling version, suited to audiences less experienced than the Globe ones, seems a needed hypothesis as well as one suggested by the title-page. Also, though often weirdly bad in detail, it is a very workmanlike object in broad planning; somebody made a drastically short version of the play which kept in all the action, and the effect is so full of action that it is almost as jerky as an early film, which no doubt some audiences would appreciate. There seems no way to decide whether or not this was done independently of the pirating reporters who forgot a lot of the poetry. The main change is that the soliloquy "To be or not to be" and its attendant scolding of Ophelia is put before the Player scene, not after it; but a producer wanting a short plain version is wise to make that change, so it is not evidence for an earlier draft by Shakespeare. The variations in names might only recall Kyd's names, perhaps more familiar in the provinces. What does seem decisive evidence, and was regularly considered so till Dover Wilson ignored rather than rebutted it, is that this text gives a sheer scene between Horatio and the Queen alone, planning what to do about Hamlet's return to Denmark; surely this would be the pirating hack. The text here seems particularly "cooked up" or misreported, and Duthie has argued convincingly that it is made out of bits vaguely remembered from

Shakespeare or Kyd in other contexts. But this only shows what the pirates did when they forgot what Shakespeare wrote, here and elsewhere; it does not prove that Shakespeare never wrote such a scene. And the adapter would not invent it, because what he wanted was action; it is less like action to have Horatio report Hamlet's adventures than to let the hero boast in person, nor is it inherently any shorter. Besides, the change fits in with a consistently different picture of the Queen, who is not only made clearly innocent of the murder but made willing to help Hamlet. Dover Wilson does not seem to deal with this familiar position beyond saying "Shakespeare is subtler than his perverters or his predecessors", assuming that the Q1 compiler is his first perverter; and he argues that the Queen is meant to appear innocent even of vague complicity in the murder in our standard text of *Hamlet*. But surely it is fair to ask what this "subtlety" may be, and why it deserves such a fine name if it only muddles a point that was meant to be clear. Why, especially, must the Queen be given an unexplained half-confession, "To my sick soul, as sin's true nature is ...", a fear of betraying guilt by too much effort to hide it? Richard Flatter, I think, did well to emphasise how completely this passage has been ignored by critics such as A. C. Bradley and Dover Wilson, whose arguments from other passages to prove that she was meant to seem innocent are very convincing. Surely the only reasonable view is that Shakespeare in the final version wanted to leave doubt in the minds of the audience about the Queen. You may say that the adapter behind Q1 just got rid of this nuisance, but you are making him do an unlikely amount of bold intelligent work. It is simpler to believe that he preferred an earlier version, which made the Queen definitively on Hamlet's side after the bedroom scene.

One might also recall, I think, that on the usually accepted dating there is a pause just after *Hamlet* in the usual speed of production by Shakespeare; here if anywhere he had time to revise a play, and this play is the one which gets the most contemporary reference, therefore would be most worth revising. It seems natural to connect the pause with the general anxiety until James became King without civil war—I take it that the revision made the play even better fitted to this growing state of public sentiment.

Dover Wilson used to believe in two versions by Shakespeare and apparently does so still, or if not he must be praised for giving the evidence against his later view with his usual firmness. Harvey's note praising a *Hamlet* by Shakespeare, he recalls, needs to predate the execution of Essex in February 1601, whereas the remarks about the War of the Theatres, and a hint at the siege of Dunkirk in the soliloquy "How all occasions do inform against me", belong to the summer of that year. This note by Harvey, written on the flyleaf of a book, in a rather affected style which could refer to dead men as if alive, has given rise to extremely confusing arguments; some of them take the play back to 1598, which I don't believe. I am not arguing that it gives strong evidence, only trying to recall that the position I take here is the normal one. If we are to believe in a revision for the 1601 season it should include these items (presumably the whole of the soliloquy, because it all refers to Dunkirk if any of it does), also the new position for "To be or not to be" and for the scolding of Ophelia, and a number of changes about the Queen, interesting for her actor but not long in bulk. The idea that the main text was written before the death of Essex and the revisions after it should perhaps have more meaning than I can find; perhaps anyway it corresponds to a certain darkening of the whole air. But there is no need to make this revision large or elaborate, and I agree with the critics who have said that the actors would have found trivial revisions merely tiresome. The points just listed seem the only ones we have direct evidence for, and are easily understood as heightening the peculiar effect of *Hamlet* for a public which had already caught onto it. May I now put the matter the other way round; I do not believe that our present text of *Hamlet*, a weirdly baffling thing, could have been written at all except for a public which had already caught on to it.

The strongest argument is from the soliloquy "How all occasions". Dover Wilson says that the Company omitted this "from the very first" from the Fortinbras scene, "which was patently written to give occasion to the soliloquy". But no producer would leave in the nuisance of an army marching across the stage after removing the only point of it. Fortinbras had anyway to march his army across the stage, as he does in Q1 as well as F, and presumably did in Kyd's version. The beginning of the play is a mobilisation against this army and the end a triumph for it; the audience thought in more practical terms than we do about these dynastic quarrels. But that made it all the more dramatic, in the 1601 version, to throw in a speech for Hamlet hinting that the troops at Dunkirk were as fatuous for too much action as he himself was for too little. It is only a final example of the process of keeping the old scenes and packing into them extra meaning. What is reckless about the speech is that it makes Hamlet say, while (presumably) surrounded by guards leading him to death, "I have cause and will and strength and means / To do it", destroying a sheer school of Hamlet Theories with each noun; the effect is so exasperating that more than one critic, after solving all his Hamlet Problem neatly except for this bit, has simply demanded the right to throw it away. Nobody is as annoying as all that except on purpose, and the only reasonable view of why this speech was added is that these Hamlet Theories had already been propounded, in discussions among the spectators, during the previous year. But the bafflement thrown in here was not the tedious one of making a psychological problem or a detective story insoluble; there was a more immediate effect in making Hamlet magnificent. He finds his immediate position not even worth reflecting on; and he does get out of this jam, so you can't blame him for his presumption at this point. His complete impotence at the moment, one might say, seems to him "only a theatrical appearance", just as his previous reasons for delay seem to have vanished like a dream. Here as elsewhere he gives a curious effect, also not unknown among his critics, of losing all interest for what has happened in the story; but it is more impressive in him than in them. By the way, I would like to have one other passage added by Shakespeare in revision, the remarks by Hamlet at the end of the bedroom scene (in Q2 but not F) to the effect that it will only cheer him up to have to outwit his old pals trying to kill him; this seems liable to sound merely boastful unless afterwards proved genuine by his private thoughts, but if the soliloquy is being added some such remark is needed first, so as to prepare the audience not to find it merely unnatural.

One might suppose that this dream-like though fierce quality in Hamlet, which becomes perhaps his chief appeal two centuries later, was not invented till the 1601 revision. I think this idea can be disproved. The moral effect is much the same, and hardly less presumptuous, when he insists at the end of the play on treating Laertes as a gentleman and a sportsman, though he has already told the audience (in high mystical terms) that he is not such a fool as to be unsuspicious; and the moral is at once drawn for us—this treatment unnerves Laertes so much that he almost drops the plot. The fencing-match no less than the Play scene is an imitation which turns out to be reality, but that is merely a thing which one should never be surprised by; Laertes ought still to be treated in the proper style. "Use them after your own honour and dignity; the less they deserve, the more merit is in your bounty"; this curious generosity of the intellect is always strong in Hamlet, and indeed his main source of charm. One reason, in fact, why he could be made so baffling without his character becoming confused was that it made him give a tremendous display of top-class behaviour, even in his secret mind as expressed in soliloquy. Now the paradoxical chivalry towards Laertes (which commentators tend to regard as a "problem" about how much Hamlet understood) is marked in Q1, whose author was clearly not bothering much about the revised version by Shakespeare, and wanted his Hamlet to be a knock-down hero. The idea was not too subtle for the audience of a simplified version of Shakespeare's *Hamlet*; on the other hand it seems clearly not due to Kyd. We feel this because of their styles, but probably a state of public feeling corresponds to it; the casual remark of Hamlet in the graveyard, that all the classes are getting mixed, has probably some bearing on his behaviour. An awareness of social change had been arising in that decade, especially of a thing which in itself had been happening for some time (encouraged though not caused by Elizabeth), the arrival of a new aristocracy which felt that grand behaviour has to be learned.

Thus another reason why there is a suggestion of theatricality about the royal behaviour of Hamlet may well be that he is presented as honestly trying to do it, like a man learning a new job. Commentators have felt it to be shifty of him to apologise to Laertes merely by saying he is mad; the audience has seen that he did not kill the man's father out of madness. No doubt, as Bradley remarked, he could hardly have said anything else; but he is still in part the Hamlet of the fairy-story, who cannot tell a lie though he can always delude by telling the truth. What he is really apologising for is the incident "I'll rant as well as thou"; there, as he has already remarked to Horatio, he is "very sorry he forgot himself". Oddly enough, neither he nor Laertes so much as mention that he has killed Laertes's father, either in the quarrel or the scene of apology for it. Hamlet of course realises that he and Laertes have the same "cause", and says so (rather obscurely) to Horatio, as a reason why he is sorry for the quarrel; and Laertes does at last mention it to him, when they are dying side by side like brothers, but even then Hamlet evades accepting forgiveness, because he recognises no guilt. The quarrel, on the surface merely about proper behaviour at a funeral, could only be recognised by the bystanders (who have not been officially told how Polonius died) as about whether Hamlet is to blame for driving Laertes's sister mad; here too he completely denies guilt, by claiming to have loved her greatly. But to have scuffled with Laertes while they both kicked her body in her grave was disgustingly theatrical; he feels it may really be described as a fit of madness, and apologises for it as such. According to Q2, he took the occasion to slip in a secret apology to his mother, for having acted theatrically on another occasion to her ("And hurt my mother" Q2, "And hurt my brother" F). I can hardly believe that this extra twist is more than a misprint, though it has been accepted by good critics; but it would be powerful if the actor could get it over, because the occasion when he was rude to *her* was when he happened to kill Polonius, for which you might suppose he was apologising to Laertes. To worry about one's style of behaviour rather than one's incidental murders now appears madly egotistical, but it would then appear as immensely princely behaviour. It seems clear that Shakespeare made Hamlet a model of princeliness as a primary element in his revivification of the play.

But one would not want Hamlet to be a complete hero all along (as in Stoll); and indeed to make obvious in the theatre that his behaviour is princely one needs sometimes to show him trying to correct it. We only know that he fought in the grave from a stage direction in the First Quarto, presumably because only a private company would need to be told it; but some critics have felt that only a vulgarised version could want anything so coarse. They are right to find it shocking, but not to assume that the shock could not be meant. There is no doubt that Laertes gets into the grave, because he demands to be buried with her, and Hamlet at once competes with his theatricality, so may naturally join him there (the graves were broader and shallower than ours). Indeed the whole suggestion of the Gravedigger scene is that Hamlet will soon get into a grave, so there is a symbolical point in having him do it at once. But to have them trampling on her corpse while they fight to prove which of them loves her most has a more powerful symbolism; the effect of their love has been to torment her and threaten her with contempt. The Hamlet of the sources descends to sordid behaviour in his pretence of madness; the great prince can only win by being more low-class than you or I dare be. We may be sure that Kyd did not want this, but Shakespeare restored about as much of it as the stage could bear. The revulsion of his Hamlet from doing it (already clear when he insists to the players that one should always be calm) was I think clear to the first audiences; they were ready for him to feel that he must have been mad to be so unprincely as to fight in the grave. There are other times, of course, when his behaviour is extravagantly princely without effort or thought.

I take it, then, that one way and another a good deal of mystery got into Shakespeare's first version of *Hamlet*, which had started with the intention of reviving the old play by making it life-like. Then, when the audiences became intrigued by this mystery, he made some quite small additions and changes which screwed up the mystery to the almost torturing point where we now have it—the sky was the limit now, not merely because the audiences wanted it, but because one need only act so much of this "shock-troops" material as a particular audience seemed ripe for. No wonder it made the play too long. The soliloquy "How all occasions" is a sort of encore planned in case an audience refuses to let the star go, and in the big days of *Hamlet* they would decide backstage how much, and which parts, of the full text to perform when they saw how a particular audience was shaping. This view gives no reason to doubt that the whole thing was sometimes acted, with the staff of the Globe extremely cross at not being allowed to go home earlier. I am not clear how much this picture alters the arguments of Dover Wilson from the surviving texts, but it clearly does to a considerable extent. Everyone says that the peculiar merit of the Elizabethan theatre was to satisfy a broad and varied clientele, with something of the variability of the Music Hall in its handling of the audience; but the experts do not seem to imagine a theatre which actually carried out this plan, instead of sticking to a text laid down rigidly beforehand. It is unlikely to have happened on any scale, to be sure, except in the very special case of *Hamlet*. But if you suppose it happened there you need no longer suppose a quarrel over some extras written in for occasional use. And there is the less reason to suppose a quarrel, on my argument, because the Company must have accepted Shakespeare's 1601 revision as regards both Ophelia and the Queen, for example treating the new position for "To be or not to be" as part of the standard Prompt Copy, eventually recorded in the Folio. (One would never swap back the order of scenes "on the night".) I imagine that this excitement about the play, which made it worth while keeping bits for special audiences, had already died down by 1605, when the Company sent plenty of Shakespeare's manuscript to the printer (as Dover Wilson says) just to outface the pirate of Q1; one no longer needed to keep extras up one's sleeve. But I should fancy that the claim on the title-page, "enlarged to almost as much again as it was", does not refer to the extreme shortness of the pirate's version; advertisements even when lying often have sources of plausibility, and it would be known that a few of the Globe performances had been remarkably long.

If, then, the First Quarto gives evidence about the first draft, the main changes for 1601 concerned Ophelia and the Queen; whom I will consider in turn. The scolding of Ophelia by Hamlet, and the soliloquy "To be or not to be" before it, were put later in the play. The main purpose in this, I think, was to screw up the paradoxes in the character of Hamlet rather than to affect Ophelia herself. I have already tried to describe a sort of Pirandello sequence in his behaviour from meeting the Players to the Recorder scene, which raises problems about whether he is very theatrical or very sincere, and this is much heightened by putting his hysterical attack on Ophelia in the middle of it; especially beside the utter detachment of "To be or not to be", which J. M. Robertson found so incredible in its new position as to demand grotesque collaboration theories. The first version by Shakespeare must have carried the main point of this sequence, because even the First Quarto makes him take an actual "pipe" after the Play scene and use it to claim he is a mystery ("though you can fret me, yet you cannot play upon me"); but this was a crucial part to "heighten" if you wanted to heighten the mystery as a whole.

One might also feel that the change had another purpose; combined with the new doubts about the Queen it gives the play a concentrated anti-woman central area. The worst behaviour of Hamlet is towards Ophelia, whether you call it theatrical or not; the critics who have turned against him usually seem to do so on her behalf, and his relations with the two women raise more obvious questions about whether he is neurotic than his delay. The first question here is how Shakespeare *expected* the audience to take the scolding of Ophelia, admitting that an audience has different parts. We can all see Hamlet has excuses for treating her badly, but if we are to think him a hero for yielding to them the thing becomes barbaric; he punishes her savagely for a plot against him when he has practically forced her to behave like a hospital nurse, beginning with his melodramatic silent visit. I feel sure that Dover Wilson is getting at something important, though as so often from a wrong angle, when he makes a fuss about adding a stage direction in II.ii, and insists that Hamlet must visibly overhear the King and Polonius plotting to use Ophelia against him. No doubt this is better for a modern audience, but we need to consider the sequence of changes in the traditional play. In our present text, even granting Dover Wilson his tiny stage direction, what Hamlet overhears is very harmless and indeed what he himself has planned for; it was he who started using Ophelia as a pawn, however much excused by passion or despair. Kyd, one would expect, gave solid ground for Hamlet's view that Ophelia is working against him; she would do it highmindedly, in ringing lines, with distress, regarding it as her duty since her lover has become mad, and never realising what deep enmity against him she is assisting; but still she would do something plain and worth making a fuss about. Hamlet's scolding of her for it would follow at once. The agile bard, with gleaming eye, merely removed the adequate motivation for the scolding of Ophelia, a habit to which he was becoming attached. Then for his revision he took the scolding far away even from the trivial bit of plotting, no more than was essential to explain the sequence, that he had left in for his Hamlet to overhear; thus making Dover Wilson's view harder for a spectator to invent. One can respect the struggle of Dover Wilson to recover one rag of the drapery so much needed by Hamlet, but if this was the development the Globe Theatre is not likely to have given any.

We should recall here, I think, the rising fashion in the theatres for the villain-hero, who staggers one by being so *outré*, and the love-poems of Donne, already famous in private circulation, which were designed to outrage the conventions about chivalrous treatment of women. Also the random indecency of lunatics, a thing the Elizabethans were more accustomed to than we are, since they seldom locked them up, is insisted on in the behaviour of Hamlet to Ophelia whether he is pretending or not. The surprising instruction of the Ghost—"Taint not thy mind"—was bound to get attention, so that one was prepared to think his mind tainted. I think the Shakespeare Hamlet was meant to be regarded by most of the audience as behaving shockingly towards Ophelia, almost too much so to remain a tragic hero; to swing round the whole audience into reverence for Hamlet before he died was something of a lion-taming act. This was part of the rule that all his behaviour must be startling, and was only slightly heightened in revision. But to see it in its right proportion we must remember another factor; the theatre, as various critics have pointed out, clung to an apparently muddled but no doubt tactical position of both grumbling against Puritans and accepting their main claims. The Victorians still felt that Hamlet was simply highminded here. D. H. Lawrence has a poem describing him with hatred as always blowing and snoring about other folks' whoring, rightly perhaps, but in Hamlet's time this would feel like the voice of lower-class complaint against upper-class luxury, as when he rebukes the Court for too much drink. All Malcontents rebuked luxury; this aspect of him would not need to be "brought out".

Here I think we have the right approach to another Victorian view of Hamlet, of which Bernard Shaw is perhaps the only representative still commonly read: that he was morally too advanced to accept feudal ideas about revenge, and felt, but could not say, that his father had given him an out-of-date duty; that was why he gave such an absurd excuse for not killing the King at prayer. (Dr Johnson thought it not absurd but too horrible to read.) Without this obscure element of "discussion drama", Shaw maintained, the nineteenth century would never have found Hamlet interesting; and of course Shaw would also feel it highminded of him to be a bit rough with the women in a Puritan manner. This Hamlet Theory has been swept away by ridicule too easily, and I was glad to see Alfred Harbage defend it with the true remark that no moral idea was "remote from the Elizabethan mind". Indeed it is not so much feudal as royal persons who cannot escape the duty of revenge by an appeal to public justice; this is one of the reasons why they have long been felt to make interesting subjects for plays. But I think Shakespeare's audiences did regard his Hamlet as taking a "modern" attitude to his situation, just as Bernard Shaw did. This indeed was one of the major dramatic effects of the new treatment. He walks out to the audience and says "You think this an absurd old play, and so it is, *but I'm in it*, and what can I do?" The theatrical device in itself expresses no theory about the duty of revenge, but it does ask the crowd to share in the question. No wonder that one of the seventeenth-century references, dropped while describing someone else, says "He is like Prince Hamlet, he pleases all."

This trait of his character has rightly irritated many critics, most recently perhaps Salvador de Madariaga, whose lively book on Hamlet has at least the merit of needing some effort to refute it. He finds him a familiar Renaissance type of the extreme "egotist", as well as a cad who had been to bed with Ophelia already. The curious indifference of Hamlet to the facts does make him what we call egotistical, but this would be viewed as part of his lordliness; "egotism", I think, is only a modern bit of popular psychology, quite as remote from medical science as the Elizabethan bit about "melancholy" and much less likely to occur to the first audiences. The argument that Hamlet has been to bed with Ophelia gives an impression of clearing the air, and I think greatly needs refuting; I am glad to have a coarse enough argument to do it without being suspected of undue chivalry. We need a little background first. Madariaga points out that the corresponding lady in the sources did enjoy Hamlet's person on a brief occasion, and argues that the audience would take the story for granted unless it was firmly changed; he then easily proves that the actress of Ophelia can make all references to her virginity seem comic, but this doesn't prove she was meant to. The only "source" which most of the audience would know is the play by Kyd which we have lost, and there is a great simplicity about the drama of Kyd which is unlikely to have allowed any questionable aspect to his hero. The legend itself, I agree, gives Hamlet a strong "Br'er Fox" smell, and Shakespeare had a nose for this, but the tradition of the theatre would let him assume that Ophelia represented pure pathos and was somehow betrayed. Kyd would be likely to introduce the idea that this lady, who needs a bit more dignity in the sources (though she loves Hamlet and was his foster-sister) was regarded as Hamlet's prospective Queen. Shakespeare gave this a further twist; he implies at her first appearance that her father and her brother are angling to make her Queen. To be sure, they don't say that to the girl, and still less to Hamlet's parents, but we need not believe their overeager protestations about the matter; the fuss made by Polonius about never having thought of such a thing seems to me just the way he would behave if he was manoeuvring for it, and I think this would be likely to occur to some members of the first audiences. The placid lament of the Queen over the grave of Ophelia, that she had expected her to marry Hamlet, sounds as if she had long known it was in the wind. (Not that this detail can have much effect on the stage, but it is a faint piece of evidence about how Shakespeare regarded the situation, and meant his actors to interpret it.) I do not know that any critic has taken it like that, but presumably the first audiences were more accustomed to such situations than we are. What her brother and her father do tell her, very firmly, is that the urgent thing is not to go to bed with him too quickly; her whole position depends on it; and she agrees to hold off in a pointed manner. Surely the audience will assume that this important family plan is being carried through; unless, of course, she leers and winks as Madariaga recommends, but that would only make her seem a fool. The impact of the poetry that introduces the character has a natural right to interpret her; it is hauntingly beautiful and rather unsuited to the brother who speaks it:

> The chariest maid is prodigal enough
> If she unmask her beauty to the moon

and so forth; the whole suggestion is that she must hold off from Hamlet, as part of her bid for grandeur, and yet that tragedy may come of it. However, I agree that these vast prophetic gestures towards all human experience could easily suggest just the opposite, that she is sure to have done what she is advised against; a more definite argument is required. In the Play scene, when Hamlet is offensively jeering at her for her supposed lust, and she is trying to laugh it off (pathetically and courageously; it is unfair of Madariaga to say this proves she is used to such talk), she says "you are keen, my lord, you are keen", meaning to praise his jokes as highminded general satire against the world, though they are flat enough bits of nastiness, and he answers:

It would cost you a groaning to take off my edge.

Now the conviction that it is fun to make a virgin scream and bleed, especially at her wedding, was far too obvious to the Elizabethans for this to mean anything else; I can imagine alternatives, but do not believe in them and will wait for them to be advanced by some opponent. The point is not that Hamlet's remark has any importance on the stage, but that the first audiences took for granted one view of her or the other, from the production if not from the tradition (an ambiguity here, I think, would only confuse the production), whereas we have to learn what they took for granted by using details which at the time merely seemed to fit in. This detail, I submit, is enough to prove they assumed her to be a virgin.

I am not trying to whitewash Hamlet; he is jeering at the desires of the virgin which he is keen to excite and not satisfy, and this is part of what sends her mad. But to jeer at a prospective Queen for having yielded to him already would be outside the code; the more loose the actual Court habits were (a point Madariaga uses) the more ungentlemanly it would seem, and Hamlet never loses class, however mad. He also keeps a curious appeal for the lower classes in the audience as a satirist on the upper class, as I have tried to describe; even here, some of the audience would probably enjoy having jeers against an aggressively pure young lady whose family are angling for a grand marriage; but for this purpose too he needs to be unworldly rather than to have been to bed with her already. What seems more important to us is his "psychology", and that gives the same answer; the whole point of his bad temper against her, which he builds up into feverish suspicions, is that it arises because she has shut him out, not because she has yielded to him. In the Nunnery scene, when he runs back for the second time onto the stage because he has just thought of a still nastier thing which he can't bear not to say, he says "I have heard of your paintings too", heard that women in general paint their faces. It is almost a Peter Arno drawing. He calls her obscene because all women are (like his mother) and a prostitute because she is plotting against him (like a nurse). To allow any truth to his accusations against her seems to me throwing away the dramatic effect.

But of course there is a grave solemn truth, never denied, which is simply that Ophelia did want to marry him and ought not to have been accused of lust for it. Madariaga regards her behaviour when mad as proof of incontinence when sane, an idea which strikes me as about equally remote from an Elizabethan audience and a modern doctor. She sings a song in which the man says to the woman "I would have married you, as I promised, if you had not come to my bed", which seems to ask for application to her own case; but many of the parallels in her mad talk work by opposites; indeed the agony of it (as in the mad speeches added to *The Spanish Tragedy*, for instance) is that we see her approaching recognition of the truth and then wincing far away again. "They say a made a good end" is her comment on the father who died unshriven, and "Bonny sweet Robin is all my joy" deals with her appalling lover before she walks out to death. Well might she reflect that the girls in the ballads, who came to a simpler kind of disaster by giving too earlier, met a less absolute frustration than the girl who held off because she was being groomed for queenhood; and surely this idea is the point of her vast farewell: "Come, my coach; ... Sweet ladies, good night." The German *Der Berstrafte Brundermorde* interprets this by making her say she wants her coach because she has to dine with the King. But we can argue more directly from the poetry of the thing. When she brings out this ballad the wicked King, who never falls below a certain breadth of sentiment, says "Pretty Ophelia", a quaintly smoking-room comment which directly tells the audience what to feel. Soon after, her brother echoes the word in a rage, saying that even in the madness forced upon her by Hamlet she turns Hell itself to favour and to prettiness, but the King saw that "pretty" is right at once. Recently I was being asked by a student in Peking what to make of the

> long purples
> Which liberal shepherds give a grosser name
> But our cold maids do Dead Men's Fingers call them.

Why are the obscene thoughts of these peasants necessary in the impossible but splendid description of her death? At the time, I could only say that the lines seemed to me very beautiful, and in the usual tone about Ophelia, so I felt sure they didn't carry any hint that would go outside it. Also, no doubt, the maids give the flower this unmentioned name "when they laugh alone", and here the Love of a maid did become Death and fumble at her, but there is a broader, and one might well say a prettier, suggestion behind all these hints at her desire; that nobody wants her to be frigid. A certain amount of teasing about the modesty required from her would be ordinary custom, but the social purpose behind both halves of this little contradiction is to make her a good wife. Indeed to struggle against these absurd theories about her is to feel as baffled as she did by the confusions of puritanism; it makes one angry with Hamlet, not only with his commentators, as I think we are meant to be. Being disagreeable in this way was part of his "mystery".

Turning now to the Queen: Dover Wilson argued that the First Quarto was merely a perversion of the single play by Shakespeare, with a less "subtle" treatment of the Queen. I do not think we need at once call it subtle of Shakespeare to make her into an extra mystery by simply cutting out all her explanations of her behaviour. The idea of a great lady who speaks nobly but is treacherous to an uncertain degree was familiar on the stage, as in Marlowe's *Edward II*, not a new idea deserving praise. No doubt the treatment is subtle; several of her replies seem unconscious proofs of complete innocence, whereas when she says her guilt "spills itself in fearing to be spilt" she must imply a guilty secret. But we must ask why the subtlety is wanted. An important factor here is the instruction of the Ghost to Hamlet, in the first Act, that he must contrive nothing against his mother. I think this was supplied by Kyd; he would see its usefulness as an excuse for the necessary delay, and would want his characters to be highminded. (It would be a natural extension of Belleforest who treats the Queen with great respect.) Also he had to give his Ghost a reason for returning later, because the audience would not want this interesting character to be dropped. In Kyd's first Act, therefore, the Ghost said Claudius must be killed and the Queen protected; then in the third Act, when Hamlet was questioning her suspiciously, the Ghost came back and said she hadn't known about his murder, supporting her own statement to that effect; meanwhile he told Hamlet that it would be dangerous to wait any longer about killing Claudius, because the Play scene has warned him. Hamlet had felt he still ought to wait till he knew how much his mother was involved. The Ghost had already forgiven her for what she had done—perhaps adultery, probably only the hasty remarriage to his brother—but had not cared to discuss it much; the tragic effect in the third Act is that he clears up too late an unfortunate bit of vagueness in his first instructions. This makes him a bit absurd, but the motives of Ghosts seldom do bear much scrutiny, and he is better than most of them. (On this account, Hamlet is still liable to have different motives in different scenes for sparing the King at prayer, but that seems a normal bit of Elizabethan confusion.) Thus there is no reason why Kyd's Queen should not have satisfied the curiosity of the audience fully; she would admit to

Hamlet that her second marriage was wrong, clear herself of anything else, offer to help him, and be shown doing it. Shakespeare, in his first treatment of the play, had no reason not to keep all this, as the First Quarto implies; his problem was to make the audience accept the delay as life-like, and once Hamlet is surrounded by guards that problem is solved. But if we next suppose him making a minor revision, for audiences who have become interested in the mystery of Hamlet, then it is clearly better to surround him with mystery and make him drive into a situation which the audience too feels to be unplumbable.

Richard Flatter, in his interesting book *Hamlet's Father*, has done useful work by taking this reinterpretation of the Ghost as far as it will go. He points out that the Ghost must be supposed to return in the bedroom scene to say something important, and yet all he does is to prevent Hamlet from learning whether the Queen helped in his murder; such then was his intention, though he had to deny it. After this Hamlet does up his buttons (stops pretending to be mad) and has nothing left but a highminded despair about his duties to his parents; that is why he talks about Fate and refuses to defend himself. In effect, he can now only kill Claudius after his mother is dead, and he has only an instant to do it in before he himself dies, but he is heroic in seizing this moment to carry out an apparently impossible duty with pedantic exactitude. To accuse him of delay, says Flatter with considerable point, is like accusing Prometheus of delay while chained to the Caucasus. This result, I think, is enough to prove that the Flatter view was never a very prominent element in a play which hides it so successfully. He produces interesting evidence from stage history that her complicity in the murder was assumed as part of the tradition; but I can't see that the German version has any claim to echo a pre-Shakespearean play, whereas the First Quarto gives evidence that it was Shakespeare who first started this hare, in his revision of 1601. He goes on to claim that the theme of a Ghost who, so far from wanting revenge, wants to save his unfaithful wife from being punished for murdering himself, wants even to save her from the pain of confessing it to their son, is an extraordinary moral invention, especially for an Elizabethan poet; and so it is, for a playwright in any period, if he keeps it so very well hidden. Here, surely, we are among the vaguely farcical "Solutions of the Hamlet Problem" which have been cropping up for generations. But we need also to consider why they crop up, why the play was so constructed as to excite them. I think the Flatter theory did cross the keen minds of some of the 1601 audiences, and was intended to; but only as a background possibility in a situation which encouraged a variety of such ideas.

Indeed, an opposite position to the Flatter one is also left open, and I have heard from people who still hold it; that the Ghost is a devil, and only comes back in the third Act to prevent the Queen from being converted by Hamlet. One might suppose that if she had been fully converted the tragedy would have been avoided, though it is not clear how. Dover Wilson has written well about the variety of views on ghosts expressed by the characters in the first Act, and therefore expected in the audience; but then he seems to assume that the whole audience, after the first Act, is swung over to one view, that the Ghost is genuine. It was not their habit to be converted so easily. The official Protestant position was that all apparent Ghosts are devils trying to instigate sin; also that Purgatory does not exist, so that this Ghost in saying it has come from Purgatory must be lying. Few of the audience would be inclined to worry about such points, but the technique of Shakespeare aims at breaking up any merely aesthetic "suspension of disbelief"—you are made to consider how people would *really* react to a Ghost. To think it a devil had both the safety of being official and the charm of being cynical; after admitting the idea at the start, the playwright could expect it to remain alive in the audience somewhere. Certainly the whole audience is meant to believe in the murder, otherwise the thing would be too confusing (this may be why the King's confession "aside" had to be added in III.i); but even a devil, for bad purposes, could "speak true". From the point of view of James I, as I understand, any usurper once legally crowned had the Divine Right, and only a devil could supernaturally encourage murder of him. That Hamlet is stirring up misery among a lot of otherwise contented people is a prominent suggestion of the play, as several critics have pointed out—he is a disease, and presumably the Ghost made him virulent. Thus you could not only think the Ghost in the bedroom scene startlingly good, but also startlingly bad; though most of the audience was not likely to think either.

We need to step back here, and consider why it is possible for such radically opposed theories to be held by careful readers; it would be trivial merely to jeer at the long history of theories about *Hamlet*, because they bear witness to its peculiar appeal. The only simple view is that the play was constructed so as to leave them open. This may seem to make it a mere trick, but the popular feeling about ghosts had always this curious ambivalence; the novelty was in getting an author who could put it directly on the stage. As for raising doubts about the Queen, I think that the fundamental reason why the change was "subtle", to recall the term of Dover Wilson, was something very close to the Freudian one which he is so quick at jumping away from; to make both parents a mystery at least pushes the audience towards fundamental childhood situations. But it would have a sufficient immediate effect from thickening the atmosphere and broadening the field.

We should now be prepared to consider the Freudian view of *Hamlet*, the most extraordinary of the claims that it means something very profound which the first audiences could not know about. I think that literary critics, when this theory first appeared, were thrown into excessive anxiety. A. C. Bradley had made the essential points before; that Hamlet's first soliloquy drives home (rather as a surprise to the first audiences, who expected something about losing the throne) that some kind of sex nausea about his mother is what is really poisoning him; also that in the sequence around the Prayer scene his failure to kill Claudius is firmly and intentionally tied up with a preference for scolding his mother instead. I have been trying to argue that his relations with the two women were made increasingly oppressive as the play was altered, but in any case the Freudian atmosphere of the final version is obvious even if distasteful. Surely the first point here is that the original legend is a kind of gift for the Freudian approach (even if Freud is wrong); it need not be painful to suppose that Shakespeare expressed this legend with a unique power. There is a fairy-story or childish fascination because Hamlet can boast of his secret and yet keep it, and because this crazy magical behaviour kills plenty of grown-ups; to base it on a conflict about killing Mother's husband is more specifically Freudian but still not secret. The Freudian theory makes a literary problem when its conclusions oppose what the author thought he intended; but it seems clear that Shakespeare wouldn't have wanted to alter the play if he had been told about Freud, whether he laughed at the theory or not. Then again, what is tiresome for the reader about the Freudian approach is that it seems to tell us we are merely deluded in the reasons we give for our preferences, because the real grounds for them are deep in the Unconscious; but here the passage to the underground is fairly open. A feeling that this hero is allowed to act in a peculiar way which is yet somehow familiar, because one has been tempted to do it oneself, is surely part of the essence of the story. There is a clear contrast with Oedipus, who had no Oedipus Complex. He had not wanted to kill his father and marry his mother, even "unconsciously"; if he came to recognise that he had wanted it, that would weaken his bleak surprise at learning he has done it. The claim is that his audiences wanted to do it unconsciously—that is why they were so deeply stirred by the play, and why Aristotle could treat it as the supreme tragedy though in logic it doesn't fit his case at all, being only a bad-luck story. This position is an uneasy one, I think; one feels there ought to be some mediation between the surface and the depths, and probably the play did mean more to its first audiences than we realise. But Hamlet is himself suffering from the Complex, in the grand treatment by Ernest Jones, though the reactions of the audience are also considered when he makes the other characters "fit in". And this is not unreasonable, because Hamlet is at least peculiar in Saxo, and Shakespeare overtly treats him as a "case" of melancholy, a specific though baffling mental disease which medical textbooks were being written about.

What does seem doubtful is whether they would think his mental disease was what made him spare the King at prayer, as is essential to the Freudian position; or, if you don't think that matters, whether they could at least suspect that the real reason was not the one he gave, as is believed by almost all modern critics. Here I want to propose a conjecture, which would put the first audiences in a much more intelligible position. In the first place, the incident is likely to have been in Kyd's version. What so many critics have felt is, not so much that the motive of Hamlet is too wicked, but that it sticks out; it is unprepared-for; and one thinks of other cases in Shakespeare where this is due to a certain strain between the story he has taken over and the characters he has invented for it. If then Kyd introduced the incident, we may presume he gave Hamlet the plain motive of wanting to send Claudius to Hell, and intended it to be believed. We have next to ask why; and we must remember that, when Kyd wrote Hamlet, the fashion for condoning revenge in the theatre had not yet arisen; besides, a revenger who killed a king was a particularly shocking one—to treat him as a hero might be positively dangerous. The immediate problem before Kyd, inventing the Elizabethan drama, is how to turn the story in Belleforest into a stage tragedy. A good deal has to be changed, because the incidents convenient for treatment don't end in tragedy; besides, to use the later formula, he needs a crisis in the third Act sufficient to give him his catastrophe in the fifth. In the structure of the play as we have it, the crisis is the refusal of Hamlet to kill the King at prayer; in no other case does he evidently refuse an opportunity, and the effect of his refusal here is the death not only of the hero but of almost the entire cast. Surely there had to be some "point" in the incident, some reason why it mattered; and for an Elizabethan moralist there would be a very obvious point, so obvious as to be hard for the dramatist to evade, even if he had wanted to. Hamlet goes too far here; he wants too much revenge. If he killed Claudius he would be impeccable (except on the theory of James I, but that was rather wild), because he is the real King, with the Divine Right, and Claudius is a murderer as well as a traitor; Hamlet would only act like an established King signing an order for execution. But even then it would be wrong not to allow the criminal the consolations of religion in the condemned cell; ordinary opinion would allow frightful cruelties against a regicide, but a plan to send him to Hell it would think outrageous. When Hamlet wants that, he goes outside his legal position; he becomes simply a wicked revenger, though he could still get sympathy for his reckless courage. He commits a tragic error of statecraft which is also a sin, forgiveable in his circumstances perhaps but his own fault, and such a fault is enough to spoil an otherwise righteous plan of revenge. Perhaps the moral was expressed by the Ghost, which gives him something to say when he reappears; but the structure of the plot made it very plain anyhow. If it is asked why we have no record of this moral, the answer is that it came to be thought unfashionably heavy; maybe that was a reason why the play was laughed at, though nobody would dare say so outright.

A number of Victorian critics, including Bernard Shaw, as I was recalling earlier, thought that Shakespeare had to write a Revenge Play for his coarse audience but that, because he was morally so "advanced", he added hints that revenge was wrong or at least out of date. One or two recent critics, sternly recalling us to the high sense of duty of a purer time, have argued that it was the unquestioned duty of Hamlet to send his father's murderer to Hell. This idea that the Elizabethans were all heathens seems to be comical; the first audiences had heard any number of sermons denouncing revenge under any circumstances. The Victorians were right in feeling there was some twist about the matter, but they got it the wrong way round; the old play was the one which would naturally have the moral, not the new one; and so far as Shakespeare seems against revenge he is "backward". But I think that, while fully realising the horror of the thing, he made positive efforts to turn Hamlet into an up-to-date revenger. G. B. Harrison has well pointed out that Hamlet happens to succeed, to an appalling degree, in his desire to kill Claudius during some act of deadly sin. Claudius knows it is the poisoned cup the Queen wants to drink from (as an intimacy with her son) and orders her not to; but she insists, and he only says (aside) "It is the poisoned cup. It is too late." When the poison takes effect he says "She swounds to see them bleed." In real life he might not have time to save her, but surely Harrison is right about the best way to act it. "Claudius could save the Queen, but that would betray himself. He has now killed the woman for whom he contrived two murders ... and can only wait for the end"—actually he is more set on life than that when he says "Oh, yet defend me, friends; I am but hurt." The actress of Gertrude, says Harrison, should make her realise what Claudius has done as she dies; she does, of course, contradict him and try to save Hamlet. I should think Shakespeare added this detail deliberately, to give Hamlet what he wanted. Also he makes Hamlet report with glee that he sent Rosencrantz and Guildenstern to their deaths positively ordering "no shriving time allowed", which might prevent discovery of his plot but would be bound to appear strikingly wicked. They are old friends against whom even he alleges nothing but meddling, not any knowledge of the order to kill him when he gets to England. I should imagine that Shakespeare both added the detail about no shriving and cut out all evidence that these characters know of the King's intention. I imagine indeed he felt a certain ironical willingness to make his revenger very bad; he could fit that in easily enough, if it would help to make Hamlet popular. At the same time, I readily agree, he was not absorbed into the fashion he was making use of; the inherent humanity of his treatment makes an eerie contrast to it. Indeed there are repeated suggestions that Hamlet is exasperated by being put into a situation so unwelcome to him, so that when he does act he plunges into his role with wilful violence. At the words "no shriving time allowed" Horatio coolly interrupts and asks "how was this sealed?", and Hamlet can boast that Heaven had provided the right seal to carry out this order, and so forth, ending after eight lines with a mention of the fight with the pirates. Horatio returns rather broodingly to the earlier detail:

> So, Guildenstern and Rosencrantz go to it.

On this mild hint Hamlet becomes boisterously self-justifying. They are not near his conscience; it was at their own risk that they came near a great man like himself. Horatio says only:

> Why, what a King is this!

and Hamlet with importunate eagerness asks him whether he doesn't now think it is "perfect conscience" to kill Claudius, who has tried to kill Hamlet as well as all his other crimes, and with such cozenage too. The repetition of "conscience", I think, shows the gleaming eye of Shakespeare. Critics, so far as I have noticed, take Horatio's remark to mean that Claudius is wicked to try to kill Hamlet, and this is perhaps what Hamlet thinks he meant; but I had always assumed, and still do, that he meant "what a King you have become"; it is Hamlet who is now acting like a king, almost too like a king, after a long period when he didn't.

I am putting in an appendix some remarks about the background of the play, which I hope support this theory about sparing the King at prayer; I want now to consider the effects on members of the first audiences, most of whom may be presumed to know the old play well enough. An idea that Hamlet doesn't realise what he is doing here in all its implications, one may say, had always been present, as part of the moral. In the new play Hamlet is no longer blamed for the motive he gives; indeed, when the Ghost says he has been neglecting to kill the King because "lapsed in time and passion" it is rather pointedly ignored. The audience is set free, I think, among other possible reactions, to regard the motive as an excuse. Also Hamlet's failure even to think of his personal danger, now that the King knows his secret, would be more glaring for Elizabethans than for ourselves (as Dover Wilson pointed out); it suits the habitual lordliness of his mind, but is evidently not justified on this decisive occasion. There is a suggestion "You thought you were going to be bored by this old moral anecdote, but you had not really considered the whole situation it describes." That there is some puzzle about it could easily occur to them, and the puzzle joins on very naturally to his mental disease.

The idea of a man grown-up in everything else who still acts like a child towards his elder relations could occur to a reflective mind, not only be sensed by the Unconscious, as soon as behaviour like Hamlet's was presented as a puzzle. The trouble with it if made prominent would be from making the hero contemptible, but Hamlet has many escapes from that besides his claim to mental disease. That his mother's marriage was considered incest made his initial disturbance seem more rational then than it does now; but his horror and jealousy are made to feel, as T. S. Eliot pointed out for purposes of complaint, a spreading miasma and in excess of this cause. I do not think Dover Wilson need have suspected that Eliot hadn't heard about incest, even for a rival effort at dodging Freud; there was admittedly an excess, because the old play was admittedly theatrical. Unconscious resistance to killing a *King* is what the audience would be likely to invent, if any; for Claudius to talk about the divinity that doth hedge a king is irony, because he has killed one, but we are still meant to feel its truth; there may be some echo of the current view of Hamlet, as one critic has suggested, in the grand scene of Chapman with the repeated line "Do anything but killing of a King." It would fit well onto the highminded aspect of Hamlet, as having an unmentioned doubt about the value of his revenge. But none of this is a rebuttal of the Freudian view; the feeling about a King is derived very directly from childhood feelings about Father.

We have to consider, not merely how a play came to be written which allows of being searched so deeply so long after, but why it has steadily continued to hold audiences who on any view do not see all round it. The Freudian view is that it satisfies the universal Unconscious, but one feels more practical in saying, as Hugh Kingsmill did, that they enjoy the imaginative release of indulging in very "theatrical" behaviour, which in this case is hard to distinguish from "neurotic" behaviour. The business of the plot is to prevent them from feeling it as an indulgence, because the assumption that Hamlet has plenty of reasons for it is always kept up. If we leave the matter there, I think, the play appears a rather offensive trick and even likely to be harmful. Indeed common sense has decided that people who feel encouraged to imitate Hamlet, or to follow what appear to be the instructions of Freud, actually are liable to behave badly. But the first audiences were being asked to consider this hero of legend as admittedly theatrical (already laughed at for it) and yet unbreakably true about life; in one way because he illustrated a recognised neurosis, in another because he extracted from it virtues which could not but be called great however much the story proved them to be fatal. So far as the spectator was tempted forward to examine the "reasons" behind Hamlet he was no longer indulging a delusion but considering a frequent and important, even if delusory, mental state, and trying to handle it. If one conceives the play as finally rewritten with that kind of purpose and that kind of audience, there is no need to be astonished that it happened to illustrate the Freudian theory. The eventual question is whether you can put up with the final Hamlet, a person who frequently appears in the modern world under various disguises, whether by Shakespeare's fault or no. I would always sympathise with anyone who says, like Hugh Kingsmill, that he can't put up with Hamlet at all. But I am afraid it is within hail of the more painful question whether you can put up with yourself and the race of man.

## HAMLET APPENDICES

I would much prefer to make this essay on *Hamlet* one consecutive piece, but as everyone has found about *Hamlet* the subject begins budding off you, and it had better be allowed to take its natural course. However, these extra little essays are intended to be subordinate; they are meant to give a tolerable amount of support to assertions which were made in the main essay. I wish that the subject was less obscure, but the fact that people at the time wanted it to be obscure does seem to me enough to make a competent historian feel less baffled; all he really needs to feel is that not he but some earlier people were baffled, and I should think they were. My remarks are therefore very comforting for him, and he need not attack me for them. It seems a fussy introduction, but I am asking to be allowed a brief glance at various learned fields. Consider the enormous fact that the books about *Hamlet* would alone completely fill a sheer house. I am rather interested in the reflection that this already defeats what is called "scholarship", because nobody has read them all. If he did, he would only be a monster. The historian of *Hamlet* is therefore already in the situation envisaged by the great Toynbee, when he said that a historian a thousand years hence, with thousands of millions of documents to choose from, could only try to write a good novel.

# Hamlet

*Hamlet* seems to be the first play of Shakespeare in which he is deliberately competing with a well-known earlier play on the same subject. We don't have the earlier play, but allusions to it tell us that it had a ghost crying "Hamlet, revenge!" One of the most popular tragedies of the time was *The Spanish Tragedy*, by Thomas Kyd, and some resemblances between it and *Hamlet* suggest that the earlier *Hamlet* was also Kyd's. The Shakespeare play has a First Quarto, a bad pirated one, which garbles the text and makes a frightful mess of such things as the "To be or not to be" speech, but still has many points of interest. In it, Polonius is called Corambis, the Queen explicitly says that she knew nothing of Hamlet senior's murder, a stage direction tells us that Hamlet leaps into Ophelia's grave to struggle with Laertes, and Hamlet's speech to the players refers to the ad-libbing of clowns. In short, it undoubtedly has some authority: how much is another question. It has been staged in its own right, and while I have not seen a performance, it's clear that it's a lively and actable play, and may well have come closer than the texts you're reading to the *Hamlet* the Elizabethan audience actually got. I don't see how an uncut *Hamlet* could ever have been performed under Elizabethan conditions. There's a seventeenth-century Hamlet play in German, called *Der Bestrafte Brudermord* (Brother-Murder Punished), probably derived from a version brought to Germany by English companies on tour there, and it's closer to Q1 than to the texts we know.

From *Northrop Frye on Shakespeare.* © 1986 by Northrop Frye.

Shakespeare's company seems to have been annoyed by Q1, and they took the unusual step of issuing an authorized Quarto, which, they said on the title page, was twice as long as Q1, and printed "according to the true and perfect copy." This Q2 is the basis of most modern editions of the play. Then there's the Folio *Hamlet*, shorter than Q2 but still containing many passages not in it. Editors assume that every line likely to have been written by Shakespeare must be preserved, and that their job is to reconstruct a monolithic *Hamlet*, containing everything in both Q2 and F that's missing from the other. No doubt they're right as editors, though whether Shakespeare really wrote such a definitive *Hamlet* is by no means certain. Anyway, when we take Q2 as a basis and add to it all the F lines not in it, the result is Shakespeare's longest play.

It's long partly because everyone, with the exception of the two women, talks too much. (That's just the dramatic effect, of course: words are not really being wasted.) "Brief let me be," says the Ghost, and goes on for another fifty lines. "I will be brief," says Polonius, after the Queen pulls him up and tells him to get on with it, but he isn't. Even the Player Queen, Gertrude says, protests too much. Hamlet, of course, talks incessantly: he wonders why he "must, like a whore, unpack my heart with words," and goes on talking about that. He talks so much that he begins to sound like a guide or commentator on the play, and one of the standard ways of misreading *Hamlet* is to accept Hamlet's views as Shakespeare's. But Hamlet's views of Polonius, of his mother's sin in marrying Claudius, of the treachery of Rosencrantz and Guildenstern, while they may often be reasonably close to what we're likely to accept, are surcharged with Hamlet's melancholy—that is, they're sick. He sees what's there, but there's an emotional excess in his perception that's reflected back to him. His self-reproaches are sick too, but it's not so hard to see that. We must never forget that while he's alienated from the other characters (except Horatio), he's still involved in the action, and not where we are in the audience.

For example: his address to the players is often read as encapsulating Shakespeare's own view of how his plays should be acted. But Hamlet's views of classical restraint in acting, his preference for plays that are caviar to the general, and the like, are views which are primarily appropriate to a university-trained highbrow. It's obvious as he goes on that Hamlet could never conceive of the possibility of such a play as *King Lear*. He's not much of a poet, he tells Ophelia, but when he's instructing the actors how to speak "my lines," we hear the voice of the amateur, concerned primarily with making sure that nobody misses a syllable of his precious speech. We can't check up on his abilities here, because we never get the speech, at least to recognize it: presumably it came after the play broke up. In short, Hamlet is one more character in Shakespeare, who contains him as he contains Peter Quince.

When I was an undergraduate, my Shakespeare teacher assigned an essay topic, "Minor Problems in *Hamlet*," by which he meant all the "problems" except two: how mad was Hamlet, and why did he delay? This was years before a very influential essay had appeared by L.C. Knights called "How Many Children Had Lady Macbeth?", an attack on pseudo-problems raised by Shakespearean critics that are not relevant to the kind of thing Shakespeare was doing. It didn't take me long, even without the benefit of that essay, to find that most of the minor problems were pseudo-problems. But I discovered two things that were useful. First, there's no boundary in the play between the actual and the pseudo-problems; second, there's no other play in Shakespeare, which probably means no other play in the world, that raises so many questions of the "problem" type. It's quite clear that problems, genuine or phony, are part of the texture of the play, and central to its meaning. I'm not saying that we get to the "real meaning" of the play by figuring out answers to its problems: I'm saying rather the opposite. Insoluble problems and unanswerable questions meet us everywhere we turn, and make *Hamlet* the most stifling and claustrophobic of plays. Not for us, because we're outside it, but for the characters caught up in its action. It used to be said that one reason for all the complexity is the older *Hamlet* play, which saddled Shakespeare with an "intractable" plot and situation much cruder than he wanted to use. There can hardly be much in that: the earlier *Hamlet* looks so mysterious because we don't have it, but we do have an earlier version of *King Lear* (spelled Leir), and it's clear from that that Shakespeare never allowed any source to become "intractable" and get in the way of his play.

Example of "problem": why does Hamlet fly into such a rage when he hears Laertes expressing a very natural and poignant grief for his dead sister, even if it includes some equally natural cursing of Hamlet? No direct answer, probably, but we can understand something of his feeling. Apart from Hamlet's sudden discovery that Ophelia is dead, as he assumes by suicide, a shock great enough to demoralize him in itself, he's seeing the reflection in Laertes of his own dilemma of words taking the place of action. "Show me what thou'lt *do*!" he screams at Laertes, although there is nothing appropriate for Laertes to do at this point except kill Hamlet. Then Hamlet says:

> What is the reason that you use me thus?
> I loved you ever.    (V.i. 313–14)

This has a ring of sincerity, but if Hamlet is only assuming madness, as we have been led to think, has he really forgotten that he's wiped out Laertes' family? Perhaps not, at least if when he says to Horatio:

> For, by the image of my cause, I see
> The portraiture of his.          (V.ii. 77–78)

he is thinking of Laertes as someone else with a murdered father. In apologizing to Laertes, however, he pleads diminished responsibility, and says that his madness and not Hamlet himself was to blame. But the worst thing Hamlet has done to Laertes is to murder Polonius, and he does that in a scene where he is swearing to his mother with the greatest vehemence that he is *not* mad. And if Hamlet can make madness a not-guilty plea for murder, why can't Ophelia be exonerated from suicide for the same reason? Yet the gravediggers agree that she was a voluntary suicide; the priest grumbles that her death was "doubtful," and has certainly no intention of giving her the benefit of any doubt; and Hamlet himself tells us that the funeral rites are those of a suicide. And so it goes: every part of the play is like this.

Take the use of the supernatural. The opening scene gets the point established that the Ghost is objective and not just a hallucination of Hamlet's. For a speculative temperament like Hamlet's there might be a certain exhilaration in the revealing of another world, in seeing for oneself that there are more things in heaven and earth than are dreamed of in Horatio's cautious and sceptical philosophy. But everything that seems to expand the horizon in the play actually limits it still further. The fact that the Ghost has to leave by dawn suggests that he could be an evil spirit, and there's enough sense of evil to make the group who first see him huddle together and try to warm themselves up, so to speak, by thinking of the "so hallowed and so gracious" time of Christmas Eve, when there are no evil spirits.

In the next scene Hamlet, in his black clothes, standing apart from the brilliant court scene, is urged by his mother not to seek his father in the dust, and by his new stepfather to throw his "unprevailing woe" to earth. Melancholy, the cold and dry humour, is being associated with earth, the cold and dry element. With Hamlet's first soliloquy a vision begins to form of a corrupt Danish court resting on a seething and heaving quicksand. This vision is embodied for us on the stage at the end of the first act, when the Ghost disappears below it and follows Hamlet and his friends *hic et ubique*, as Hamlet says, saying "swear" at intervals, the perfect image for an unresting spirit whose unresolved murder is threatening the whole Danish world with destruction from below. Quite a contrast with the language of the opening scene, which begins (practically) with the words "Long live the king!", meaning Claudius, and where the first line addressed to the Ghost by Horatio contains the word "usurp." Usurpation, kingship and the source of evil are reversing their locations.

Hamlet's real difficulty with the Ghost is: if purgatory is a place of purification, why does a ghost come from it shrieking for vengeance? And why does purgatory, as the Ghost describes it, sound so much as though it were hell? The Ghost's credentials are very doubtful, by all Elizabethan tests for such things, and although Hamlet is in a state close to hysteria when he calls the Ghost "old mole," "this fellow in the cellarage," and the like, it is still unlikely that he would use such phrases if he had firmly identified the Ghost with his father at that point. On the other hand, he has always despised and distrusted Claudius, and is inclined to think the story authentic whether the teller of it is or not. There are two elements, in any case, in the message the Ghost brings him that increase to an unbearable pitch what I've called the sense of claustrophobia.

The first element is the role of religion in the play. The Ghost suffers so much in purgatory because he was killed before he had time to be confessed and shriven. So Hamlet decides that he won't kill Claudius while he's at prayer because he wants him to go to hell and not to purgatory. Never mind how genuine this feeling is just now: the implication is that when we enter the next world we run on a mindless railway switch that will automatically send Claudius to hell if he dies drunk, and to purgatory if he dies praying. We could write this off as an excuse, of course, if it stood alone; but the notion is deeply rooted in Hamlet's mind, whether implanted by the Ghost or already there. He makes a point of the fact that Rosencrantz and Guildenstern were to be killed with "not shriving-time allowed," and when he discovers that the man behind the arras is Polonius and not Claudius he says "take thy fortune." Apparently everything depends on whether the priest gets there in time or not. So it's not very reassuring to find that the only accredited priest in the play is that horrible creature who presides over Ophelia's funeral, and who gets a concentration of malice and spite into an eight-line speech that would do credit to the Devil himself, who doubtless inspired it.

The supernatural dimension of the play, then, doesn't expand our vision: on the contrary, it seals it in by surrounding us with an "afterlife" that has no infinite presence in it, only the clicking and whirring of a sacramental machine. Hamlet's weariness with his life and his longing for death, if necessary by suicide, are expressed many times in the play. Suicide is an obvious way out for someone who feels that the world is a prison, even if "a goodly one." But the machine cuts that escape off too: if you kill yourself you won't get the release of death; you'll simply lose what chance there is of ever being released.

The second element in the Ghost's message that squeezes Hamlet's life into narrowing limits is the interruption of the habits, such as they are, of Hamlet's life. At first, though he has no use for Claudius, he has no great hatred for him either, and the real cause of his melancholy is not the loss of his father but the remarriage of his mother. The Ghost tells him that he must focus on Claudius and stop brooding about Gertrude. "Taint not thy mind," he says, apparently not realizing how much it's tainted already, and "leave her to heaven," again not a reassuring recommendation coming from him. But Hamlet's feelings are still fixated on his mother, and he has to keep working up his hatred of Claudius.

It is a little unusual for someone who has an appointment to see his mother to stop on the way and remind himself in a soliloquy that he must be careful not to murder her, especially when he's about to pass up a chance to kill Claudius and get rid of his ghostly incubus. One reason why it's Gertrude rather than Claudius who drives Hamlet up the wall is her total unconsciousness of having done anything wrong. She is a soft, easygoing, sentimental woman who "would hang on" her late husband and be treated with the greatest solicitude in response, and Hamlet does not see that the instinct to hang on his father was the same one that prompted her to attach herself after his death to the nearest strong-looking man who presented himself. Because of her compliant nature, Hamlet finds her delightfully easy to bully, and she keeps crumpling under his ranting until the exasperated Ghost comes in to derail him again. We notice that the Ghost is still solicitous about her, in spite of his purgatorial preoccupations.

Hamlet keeps calling the marriage incestuous, as technically perhaps it was: marriage with deceased husband's brother was the other half of the great Victorian anxiety symbol of marriage with deceased wife's sister. The *Hamlet* situation was the one that brought the Reformation to England, when Henry VIII asked the Pope to dissolve his marriage to Catherine of Aragon on the ground that she had been previously married to his deceased older brother. But no one else, even the Ghost, seems much concerned about that side of it, although the Ghost does call Claudius an incestuous and adulterate beast, along with many other epithets that he had after all some provocation for using. But the incest theme is really another stick to beat Claudius with: the real centre of Hamlet's distress is the "wicked speed" of the marriage; it seems almost to suggest some prearrangement.

Freudian critics have been quick to notice that Hamlet is in the classic Oedipus situation in regard to his parents, and have suggested that Hamlet is paralyzed in trying to move against Claudius because Claudius has fulfilled

Hamlet's own Oedipal desires by killing his father and marrying his mother. It would not be reasonable to ignore the Oedipal element in the set-up, but, as always in Shakespeare, there are many other factors involved. Hamlet is a student whose few pleasures have to do with the life of the mind. It is pathetic, almost humorous, that after he hears the Ghost his conditioned impulse is to reach for what we would call his notebook and make a memorandum about the hypocrisy of villains. I am not saying that Hamlet has a studious temperament averse to action, though he does have the student's disease of melancholy, which means that his actions are apt to be out of synchronization, being either delayed, like his revenge on Claudius, or hasty and rash, like his killing of Polonius. This fact has a good deal to do, naturally, with his horror at seeing his amiable mother moving so much faster to remarry than one would expect.

What I am saying is that the cold, bleak, primitive call to revenge does not give Hamlet's life a positive purpose: it merely impoverishes still further what life he has. Among the conflict of emotions in his mind when he watches Claudius praying and wonders if he should kill him now, one is undoubtedly a strong distaste for a treacherous and rather cowardly act, which is what sticking a rapier into a man's turned back really amounts to, whatever the urgency of the revenge ethic. It is, as he says, "hire and salary, not revenge." O.K., Claudius started it, but if you adopt the methods of your enemies you become like your enemies, and Hamlet has no wish to become like Claudius at his worst. Revenge, said Francis Bacon in his essay on the subject, is a kind of wild justice, and something in Hamlet is too civilized for stealthy murder, though he clearly would stand up to any kind of open conflict.

In all revenge tragedies we need three characters (sometimes doubled or in groups): a character to be killed, a character to kill him, and an avenger to kill the killer. The revenge is usually regarded by an audience as a positive act of retribution that brings the moral norms of society into balance again, and it usually sympathizes with the avenger accordingly. Because in the Bible God is represented as saying "Vengeance is mine," the avenger is often regarded, in the tragedies of the period, as an agent of divine vengeance, whatever his own moral status. It is in tragedy particularly that we see how persistently man creates his gods in his own image, and finds nothing incongruous when a ferocious and panic-stricken human revenge is called the carrying out of God's own will. Shakespeare has two revenge tragedies apart from *Hamlet*: *Julius Caesar* and *Macbeth*. Julius Caesar and Duncan are, murdered; Brutus (with others) and Macbeth are the murderers; the avengers are Mark Antony, with Octavius Caesar, and Malcolm and Macduff.

In *Hamlet*, however, there are three concentric rings of revenge tragedies. In the centre is Polonius murdered by Hamlet and avenged by Laertes. Around it is the main action of the play, Hamlet senior murdered by Claudius and avenged by Hamlet junior. Around that again is the background story of Fortinbras senior, killed by Hamlet senior in a duel on the day that Hamlet junior was born and the first gravedigger entered into his occupation. Fortinbras junior, at the beginning of the play, is planning a revenge on Denmark: Claudius manages to avoid this threat, but Fortinbras comes in at the end of the play, achieving precisely what a successful revenge would have achieved, the crown of Denmark. The final result of all the to-do the Ghost of Hamlet senior starts is that the successor of Claudius on the throne of Denmark is the son of the man he had killed long before the play began. Naturally, the simultaneous existence of these three revenge themes produces a fantastically complex play, especially when Hamlet has both the murderer's role in the Polonius tragedy and the avenger role in the main story. Their total effect is to neutralize the sense of the restoring of moral balance that a revenge is supposed to give us as a rule. Revenge does not complete anything, it merely counters something, and a second vengeance pattern will grow up in opposition to it. Of Fortinbras, on whom the hopes and expectations of the few survivors of the play are fixed, we know nothing except that he will fight for anything. In tragedy the typical effect on the audience is traditionally assumed to be a catharsis, a word that has something to do with purification, whatever else it means. *Hamlet* seems to me a tragedy without a catharsis, a tragedy in which everything noble and heroic is smothered under ferocious revenge codes, treachery, spying and the consequences of weak actions by broken wills.

Let us look first at the inner circle of Polonius, Laertes and Ophelia. At the beginning we have a contrast between Hamlet, forbidden to leave Denmark and become a student again at Wittenberg, and Laertes, who has finally persuaded his father to let him go to France. So we have a scene of leave-taking, with Polonius sounding off with a number of maxims (we get an impression that Laertes has heard them all before, and perhaps not very long before), and ending with the noble and resonant "This above all," etc. After which he gets a servant to follow Laertes to Paris to snoop and spy and encourage talebearing from his friends. That's one of the first examples of how any opening in the thick fog surrounding the court of Denmark gets sealed up again. In the same scene Polonius tells Ophelia not to encourage Hamlet's advances, because he's too high in rank to want to marry her. Ophelia says that Hamlet's wooing has been "honourable," and we gather later on that Claudius and Gertrude would have approved of the match and that Gertrude at least expected it. Polonius may be simply an obstinate ass, but it's more likely that he's rationalizing something, and that we have to add him to the Shakespearean fathers with grown-up daughters who won't let go, except on their own terms. Laertes weighs in with a remarkably priggish speech about maidenly virtue, and Ophelia tells him, very politely and demurely, that he just might try to mind his own business and look after his own morals. "Oh, fear me not," snaps Laertes: sisters are not supposed to answer back. The point of this is, apparently, to establish Laertes as already suspicious of Hamlet.

After Hamlet learns the truth about how Claudius became king, he conceals his feelings under the disguise of madness, and Claudius feels that there is something dangerous there to be investigated, something more than just the shock of his father's death and mother's remarriage. Polonius is all ready with a theory. In speaking of the love conventions that come into *Romeo and Juliet*, I said that those who died for love were saints and martyrs in the God of Love's calendar. It was also in the convention that great lovers frequently went mad when frustrated in love: one of the best-known poems of the age was Ariosto's *Orlando Furioso*, about the great knight Roland, or Orlando, of Charlemagne's court, driven mad by the infidelity of his mistress, Angelica. Polonius, a wide if not always critical reader, has decided that the frustration of Hamlet's courtship of Ophelia, the result of his own piercing insight into the situation, has driven Hamlet mad. Must be true: he read about it in a book somewhere. He has one piece of evidence: Hamlet, Ophelia reports, had burst into her room, stared hard at her face, and then left. We can see that he was wondering if he could possibly make Ophelia a friend and confidante in his situation, as Horatio is, and saw nothing but immaturity and weakness in her face. However, Polonius proposes setting a booby trap for Hamlet, using Ophelia as a decoy, and Ophelia has no power to resist this scheme. So there's a conversation between Hamlet and Ophelia, with Claudius and Polonius eavesdropping, as Hamlet realizes near the end of the interview (at least, that's how the scene is usually played, and it seems to fit everything). That's the end of any luck Ophelia might have in future. "Am I not right, old Jephthah?" Hamlet says to Polonius. "If you call me Jephthah, my lord," says Polonius, "I have a daughter whom I love passing well" (congratulating himself on his astuteness in picking up another reference to his daughter). Sure, but what Jephthah did to his daughter was sacrifice her. The women in this play are heroines in a tragedy, but not tragic heroines, like Juliet or Cleopatra: they're pathetic rather, crushed under the wheels of all the male egos.

To look briefly now at the struggle with Claudius: if we could manage to forget what Claudius did to become king, we could see what everybody except Hamlet and Horatio sees, a strong and attractive monarch. He shows the greatest coolness and shrewdness in dealing with the Fortinbras threat, preparing to meet it if it comes, but deflecting it nonetheless. Apparently there's no question of any de jure line of succession in so turbulent a time, and the new king is elected by the nobles. Hamlet says late in the play that Claudius "Popped in between the election and my hopes," but there might have been a quite sensible decision that Hamlet was too young and untried: in any case, Claudius not only treats him like a son, but publicly supports him as his own successor. And while in such a time Claudius may have strengthened his position by marrying Gertrude, there seems no reason to doubt the sincerity of his affection for her.

In fact, once the play starts, he does no harm to anyone except Hamlet, and even against him he proceeds very unwillingly. The delay in Hamlet meets a corresponding delay, with equally unconvincing excuses, in Claudius. An uncomplicated villain, like Richard III, would have wiped Hamlet out of his life at the first hint of danger, and slept all the better for it. Claudius seems a sensuous, even coarse, physical type, with an abounding vitality that makes for a lot of noisy partying. When Hamlet is freezing on the ramparts of Elsinore he hears such a party going on, and makes a disapproving speech about how a heavily drinking king is bad for Denmark's reputation. Two points to note here: first, Hamlet doesn't yet know why Claudius has to drink so much; second, the party, judging from what Claudius has said, is at least partly in honour of Hamlet and the fact that he's staying in Denmark. Even the final scene, in which Hamlet, Claudius, Gertrude and Laertes all die, is essentially a party in honour of Hamlet. We're told (by Claudius) that Hamlet is a great favourite with the "general gender" offstage, who evidently don't trust Claudius completely—at any rate, Laertes is hailed as a possible new king on his return from France. But Shakespeare's portrayal of crowds is not very flattering in any of the plays in which crowds are featured.

So Claudius keeps his distance from Hamlet, not wanting to harm him as yet, only watching. And as he does so the "mousetrap" play suddenly closes on him. There are dozens of confrontations with pictures and mirrors and images in this play, but of course the central one is the mirror that, in the dumb show, holds up to Claudius the image of his crime. It takes all the nerve of a very strong man not to break right there: when he speaks (and it's a long time before he speaks), he says: "Have you heard the argument? Is there no offence in it?" It's the question of a suspicious tyrant, not of the affable and gracious king that Claudius still is to everyone except Hamlet and Horatio. When the image is repeated, that does it. But it isn't every murdering villain who would take to prayer in such circumstances. The prayer wouldn't be very effective unless he did what he still could to undo his crime, such as surrendering the crown. But the cold little voice in possession of Claudius says very clearly, "Don't be silly," and there's nothing to do but get up and start planning the death of Hamlet. After all, the mousetrap play depicts a nephew killing his uncle, not a usurper killing his brother.

I think it was the critic Wilson Knight, at one time a colleague of mine here in Toronto, who first pointed out how healthy a man Claudius was, except for his crime, and how sick a man Hamlet was, even with his cause. Rosencrantz and Guildenstern, for example, are old friends whom Hamlet is at first delighted to see: he soon realizes that they have been "sent for," which they immediately admit, and the discovery doesn't bother him too much. They are serving the king, whom they assume is the rightful king—Hamlet hasn't taken them into his confidence to that extent—and it never occurs to them that they are not acting in Hamlet's own best interests. "My lord, you once did love me," Guildenstern says with simple dignity. For Hamlet to describe them so contemptuously to Horatio as the shabbiest kind of spies, whose death is simply a good riddance, is one of those bewildering shifts of perspective that make what broadcasters call "easy listening" impossible.

I've spoken of the number of mirrors and confronting images that we meet everywhere in the play. Hamlet, for example, finds himself watching the recruits of Fortinbras, who, deflected from Denmark, are going off to attack Poland, free at least to get out of Denmark and engage in some positive action. Then we hear that the territory to be fought over is hardly big enough to hold the contending armies. One doesn't escape claustrophobia even by avoiding Denmark. Hamlet eventually leaves Denmark and is sent to England, but in his journey there he is "be-netted round with villainies," and is as unable to sleep as fettered mutineers. Polonius spies on him; Claudius spies on him; Rosencrantz and Guildenstern spy on him, and he has the additional difficulty of pretending to be mad when with them and sane when with Horatio. He tells Rosencrantz and Guildenstern that he has of late "foregone all my exercises," but tells Horatio that since Laertes went into France he has been in continual fencing practice.

Gertrude is forced by Hamlet to "look upon this picture, and on this," to compare Hamlet senior with Claudius, in the process of having also to contemplate the very unflattering portrait of herself that Hamlet is drawing. Claudius says of the mad Ophelia that without our reason we are mere "pictures," or else beasts, and as Ophelia isn't a beast she must be a picture, a terrible but quite recognizable picture of what she could have been. The function of a play, says Hamlet, is to hold the mirror up to nature. He should know; he asks a player for a speech about Pyrrhus, the ferocious Greek warrior about to kill Priam, and hears how:

> As a painted tyrant, Pyrrhus stood,
> And like a neutral to his will and matter,
> Did nothing.        (II.ii. 510–12)

I said that in the first act we get a vision of the court of Denmark as rocking and heaving on the quicksand of the murder of Hamlet's father, and that this vision is to some degree physically presented to us when the Ghost disappears below the stage and speaks from there. At the beginning of the fifth act the lower world suddenly yawns open on the stage, as the gravediggers are preparing a grave for Ophelia.

This episode is particularly one that the more conservative humanist critics I spoke of earlier regarded as barbaric. It is a type of grotesque scene that Shakespeare occasionally throws into a tragedy: the porter answering the knocking at the gate in *Macbeth* and the clown coming in with the basket of figs and the serpent in *Antony and Cleopatra* are other examples. The word "grotesque" is connected with the word "grotto," a cave or opening in the ground, and it usually has some connection with the ironic aspect of death, death as the decaying of the body into other elements. These grotesque death scenes became particularly popular in the Middle Ages, when a form appeared in literature known as the *danse macabre*, the figure of Death coming to take away a great variety of social types from king to beggar. The popularity of the *danse macabre* was based on the fact that in a hopelessly unjust society death is the only impartial figure, and the only genuine democrat: in fact, all we can see of the God who is supposed to be no respecter of persons. The reasons why such scenes as this were disapproved of by highbrows are all connected with the incessant self-idealizing of ascendant classes, whether aristocratic or bourgeois. We feel sympathy with Laertes when he speaks of Ophelia's "fair and unpolluted flesh," and when we hear the gravedigger telling us that "your water is a sore decayer of your whoreson dead body," we dislike the implication that Ophelia's fair and unpolluted flesh wouldn't stay that way very long.

In this scene we're at the opposite end from the mood of sinister chill in which the play opened. In that opening scene we heard Horatio explain how:

> A little ere the mightiest Julius fell,
> The graves stood tenantless and the sheeted dead
> Did squeak and gibber in the Roman streets. (I.i. 114–16)

Here the atmosphere is not simply ghostly, but heroic as well: the great Caesar cannot just die; prodigies occur when he does. In the present scene we get a very different tone:

> Imperious Caesar, dead and turn'd to clay,
> Might stop a hole to keep the wind away.     (V.i. 233–34)

And there are no ghosts in this scene: characters are either alive, like Hamlet and Horatio and the gravediggers, or dead, like Yorick and Ophelia. The terrible ambiguity of life in death, which the Ghost has brought into the action, and which has transformed the action of the play into this nightmarish sealed labyrinth, is resolving into its primary elements.

Then we come to the funeral of Ophelia, which Hamlet recognizes to be the funeral of a suicide as soon as he sees it. There follows the struggle between Hamlet and Laertes I spoke of, where probably both men are in Ophelia's still open grave. Both profess a deep love for her: Laertes clearly means what he says, and Hamlet, though ranting, probably does too. All this affection comes a little late in the day for poor Ophelia, who has hardly had a decent word thrown at her since the beginning of the play. She is bullied by her father, and humiliated by being made a decoy for Hamlet; she has been treated, during the play scene, to a conversation with Hamlet that would have been more appropriate in a whorehouse; and even Gertrude, who seems genuinely attached to her, panics when she comes in for the mad scene, and refuses to speak with her. But something connected with her death brings about a sudden sobering of the action, especially in Hamlet, who all through the gravedigger scene has been in a mood in which his melancholy is never quite under control, and his far-ranging associations "consider too curiously," as Horatio observes. It is as though Ophelia's suicide, to the extent that Hamlet assumes her death to be that, has broken the longing for death in Hamlet's mind that has been burdening it from the beginning.

As the play slowly makes its transition to the final duelling scene, Hamlet modulates to a mood of complete acceptance and resignation. He realizes he has not long to live, but commends himself to providence—the first indication we have had that such a thing is in his world—and says simply "the readiness is all." Horatio tries to tell him that he is still a free agent, and could decline the contest with Laertes if he liked, but Hamlet has already asked Osric "How if I answer no?" and Osric has said "I mean, my lord, the opposition of your person in trial." Sometimes a no-answer is more informative than any pretence of an answer: Hamlet's enemies will not wait very long now.

The sudden quieting of mood affects Laertes as well as Hamlet. Just as Hamlet, in spite of the powerful push to revenge given by the Ghost, could not bring himself to assassinate Claudius without warning, so Laertes, with both father and sister to avenge, feels ashamed of his poisoning scheme. Laertes and Hamlet die mutually forgiven, and with "heaven" absolving them of mortal sins. This does not mean that the machine-god of the earlier action has suddenly turned sentimental, in spite of Horatio's speech about flights of angels—angels who can hardly have read the first four acts. It means rather that the two elements of tragedy, the heroic and the ironic, have reached their final stage.

On the heroic side, the last scene reminds us what a tremendous power of mental vitality is now flowing into its delta. Against the sheer fact of Hamlet's personality, all the reminiscences of his indecision and brutality and arrogance seem merely carping: the death of so great a man is still portentous, even if he doesn't have Julius Caesar's comets. On the ironic side, the immense futility of the whole action takes such possession of us that we feel, not that the action has been ridiculous, but that we can look at it impartially because it has no justifications of its own. Horatio, obeying Hamlet's charge to tell the story again—a charge far more weighty than any ghostly command to revenge—promises:

> So shall you hear
> Of carnal, bloody, and unnatural acts,
> Of accidental judgments, casual slaughters,
> Of deaths put on by cunning and forced cause,
> And, in this upshot, purposes mistook
> Fall'n on th' inventors' heads.          (V.ii. 394–99)

This is a summary of what I called earlier a tragedy without a catharsis. The ironic side of the play relates to what has been done, which is precisely nothing, unless we call violent death something. The heroic side of it relates to what has been manifested. Hamlet has manifested such a torrent of abilities and qualities that Fortinbras assumes that he would have been a great king and warrior too: two roles in which we've never seen him. Hamlet's earnest injunction to Horatio to tell his story expresses something that we frequently meet in the resolution of tragedies. Othello's last speech contains a similar injunction. The effect of this imaginary retelling is in part to present what the tragic hero has done in relation to what he has been: it asks for a totally conscious judgment, not just a subtracting of bad deeds from good ones.

The contrast between judging from actions and judging from character comes into the central struggle between Hamlet and Claudius. A man's quality may be inferred from the record of what he has done, or it may be inferred from what he is trying to make of himself at any given moment. The former is, so to speak, the case for the prosecution: you've done such and such, so that's forever what you are. Most of us are aware that our potential of interests and abilities steadily narrows as we get older, and that what we can still do becomes increasingly predictable. But we tend to resign ourselves to that, unless, like Claudius, we're blocked by some major crime and we have enough intelligence and sensitivity to know that it is a major crime. Claudius is someone of great potential fatally blocked by something he has done and can never undo.

Hamlet has an even greater potential, and has not blocked him self in the same way. He is aware of the infinite possibilities inherent, at least in theory, in being human and conscious, but, of course, knows also that even someone as versatile as he still has only a limited repertoire. It takes a very unusual mind to feel that simply to be a finite human being is to be in some sense a prisoner. We all build secondary prisons out of our actions; but these are projections of the deeper prison of what we are, the limits of our powers imposed at and by birth. *Hamlet*, so far as it's a study of its chief character, is perhaps the most impressive example in literature of a titanic spirit thrashing around in the prison of what it is. A naive consciousness would say that, although bounded in a nutshell, it was also king of infinite space, but Hamlet's consciousness is not naive, and it dreams.

The stock remedy for the claustrophobia of consciousness is action, even though human action is so often destructive or murderous. But consciousness is also a kind of death principle, a withdrawing from action that kills action itself, before action can get around to killing something else. Hamlet himself often comments on his own inaction in these terms, often with a kind of half-realized sense that the Ghost cannot stimulate any form of vitality, however destructive, in the living world, but can only draw everything it touches down with itself into the shades below.

The "to be or not to be" soliloquy, hackneyed as it is, is still the kernel of the play. It's organized largely on a stream of infinitives, that mysterious part of speech that's neither a verb nor a noun, neither action nor thing, and it's a vision that sees consciousness as a kind of vacuum, a nothingness, at the centre of being. Sooner or later we have to commit ourselves to nothingness, and why should so much merit be attached to dying involuntarily? The Ghost insists that Hamlet mustn't die before he's killed Claudius, and the one thing that prevents Hamlet from voluntary death is the fear that he might become just another such ghost. Until the death of Ophelia releases him, he sees no form of detachment that would achieve the kind of death he wants: freedom from the world.

During the nineteenth century, and through much of the early twentieth, *Hamlet* was regarded as Shakespeare's central and most significant play, because it dramatized a central preoccupation of the age of Romanticism: the conflict of consciousness and action, the sense of consciousness as a withdrawal from action which could make for futility, and yet was all that could prevent action from becoming totally mindless. No other play has explored the paradoxes of action and thinking about action so deeply, but because it did explore them, literature ever since has been immeasurably deepened and made bolder. Perhaps, if we had not had *Hamlet*, we might not have had the Romantic movement at all, or the works of Dostoyevsky and Nietzsche and Kierkegaard that follow it, and recast the *Hamlet* situation in ways that come progressively nearer to us. Nearer to us in cultural conditions, that is, not in imaginative impact: there, Shakespeare will always be first.

YVES BONNEFOY

# *Readiness, Ripeness:* Hamlet, Lear

I

Just after he agrees to fight with Laertes—but not without a sense of foreboding that he tries to suppress—Hamlet concludes that "the readiness is all." And toward the end of *King Lear*, Edgar, son of the Earl of Gloucester, persisting in his efforts to dissuade his father from suicide, asserts that "ripeness is all." And shouldn't we suppose that Shakespeare established consciously the opposition in these two phrases that are so closely related and that come at two moments so dense with meaning—and that they therefore speak of one of the tensions at the very heart of his poetics? I would like to try to understand more clearly the "readiness" in *Hamlet* and the "ripeness" in *King Lear*.

But first a preliminary remark which, though it has been made before, seems nevertheless useful to bear in mind when we raise questions about Shakespeare's work. As one studies the history of Western society, one discovers at one moment or another, and on every level of life, especially on the level of self-awareness, a deep fissure whose line marks the point of separation between a previous and now seemingly archaic era and what one might already call the modern world. The time "before"—that was when a conception of oneness, of unity, experienced as life, as presence, governed every relationship one could have with specific realities. Each of these

From *New Literary History* 17, no. 3 (Spring 1986). © 1986 by Yves Bonnefoy.

realities thus found its place in a precisely defined order which in turn matte
of each a presence, a kind of soul alive to itself and to the world, among the
other realities endowed with the same life, and assured to each a meaning of
which there could be no doubt. The most important and the most fortunate
consequence of this fact of an order and a meaning was that the human
person, who knew himself to be an element in this world and who sometimes
even thought himself the center of it, also had no occasion to call his own
being into doubt or the fact that he stood for the absolute. Whatever may
have been the high and low points of his existence, in which chance often
came into play, the human person still could and had to honor his essence,
which preserved a divine spark—herein is the whole substance of the
teaching of the Christian Middle Ages with its theology of salvation. But a
day came when technology and science began to mark out—in what as a
result became simply objects—features that could not be integrated into the
structures of traditional meaning. The established order fell into
fragmentation, the earth of signs and promises became nature once again,
and life matter; the relation of the person to himself was all at once in
enigma, and destiny a solitude. This is the fracture I was speaking of, the final
settlings of which have riot yet been determined.

And it should also be noticed that the first truly irrevocable
manifestations of this crisis out of which was born the civilization—if this
word still applies—that today we oppose to the rest of the planet, this first
manifestation took place, according to the country and according to the
social milieu as well, at various moments of the end of the sixteenth and
beginning of the seventeenth century, which in England corresponds to the
years during which Shakespeare wrote his plays. The fracture line that broke
the horizon of atemporality and gave over the history of the world to its ever
more uncertain and precipitous development, this fracture line passes
through *Hamlet*—this is obviously one of the causes of the play—and I would
even say runs right through the heart of the work. Without attempting a
detailed analysis, for these few pages would hardly be the place for it, I can
at least emphasize, as an example of what I mean, the central importance of
the opposition of two beings who clearly represent the succession of the two
eras, a contrast which is all the more striking for being established between
a father and son who bear the same name. On this scarcely realistic stage,
where aspects of the high Middle Ages are boldly combined with others that
reflect the life of Shakespeare's own time and even its philosophical avant-
garde—the references to Wittenberg, for instance, the stoicism of Horatio—
the old Hamlet, the King who furthermore is already dead, although he
continues to make himself heard, the old King represents, and this is obvious
and even explicitly expressed, the archaic mode of being. Not only does he

wear the dress and bear witness to the customs of feudal society, even his need for vengeance signifies his adherence to the dying tradition, since this demand that is so full of the conviction of sacred right, implies, among other things, the certainty that the entire state suffers when legitimacy is violated. And beyond this, his status as battling and triumphant sovereign of being is an excellent metaphor for the domination that the Christian of the era before the new astronomy thought he exercised over a world on the peripheries of which the devil might nonetheless be prowling. And finally, the first Hamlet is a father, without the slightest apprehension, with hope even—which means that he has confidence in established values, in continuity. Claudius, who puts an end to the reign, has no children.

And as for the other Hamlet, as for this son called upon to reestablish the traditional order and thus to assume his royal function, it is easy to see that if he is the hero of Shakespeare's tragedy, it is because the values evoked by the Ghost, which Hamlet tries at once to inscribe in the "book" of his memory, have now almost no reality in his eyes. His good will is nevertheless quite real; he burns with the desire to vindicate his father, and he admires two other sons who do not hesitate to take their place in the society they believe still exists; and if for a moment he thinks of marriage, he who had been filled with disgust for things sexual by his mother's new relationship, in my opinion it is in the hope that the very real love he feels for Ophelia might reconcile him to life as it is, and to the idea of generation, which in turn could help him to vanquish the skepticism that saps his energy and turns him from action. But this desire to do what is right sets off even more strikingly the extent to which his vision of the world, like a paralyzing, if not completely destructive fatality, no longer recognizes its once perfect organization—that organization which is, in fact, already in disarray in the comportment of the "Danish" court, prey to a symptomatic corruption. One remembers his moving words on the earth, that sterile promontory, on the heavens, that foul and pestilent congregation of vapors. Similarly, if he fails as he does with Ophelia, although there is nothing really wrong with their personal relationship, it is because he has not managed to spare her from that vision that seizes everything and everybody from the outside—as is indicated by his mocking cry, "words, words, words"—and he therefore can see nothing but opacity and lies in every manner of thinking and speaking, including those of young girls. Even if one feels obligated to try other keys—the oedipal motivations, for instance—for understanding the suspicion with which Hamlet persecutes Ophelia, it remains nonetheless true that this suspicion betrays, in its difference from the simple faith of Hamlet's father, the presence of an alienation, of an isolation, a vertigo which the earlier, snore united society could never have imagined and would not have tolerated. And it is, furthermore, in his ambiguous relation to his father, who represents—who is, in fact, the former world—that Hamlet's revulsions most clearly appear. He does not want to doubt that he admires and even loves his father; but when he calls him the "old mole" or thinks he sees him in his nightgown the second time he appears, or lets himself be carried away by the thought of those sins which keep him in Purgatory—the reference to him as "gross" and "full of bread," for instance—aren't these simply more signs of his inability to understand the ways of the world and the beings in it, as the old way of looking at life would have allowed him to?

This inability to recognize his father for what he truly is, although he will affirm his worth at every chance he gets, is doubtless one of the most painful of Hamlet's secrets and one of the unacknowledged elements with which he nourishes what is obviously his sense of remorse, and it explains a number of the most obscure aspects of the play, beginning with the other great obsession that structures it. There are certainly many reasons that explain Hamlet's rages against Gertrude—and once again I am not attempting for the moment anything like a systematic analysis—but it seems obvious to me that if the son accuses his mother so violently of betrayal, it is because he himself has betrayed—although he does not realize it—the very person whom, according to Hamlet, she should have kept without rival in her heart. He always insists that it is the majesty of the old Hamlet, his twofold greatness of man and prince, that has been insulted by the new marriage; he vehemently denounces Claudius's vices, especially as they show him to be unworthy of the role he has usurped; but the whole scene of the "two pictures," during which Hamlet would prove to Gertrude the grandeur of the one and the ignominy and even the ridiculousness of the other, serves only to show that rhetorical device plays a large role in the emotion he tries to feel. Once again in this play we are at the theater, and perhaps much more so during these moments of accusation and introspection than when the player recites those rather bombastic, if deeply felt, verses on the death of Queen Hecuba. Hamlet tries to live according to the values which have been handed down to him from the past, but he can only do so on the level of "words, words, words," the obsession with the emptiness of which one now begins to better understand. He who, in order to wreak his vengeance, in order to restore the threatened order, in short, in order to proclaim meaning, feels it necessary to disguise himself for a brief interval that in fact becomes endless, is merely an actor on this level as well—so that his true double in the play is, alas, neither Laertes, nor Fortinbras, nor even Gertrude, who is only guilty of weakness—and Hamlet knows this, as does his father who reminds him of it with insistence—but rather the character who says one thing and thinks another, and merely pretends to respect and observe values in which he certainly no longer believes: Claudius, the destroyer, the enemy.... This is the true core of *Hamlet*, as well as the necessary consequence of that crisis in society of which the murder of the king is only the symbol. Those who appear now, and who can be seen to exist beyond the boundaries of the broken social order, are more deeply imbued with reality, more fully steeped in the denseness of life than their fellow men, whose obedience to the categories of former times seems only backward and obtuse. They live in anguish and confusion; their survival reactions are cynical and ignominious—as is certainly the case with that opaque being, Claudius, for such a long time the shadow of his brother. He is all undeniably covetous man, as there have always been covetous men, but he is also one who has consciously transgressed the strictest social codes.

All through *Hamlet* there are a thousand signs of the fascinated interest—sometimes bordering on the equivocal, it seems so affectionate—the nephew has in his uncle. One senses that something attracts him in the very person he thinks he detests, without it being necessary to infer from this strange obsession, at least as its essential reason, some ambiguous extension of the complex algebra of the oedipal relations to be deciphered by the psychoanalyst. I would say that Hamlet less loves, than he simply *understands* Claudius for what he is, and that he understands him more intimately than he can understand others, because it is his contemporary he is encountering, and his only contemporary, in these changing times that have suddenly become a thundering storm, a sinking ship. He feels for this man who is nonetheless his adversary according to the reasoning of days gone by—and certainly his enemy according to values that are eternal—that instinctive solidarity that binds together shipwrecked men.

## II

In short, *Hamlet* is clearly, deeply, specifically the problematics of a consciousness awakening to a condition that was undreamt of and unimaginable only the day before: a world without structure, truths which henceforth are only partial, contradictory, in competition with one another—as many signs as one would wish, and quickly far too many, but nothing that will resemble a sacred order or meaning. And it is from this perspective that we have to try to examine the idea of "readiness," as Hamlet advances it, at a moment, it should be noted, that is late in the play—in the fifth act—when Hamlet has had the chance to measure the extent of a disaster that he experiences at first as an endless tangle of insoluble contradictions. And what about Claudius? Hamlet had been so filled with the desire to kill him, and yet here he is still hesitating to do so, apparently resolute, as resolute as ever, but distracted in every situation by some new consideration—this time, for instance, by his interest in Laertes. And Ophelia? It is certain now that he did love her, the news of her suicide has given him absolute proof of it—he loved her, he says at the time, more than forty thousand brothers, and more in any case than Laertes whose grandiloquence is clearly open to criticism; and yet this strange love, poisoned by suspicion, disguised in insult, has only thrown her into despair and death. It is clear now that he is suffering deeply from an evil the cure for which is beyond him, and that he has lost all hope in his ability to arrest the collapse of meaning. Hamlet is acutely conscious of his own powerlessness as he gives expression to his deepest thoughts on the last day of his life in the presence of Horatio, who always seems to incite him to profound reflection and exigency.

What does Hamlet say to Horatio in this scene—preceded, it should be remembered, by their long meditation in the cemetery beside the skull of Yorick, the King's jester, he who knew better than anyone the falseness of appearances? He says that even the fall of a sparrow is ruled by Providence, that "if it be now, 'tis not to come; if it be not to come, it will be now," and that if it be not now, let there be no doubt about it, "yet it will come." And as we do not know this moment, and never can, the important thing is to be ready.... One might suppose that Hamlet is talking about death here, and in a way that does not seem in contradiction with traditional teaching, since the medieval mind loved to insist that God had the final decision about the fate of man's undertakings. Should we draw the conclusion that Hamlet—who has obviously thought a great deal during his trip to England, and after it as well—is in the process of rediscovering the truth of the ancient precepts and is referring, in any case, to those fundamental structures of being of which they were the expression? But Christianity confided to Providence only the final result of an act and not its preparation which, on the contrary, it asked one to subject to careful consideration and to bring within the bounds of established values. Hamlet, however, is taking advantage of what seems fatalistic in the traditional way of looking at things in order to dispense with the necessity of examining what he has been compelled to accept in this situation which could be decisive for him—his swordfight with a master duelist—an encounter which could easily be refused, especially as it clearly seems to be part of a trap. Why does he consent to risk his life before having brought to successful conclusion his grand scheme to reestablish justice? Neither the ethics, nor the religion of the Middle Ages would have accepted this way of behaving that seems to suggest that a prince is indifferent to his cause, a son to the wishes of his father.

In spite of how it might seem, therefore, Hamlet has not really taken up for himself an adage which in its true significance—"Heaven helps those who help themselves"—gave such apt expression, in fact, to the old universe with its contrasting poles of transcendence and chance. If he has recourse to a traditional formula, it is to turn it toward aims of an entirely different nature, and this time authentically, totally, fatalistic. The "readiness" he proposes is not reliance on the will of God as the guarantor of our efforts, the protector of our meaning, it is rather cessation of what the God of former times expected of us: the fearless and unflagging exercise of our judgment in the world he created, the discrimination between good and evil. In place of the discernment that tries to organize and provide, and does so through awareness of values, he substitutes the welcoming acceptance of things as they come along, however disorderly and contradictory they might be, and the acceptance of chance: from the perspective of this philosophy of pessimism, our acts seem as thoroughly devoid of a reason for being as the necessity that comes into play with them. Our condition is in nonmeaning, nothingness, and it is just as well to realize it at moments that seem moments of action, when normally our naivete is summoned. In a word, a single act still has some logic and is worthy of being carried out: and that is to take great pains to detach oneself from every illusion and to be ready to accept everything—everything, but first of all, and especially, death, the essence of all life—with irony and indifference.

And yet it cannot be denied that the Hamlet who proposes this surrender is, as the whole scene will show, also a man who is now much more alert than at other moments of the play, and much more attentive than he once was to the ways in which others behave, for example, even if his observation leads only to mocking and scorn. He can even be seen to prepare himself for a sport which nothing in his past has allowed us to expect from him, a sport that demands swiftness of eye and quickness of hand—and also the encounter with the other, in that true and not entirely heartless intimacy which can exist in hand-to-hand combat. These characteristics, so unexpected in the one once covered by the inky cloak, act, of course, to pave the way for the denouement of the play which must pass through the battle of two sons who are, as Hamlet himself remarks, the image of one another; and yet, so striking and so present are they, that they must be said to play a role as well in the implicit characterization of the ethics that is developed, and thus it would be a mistake to think that this *readiness*, which is a form of renunciation, is so in a passive or discouraged way. Doubtless because the conclusion reached by Hamlet has freed him from his earlier self-absorption, from his recriminations and his endless reverie, his new mode of being seems also to take on a body, a capacity for sport, an interest, if perhaps a cruel one, for those things in the world he once had fled. This is now an all-embracing consciousness, an immediacy in the way the world is received that is already response, return: and this "readiness" is in truth so active, one can feel so intensely the need to bring together everything in the experience of the void, that one is tempted to compare it to other undertakings which, though they too seem pessimistic, are nonetheless of a spiritual nature and another form of the absolute. Is the "readiness" of Hamlet an Elizabethan equivalent of the Buddhist discipline, of the way in which the samurai, for instance, prepares himself—another swordsman at the end of another Middle Age—to accept the moment of death without a shadow of resistance? A way of recovering positivity and plenitude in the very heart of an empty world?

But with the Oriental—be he warrior or monk—the critique of appearances, of the manifestations of illusion, is also, and even first of all, brought to bear on the self, which has appeared to him, not without good reason, as the supreme form of illusion, whereas Hamlet's lucidity, however radical it may wish to be, is the reaction of a man who has considered himself the depository of the absolute, who hasn't as yet resigned himself to the dislocation of that heritage which remains centered on the self; and I see it therefore as the ultimate response of an unrelenting "personality," a kind of doleful, yet not entirely hopeless meditation on the meaninglessness he himself has tried to prove. Hamlet's "readiness" is not the Oriental's effort to go beyond the very idea of meaning to attain to the plenitude of immediacy—the person who recognizes that he has no more importance than the fleeting blossoms of the cherry tree; no, it is rather the degree zero of a meaning, an order, still vividly recalled—the fundamental structures of which, though lost, are still considered desirable, and the need for which is still secretly acknowledged by that very complexity of consciousness in which all the language existing only for the purpose of hoping and organizing still remains in reserve for the possibility of some future miracle. The new relation to the self of this king without a kingdom is therefore not a peaceful one; it is not the great bright burst of laughter that tears apart ancient woe. What should be seen, on the contrary, is a sharpening of unvanquished suffering, its reduction to a single shrill note—almost inaudible and yet ever present—a form of irony not unlike that of which Kierkegaard will write, in which the moments of spiritedness or laughter are always chilled by nostalgia. Not the liberation, but the celibacy of the soul—taken on as a last sign, a challenge full of desire, offered to the God who has withdrawn from his Word. An appeal, and in this sense a recognition of the existence of others, a sign that he who pretends to prefer solitude is in fact lying to himself—in all of which is prefigured, as the enormous vogue of *Hamlet* throughout the entire nineteenth century bears witness, the dandyism of Delacroix and Baudelaire.

I therefore see the "readiness" that emerges in Hamlet as quite simply a negative strategy for the preservation of the soul, a technique useful at all times when humanity strives to recall what its hopes once were. And I think it necessary, of course, to try to understand whether this state of mind applies only to the prince of Denmark and to a few others like him in Shakespeare's bountiful and polyphonous universe, or whether one should ascribe it, in one way or another, to Shakespeare himself and therefore consider it as one of the possible "solutions" proposed by the poetry of the Elizabethan era for the great crisis in values it was beginning to analyze. One could easily imagine it as such—*Hamlet* is so obviously a personal play, and one can feel so intensely, in phrase after phrase of his hero, a poet's effort to stand in place of rhetorical conventions. But let us be careful to notice that nothing has really been definitively undertaken, even in the play itself, when Hamlet, at the very last moment, affirms and assumes his new philosophy. That he takes it seriously, that he would like to truly live it, can scarcely be doubted, since it is to Horatio, to whom he never lies, that he confides his deepest thoughts on the matter. But mortally wounded an hour later, it is to Fortinbras that he casts his "dying voice"—and beyond him to traditional values, or at least to the attitude that wills the preservation of their fiction. One therefore has the right to wonder if "readiness" isn't for Shakespeare simply one phase of psychological insight and in Hamlet the whimsical stance that masks the even more disastrous reason that has led him to accept Laertes' strange challenge so lightly, and with it the possibility of dying.

### III

But let us not forget that it is in *Lear*, not more than five or six years later, that one sees clearly designated that "ripeness" which Shakespeare seems to have wanted to place against the "readiness" of the earlier work.

The historical context of Lear is not without certain resemblances to the earlier play, since the work is set in an England at least as archaic as the Denmark of Hamlet's father—it is even a pagan world, closely watched over by its gods—and yet here, too, one discovers signs that seem to announce new modes of being. And in *Lear* there also emerges a character one can sense from the outset incapable of recognizing that the world is an order, rich in meaning—Edmund, second son of the Earl of Gloucester. A son, then, like the prince of Denmark, and one who has, like Hamlet, reasons for doubt about what will be his heritage. But the resemblance between Edmund and Hamlet stops there, for the painful plight of the son, which Hamlet has lived through with honesty and with the burning desire to do what is right, is now studied in one who is clearly evil, and with conceptual categories that remain essentially medieval. One might, at first sight, consider modern this certainly nonconformist personality who scoffs at astrological explanations, at the superstitions of those who surround him, and even at the values of common morality. But it should be observed that Edmund's speeches are accompanied by none of those indications—such as the actors, Wittenberg, the presence of Horatio—which in *Hamlet* serve to mark, by outward sign, that one is approaching the modern era. What makes Edmund an outsider, far from being seen as symptomatic of crisis, is rather set very explicitly by Shakespeare in the context of one of the convictions advanced by the medieval understanding of man: if Edmund would usurp his brother's place, if he longs to see his father dead, if he thus shows how far he is from the most universal human feelings, it is because he is a bastard, born out of wedlock, the fruit himself of sin. And it is in complete agreement with traditional Christian teaching that *King Lear* asks us to understand that this sin, this adultery, is precisely the occasion that evil, ever unvanquished, even if always repelled, has been waiting for—the chance to invade once again the order established by God, which order will nonetheless in the end emerge triumphant once more, thanks to the intervention of a few righteous souls. And this being the case, if Edmund evokes nature as his one guiding principle, as the law to which his services are bound, one should not see in this a reflection of the Renaissance humanist for whom the study of matter is unbiased activity of mind, but rather the revelation of the baseness of a soul, influenced, on the contrary, by black magic—a soul that feels at home nowhere so much as amidst the most frankly animal realities. Edmund's actions do not disclose the ultimate crisis of sacred order, but rather its innermost weakness. And one knows from the very outset of the action that he will perish—unmistakably, without a trace of uneasiness or regret, without a future in the new forms of consciousness, as soon as the forces of goodness he has caught off guard have reestablished their power.

Far from signifying, then, that Shakespeare's attention is focused on the problems of modernity as such, as was the case in *Hamlet*, the character of the son in *King Lear* serves rather to reinforce the notion that the old order remains the uncontested frame of reference in the play, the determining factor in the outcome of the drama, the truth that will be reaffirmed after a moment of crisis. And it is clearly for this reason that there emerges in the foreground of the play a figure missing in *Hamlet*, since neither Laertes nor Fortinbras ever attains truly spiritual stature, the figure of the child—girl or boy, since it is as true of Cordelia, third daughter of Lear, as of Edgar, firstborn son of Gloucester—whose purity and moral determination find the means of thwarting the traitors' schemes. In fact, more even than Cordelia, whose somewhat cool and arid virtuousness keeps a certain distance from those violent, contradictory words, mingled with both love and hatred, through which the action of the play is developed and resolved, the agent of redemption for the imperilled group is Edgar who, at the very moment when he might have yielded to despair or given in to cynicism—hasn't he been falsely accused, attacked by his own brother, misjudged, without cause, by his father?—gives proof, on the contrary, to those reserves of compassion, of lucidity, of resolute understanding of the darkest depths of the souls of others, that can be found in anyone, even quite early in life and without special preparation. Struck in a completely unforseeable way by what appears to be the purest form of evil, this still very young man, who only the day before was rich, pampered, assured of a future place among the most powerful of the land, chooses at once to plunge into the very depths of adversity, taking on the semblance of a beggar and the speech of a fool to shatter at the outset the too narrow framework of his own personal drama and to bring his inquiry to bear on all the injustices, all the miseries, all the forms of madness that afflict society. He understands instinctively—and here is clearly a sign that this world is still alive—that he will be able to achieve his salvation only by working for the salvation of others, each man needing as much as another to free himself from his egotism, froth his excesses, from his pride so that true exchange might begin once more.

In spite of everything, however, the hero of *King Lear* remains the one for whom the play is named—the old King—since unlike Edmund who has been marked from the outset by the sin involved in his birth, and in contrast to Edgar who emerges into his maturity through the crimes of another, Lear is thrown into his troubles by his own free act, and thus his punishment and his folly, his gradual discovery of those truths and realities he had neglected before, become a succession of events all the more deeply convincing and touching. Lear begins, not with something rotten in the state, as was the case for Hamlet, but rather with a mysterious sickness in the soul, and in this case, with pride. Lear admires himself, prefers himself; he is interested in others only to the extent that they are interested in him, and thus he is blind to their own true being; he therefore does not truly love others, in spite of what he might think: and so the ground is laid for the catastrophic act that will refuse to recognize true value, that will deprive the righteous of their due, and that will spread disorder and sorrow everywhere and give the devil the chance he has been waiting for in the son born of adultery. Lear—even more than Gloucester whose only sins are sins of the flesh—has relived, has reactivated the original sin of men, and thus he represents, more than any other character in the play, our condition in its most radical form, which is imperfection, but also struggle, the will to self-mastery. When, on the basis of those values he has never denied but has understood so poorly and lived so little, he learns to recognize that his kingly self-assurance is pure pretension, his love a mere illusion, and when he learns what true love is, what happiness could be, one feels all the more deeply moved as his initial blindness belongs to all of us, more or less: he speaks to the universal. And yet, even though he occupies the foreground from beginning to end of the play, Lear cannot and must not hold our attention simply because of what he is, or merely on the basis of his own particular individuality, since his spiritual progress comes precisely from having rediscovered the path toward others and from having thereafter forgotten about himself in the fullness of this exchange. It is in the modern era, the era of Hamlet, that the individual—separated from everything and from everybody, incapable of checking his solitude, and trying to remedy what is missing through the proliferation of his desires, his dreams, and his thoughts—will slowly assume that extraordinary prominence, the end point of which is Romanticism. In *King Lear*—as on the gothic fresco which is always more or less the *danse macabre*—no one has greater worth merely because of what sets him apart from others, however singular or extreme this difference might be. The soul, studied from the point of view of its free will, which is the same in every man, is less the object of descriptions that note differences than it is the very stage of the action, and from the outset the only stage: and what appears in the play, what finds expression there, are the great key figures of the society, such as the king and his fool, the powerful lord and the poor man, and those categories of common experience such as Fortune or charity, or the deadly sins that Marlowe, in his *Doctor Faustus*, scarcely ten years earlier, had not been reluctant to keep on stage. In short, behind this character who is remarkable, but whose uncommon sides are above all signs of the extent of the dangers that menace us—and the extent of the resources at our disposition as well—the true object of Shakespeare's attention, the true presence that emerges and runs the risk of being overwhelmed, but triumphs in the end, is that life of the spirit to which Lear, and Edgar as well, and also to a certain extent Gloucester and even Albany all bear witness—what is designated by the word *ripeness*.

*Ripeness*, maturation, the acceptance of death as in *Hamlet*, but no longer in this case because death would be the sign, par excellence, of the indifference of the world, of the lack of meaning—no, rather because acceptance of death could be the occasion for rising to a truly inner understanding of the real laws governing being, for freeing oneself from illusion, from vain pursuits, for opening oneself to a conception of Presence which, mirrored in our fundamental acts, will guarantee a living place to the individual in the evidence of All. One can only understand *King Lear* if one has learned to place this consideration in the foreground, if one has come to see that this is the thread that binds everything together, not only, the young man with the old one whose soul is ravaged but intact, but with them the Fool, for instance, who represents in medieval thought the outermost edge of our uncertain condition; and this consideration must be seen to dominate even in a context in which the forces of night seem so powerful, in which the Christian promise has not as yet resounded—although its structures are already there, since it is Shakespeare who is writing; one can therefore sense in them an indication of change, a reason for hope. *Ripeness* emerges in *Lear* as a potentiality for everyone, as the existential starting point from which the protagonists of this tragedy of false appearances begin to be something more than mere shadows; and from the Fool to Lear, from Edgar to his father, from Cordelia, from Kent, from Gloucester to their sovereign, even from an obscure servant to his lord when the latter has his eyes plucked out, it is what gives the only real substance to human exchange which is otherwise reduced to concerns and desires that are only hypocrisy or illusion. This primacy accorded to the inner life of men, with the inevitable shaking of the foundations that comes with it, is what gives meaning to the most famous scene in *Lear* in which one sees Edgar, disguised as a fool, with the fool who is a fool by profession, and Lear, who is losing his mind, all raving together— or at least so it seems—beneath the stormy skies. "Those blasting winds and bursts of lightning, that cracking of the cosmos, might well seem to suggest the collapse of meaning, the true state of a world we once had thought of as our home; but let us not forget that in that hovel, and under the semblance of solitude, misfortune, and weariness, the irrational powers that tend to reestablish truth are working much more freely than ever they could in the castles of only a moment before. It is here that true reflection begins again, here that the idea of justice takes shape once more. This stormy night speaks to us of dawn. The brutality of the gods and of men, the fragility of life, are as nothing against a showing of instinctive solidarity that brings things together and provides comfort. And let us also remember that nothing of this sort appears in *Hamlet*, where, if one excepts Horatio, who in fact withdraws from the action, and Ophelia, who, unable to be what she truly wants to be, becomes mad and kills herself, everything in the relationship between people is cynical, harsh, and joyless: let us not forget, for instance, the way in which Hamlet himself gets rid of Rosencrantz and Guildenstern—"They are not near my conscience." It is not the universe of Lear—however bloody it might seem—that contains the most darkness. This "tragedy"—but in an entirely different sense from the Greek understanding of the term—is, with comparison to *Hamlet*, an act of faith. We meet in an arena of error, of crime, of dreadfully unjust death, in which even the very idea of Heaven seems missing; and yet, "the center holds," meaning manages to survive and even to take on new depth, assuring values, calling forth sacrifice and devotion, allowing for moral integrity, for dignity, and for a relation to oneself that one might term plenary if not blissful. Here we learn that the structures of meaning are but a bridge of thread thrown over frightful depths; but these threads are made of steel.

## IV

*Ripeness, readiness....* Consequently, the two irreducible attitudes. One, the quintessence of the world's order, the unity of which one seems to breath; the other, the reverse side of that order, when one no longer sees anything in the greyness of the passing days but the incomprehensible weave.

And the most important question that one might raise about Shakespeare's entire work, it seems to me, is the significance that this absolutely fundamental opposition he has now formulated took on for the playwright himself, in terms of the practical possibilities for the future of the mind and spirit. In other words, when he writes *King Lear* and speaks of *ripeness*, is it simply a question of trying to restore a past mode of being that our present state dooms to failure, and perhaps even renders unthinkable, at least past a certain point: the only path for people living after the end of sacred tradition being rather the *readiness* conceived of by Hamlet, the Elizabethan intellectual? Or, taking into consideration the emotion and the lucidity that characterize the play—as if its author did in fact know precisely what he was talking about—should we ask ourselves if Shakespeare doesn't, in one way or another, believe that the "maturation" of Edgar and Lear is still valid even for the present, the order, the system of evidence and value which is the necessary condition for this maturation, having perhaps not so completely or definitively disappeared in his eyes, in spite of the crisis of modern times, as it seems to his most famous but scarcely his most representative character? An essential question, certainly, since it determines the ultimate meaning of the relation of a great poetic work to its historic moment. The answer to which must doubtless be sought in the other plays of Shakespeare, and in particular in those that come at the end, after *Hamlet* and the great tragedies.

One will find there—at least this is my hypothesis—that in spite of the collapse of the "goodly frame" which the Christian Middle Ages had built with heaven and earth around man created by God, this poet of a harsher time felt. that an order still remained in place, in nature and in us—a deep, universal order, the order of life, which, when understood, when recognized in its simple forms, when loved and accepted, can give new meaning through its unity and its sufficiency to our condition of exiles from the world of the

Promise—just as grass springs up among the ruins. One will also find here that Shakespeare has understood that, with this recognition, the function of poetry has changed as well: it will no longer be the simple formulation of an already obvious truth, already tested to the depths by others than the poet; rather it will have as task to remember, to hope, to search by itself, to make manifest what is hidden beneath the impoverished forms of everyday thinking, beneath the dissociations and alienations imposed by science and culture—and thus it will be an intervention, the assumption of a neglected responsibility, that "reinvention" of which Rimbaud in turn will speak. Great thoughts that make for the endless richness of *The Winter's Tale*, that play which is, in fact, solar, and which may be superimposed on *Hamlet* point by point—someday I would like to come back to this idea—like the developed photograph—zones of shadow becoming clear, the bright reality as opposed to its negative. The great vistas, also, joyfully dreamt of in *The Tempest*—luminous double of *King Lear*. And grand opportunities, of course, for a resolute spirit, which explains, retrospectively, what has from the outset constituted the exceptional quality of the poetry of Shakespeare—first in the West to measure the extent of a disaster, and first also, and especially, to seek to remedy it.

JULIA LUPTON

# Truant dispositions:
# Hamlet *and Machiavelli*

### I. *Machiavellism and Elizabethan Readers*

*Hamlet's* play-within-a-play uses the notorious language of English
Machiavellism to identify faith in marriage and faith in language as
interwoven political imperatives. The interchange between the Player-King
and his Queen elaborates the themes of fear and love, promising, and
friendship addressed in Machiavelli's *The Prince*. This thematic overlap with
Machiavellism is reproduced in the poisoning of King Hamlet, a murder
which literalizes the rhetoric of the contemporary attack against theatre: the
representation of drama as seductive, violent, poisonous, contagious. Similar
invective was fired against Machiavelli, sometimes in the same works as the
anti-theatrical arguments. Machiavelli's analysis of dissembling, which
encompassed his definition of religion as a political tool, prompted the
greatest vituperation—and the deepest interest—in Elizabethan readers.
Theatre and Machiavelli raised similar threats to linguistic, moral and
psychological stability. This essay will first read Hamlet's "mirror up to
nature" as a Machiavellian mirror for the prince, and will then turn to the
chiastic figurations of theatre as politics, politics as theatre. Finally, the
Machiavel, vice, villain and villein, not only characterizes Claudius, "vice of
kings," but Prince Hamlet as well.

It was once an academic commonplace that the ubiquitous stage

From *The Journal of Medieval and Renaissance Studies* 17, no. 1 (Spring 1987). © 1987 by Duke
University Press.

125

Machiavel, typically a villainous dissembler and atheist, overshadowed Machiavelli's republicanism or the ethics of his statecraft in the Elizabethan period. Moreover, the argument went, Machiavelli himself was not read; *The Discourses* was not published in English until 1636, and *The Prince* in 1640, although the *Florentine History* (1598) and *The Art of War* (1563, 1573, 1588) had appeared much earlier. The major source for his ideas in England was Innocent Gentillet's 1575 *A Discourse upon the Meanes of Wel Governing...; Against Nicholas Machiavell the Florentine*, a polemical Protestant tract translated from the French in 1577 and published in 1602.

In the last thirty years, scholars have argued increasingly that Machiavelli's texts were available to Elizabethan and Jacobean England: through French and Italian editions; through continental tracts and pamphlets sympathetic to Machiavelli; through works by less dangerous figures like Tacitus, Jean Bodin, Guicciardini, Castiglione, or Botero.[1] In addition, seven manuscript translations of *The Prince* have been discovered. Felix Raab, George Mosse, and J. G. A. Pocock have argued for an intense and well-informed interest in Machiavelli on the part of Elizabethans, especially courtiers, such as Spenser, Sidney, Raleigh, and Bacon.

While English Machiavellism is now represented as a more or less legitimate phenomenon in the history of ideas, the stage Machiavel continues to be understood as a spurious and crude caricature of Italian political theory. This essay, however, which departs from traditional intellectual history by emphasizing the role of rhetorical and dramatic presentation in articulating and disseminating ideas, will attempt to take seriously the incessant conjunction of 'Machiavelli' and 'theatre' in the Elizabethan period. This analysis not only reassesses the Italianate villain and his circulating stock of politic maxims but also diagnoses the spread of Machiavellism into adjacent arenas affected by the intersection of politics and theatre: Renaissance notions of passion and love, self and time, social order and mobility. The strategies of dissembling which Machiavelli describes in *The Prince* are *theatrical*, based on a split between person and role, intention and language, and hence of great interest to dramatists, and to courtiers-as-dramatists, in a period when rhetorical rather than military modes of political expression were becoming increasingly important.[2] This coalescence of political and dramatic modes in Machiavellism indicates the Renaissance understanding of language as an interested expression of social and political relations. The casting of Machiavelli as vice or villain thus constitutes an important reflection on and of power and its representation in the Elizabethan period.

The appearance of Machiavellism at the center of *Hamlet* necessarily changes our structural and thematic understanding of the play. In what way does the scene of murder replayed in Hamlet's mousetrap configure issues of language and politics? When does the didactic mirror, selectively imaging the world as a theatre of moral *exempla*, become a dangerously unselective historical mirror that blurs ethical categories? When are foils foiled? The analysis of love, promises and friendship threatens both to contradict the larger play's apparent argument against remarriage and to qualify the antinomy between Claudius as illegitimate politician and his brother as Christian king. In *Hamlet's* exemplary mirror, virtue's feature and scorn's image fail to coincide with the very age and body of the time.

## II. *"Wisest Sorrow"*

The Prologue character, submitting the play-within-a-play to his royal audience's "clemency," gentleness in exercising power, suggests a relation between literary and legal judgment. Then the Player-King in heavily archaic language announces to his wife the length of their marriage. The Player-Queen is disturbed:

> But woe is me, you are so sick of late,
> So far from cheer and from your former state,
> That I distrust you.
>
> (III.ii.158–60)[3]

The Player-Queen, disparaging her worries, reassures the King:

> Yet though I distrust,
> Discomfort you, my lord, it nothing must;
> For women's fear and love hold quantity,
> In neither aught, or in extremity.
> Now what my love is, proof hath made you know,
> And as my love is siz'd, my fear is so.
> Where love is great, the littlest doubts are fear;
> Where little fears grow great, great love grows there.
>
> (160–69)

So sick of late, so far from former state: in *Hamlet*, the proliferating medical metaphors picture political corruption as disease and use the word 'state' to indicate both body and body politic, social as well as personal constitution: the ghost, says Horatio, "Bodes some strange eruption to our state" (I.i.72). Here, too, appears a change in state. Similarly, the Player-Queen seems to have found a clever formula for describing a woman's anxiety: she fears for her husband insomuch as she loves him. At the same time, fear and love form a coupling, at once political and psychological, common to discourse on government, and made especially current by Machiavellism.

Chapter 17 of *The Prince* develops one of the most infamous Machiavellian themes: "Of crueltie and gentlenes, and whether it be better to be loued or Feared" (Craig, 71). In a more traditional Christian account, love, induced by a ruler's liberality, magnanimity and justice, is superior to fear, inspired by punishment, as a motive of obedience. Such a view depends on a natural order represented by the king yet separate from him, an order which is the final object and guide of the people's loving submission. Yet fear, admit Christian commentators and theorists, is often necessary to bring men to love.[4] In the *Arcadia*, Sir Philip Sidney aptly represents the mechanics of Christian government in the aftermath of a suppressed rebellion: "But then shined foorth indeede all love among them, when an awfull feare, ingendred by justice, did make that love most lovely."[5] Fear is the dynamic, coercive principle in creating loving subjects.

In Machiavelli's politics, the transcendental signified of God and divine law has ceded to the shuffling signifiers of a temporal world. Unlike earlier theorists, Machiavelli clarifies both love and fear as relations of power between the prince and his subjects. Techniques for inspiring obedience are evaluated in terms of expediency, situation. In *The Prince* Machiavelli subordinates love to fear as a more dependable motive for obedience, since it requires less reliance on a fickle and self-interested populace:

> love is conteyned under dutie, which for verie lighte occasion wicked men will violate, abusinge all meanes of pietie for anie kynde of proffitte. But dread of punishment causethe them not onlie to shake for feare, but to stande faste in obedience [Craig, 72–73].

This privileging of fear over love, however abhorrent to Elizabethans, is less important than Machiavelli's insight into each as expressed relations of power whose effectiveness depends on political system and situation. Traditional virtue is significant as appearance, "face and shewe," which, while often eloquent, in no way insures rhetorical success; political innovation, the topic of *The Prince*, presumes the precariousness of meaning, the instability of ethical systems (Craig, 68).

Love and fear, popularized by Machiavelli's infamous discussion, appear increasingly in Elizabethan texts as the intermingled and potentially fickle conditions of political legitimacy. Legitimacy is itself conceived in theatrical terms, a question of performance and persuasion. In *Measure for*

*Measure* Shakespeare indicates the foundation of power in public display, the theatrical nature of fear and love. The Duke Viscentio wonders about Angelo's representation of his sovereignty:

> What figure of us think you he will bear?
> For you must know, we have with special soul
> Elected him our absence to supply,
> Lent him our terror, dress'd him with our love,
> And given his deputation all the organs
> Of our own pow'r.
>
> (I.i.16–21)

Appropriately, the Duke uses a ploy recommended by Machiavelli, one which conceives of politician as both actor and director: delegation of odious tasks to a representative.[6] In *The Spanish Tragedy*, love and fear first evoke the tragic precariousness of unfortunate kings (III.i.9–11) and then appear in the more personal encounter between Belimperia (beautiful power) and the stage Machiavel Lorenzo (III.x.94–99). "Love and fear" bridge the two scenes, at once political and sexual, public and private.

Fear and love, then, are personal emotions with a distinctly political coloring which popular Elizabethan conceptions of Machiavelli had heightened. In *Hamlet's* play-within-a-play, the Player-Queen's equation of fear and love is symptomatic of her own "distrust": the insecurity, political and psychological, brought about by historical deviation, the diseased fall from "former state." The Player-Queen's attempt to make fears groundless by grounding them in love destabilizes both, since love is bound up in fear—"Where little fears grow great, great love grows there" (167)—and fear is a reaction to change: "So far from cheer and from your former state, / That I distrust you" (159–60). Fear and love threaten to become interchangeable, a contrast-turned-equation encouraged by chiasmus. Love, grafted to fear, appears not as the sign of plenty but the sign of loss, a melancholic love for what has already disappeared, an anxious love which clutches the passing. Fear of loss, fear in losing: a love coupled with fear indicates the instability or illegitimacy of the object loved. Fear makes love lovely, or rather, desperate. The Player-Queen's speech appropriately presents insecurity in both psychological and political terms: as anxiety, as illegitimacy. That love and fear bridge personal and political realms befits her status as queen, repeating the special pressures on feminine virtue as political imperative throughout the play, and the period.

The Player-Queen's words signal a political context rather than specify one. The Player-King counters his wife's declaration of fidelity by reasoning the mutability of promises. The passage is often understood as a rephrasing of Hamlet's inability to carry out the promise made to the ghost earlier in the play. Yet it is also a Machiavellian account of faith and the requirements of its breaking, a theme which does not separate the passage from Hamlet's irresoluteness so much as underline the political frame of his inaction.

The Player-King's first lines, apparently an avowal of belief, reinstates "distrust" as the shaky foundation of political discourse. His assurance "I do believe you think what now you speak" asserts the instability of the self even as it declares its faith in present sincerity. He goes on to establish a link between purpose and memory:

> I do believe you think what now you speak;
> But what we do determine, oft we break,
> Purpose is but the slave to memory,
> Of violent birth but poor validity,
> Which now, the fruit unripe, sticks on the tree,
> But fall unshaken when they mellow be.
>
> (181–86)

The Player-King ties promises to the immediate intentions which inspire them. The signified of a promise, he argues, is not the deed it purports to fulfill but the private reason for committing oneself to a future act. Hence the sly reasoning that promises are made to ourselves, not to others: "Most necessary 'tis that we forget / To pay ourselves what to ourselves is debt" (187–88). The natural metaphor, perversely picturing an oath ripe not at the moment of fulfillment, or even at the point of breaking, but at the death of its occasion, isolates and privatizes the trajectory of a failed promise. The Player-King's account assumes and exacerbates a split between inside and outside, intention and discourse, a disjunction which aggravates rather than secures the inconstancy of each. Both promising and memory, traditionally the Janus-faced insurances of identity over time, are subject to repeated politic revision.

In the chapter immediately following the discussion of fear and love, Machiavelli approaches the topic "Howe princes owght to keepe their faythe and promises." The new prince must learn the ways of both beasts ("force and subtility") and of men ("faythe and sincerenes"). In Machiavelli's anthropology, the bestial includes a good measure of reason, for it in turn is split between lion and fox, force and cunning, a Plutarchan dualism that would become notoriously Machiavellian. The prudent prince "shoulde sticke noe longer to his promise then maye stande well with his proffitt, nor thincke himself noe longer bownde, to keape his othe then the cause remaynes that moved him to sweare" (Craig, 75). As in the Player-King's speech, a promise is "bound" to its usefulness ("profitt" or "cause"), not its addressee. In a world of shifting expediencies, the useful is open to continual redefinition, and so, too, as Machiavelli points out in the same chapter, is the face and word of the prince (Craig, 77). The new prince must at once respond to and control the string of events which he had helped to author.

Initially, however, the Player-King addresses not political expediency but passion as the root of these disposable, deposable promises: "What to ourselves in passion we propose, / The passion ending, doth the purpose lose" (189–90). This is in keeping with a general—and perhaps astute— Elizabethan reading of Machiavellian politics as an exercise of sexual desire. Reginald Pole, perhaps the earliest English polemicist against Machiavelli, casts Henry VIII as a libidinous tyrant; the Elizabethans added the boar, badge of sensuality, to the Machiavellian menagerie of lion and fox, renaming political self-interest as lust (Meyer, 25).[7] The characterization of Claudius throughout *Hamlet* as a lascivious king, an "adulterate beast" (I.v.42), corresponds to this derivation of Machiavellian politics from "desideriis et cupiditatibus" (Pole, 145). Passion so understood is not blindly reactive or instinctual: it shares violence with the lion, but cunning with the fox. Hence lovers' discourse continually appears in *Hamlet* as a duplicitous language of persuasion inseparable from political interests; the Machiavellian emblem fear and love bridges eros and civilization.

In the Player-King's speech, the word "violent" occurs twice—"Of violent birth," "The violence of either grief or joy"—to indicate the passionate provenance of promises that die. Such declarations, far from being cries prompted in the heat of mindless emotion, are highly motivated, the degree of their purposiveness signalling the brevity of their employment:

> The violence of either grief or joy
> Their own enactures with themselves destroy.
> Where joy most revels, grief doth most lament;
> Grief joys, joy grieves, on slender accident.
>
> (191–94)

Seeming to argue for the arbitrary fickleness of passionate extremes, the Player-King at the same time repeats an earlier relay of grief into joy: Claudius' formula for remarriage: "With mirth in funeral and with dirge in marriage" (I.ii.12). Claudius himself establishes the political nature of his topsy-turvy emotions:

Yet so far hath discretion fought with nature
That we with wisest sorrow think on him
Together with remembrance of ourselves.

(I.ii.6–7)

Discretion, the "wisdom" of political prudence, self-interest: Claudius uses an elevated version of Machiavellism to describe his marital motives. In the heights of emotion, there is method in madness. Like the Player-Queen's ratio of fear and love, shifting circumstance counter-changes laughter and tears: "Grief joys, joy grieves, on slender accident." Claudius and the Player-King, each defending remarriage, point to both the mutability and the rationality of emotion.

Fittingly, the Player-King turns from passion, with its presumably marital connotations, to the court:

This world is not for aye, nor 'tis not strange
That even our loves should with our fortunes change,
For 'tis a question left us yet to prove,
Whether love lead fortune or else fortune love.
The great man down, you mark his favourite flies;
The poor advanc'd makes friends of enemies;
And hitherto doth love on fortune tend:
For who not needs shall never lack a friend,
And who in want a hollow friend doth try
Directly seasons him his enemy.

(196–204)

Here, the Player-King defines the fickleness of love in unequivocally political terms.[8] Fortune and love replace the earlier ratios of fear and love, joy and grief, with historical contingency now a term in its own right rather than the suppressed hinge of "slender accident" or fall from "former state."

The wry reduction of love to fickleness parallels numerous passages in Machiavelli, who counters an amoral social domain with a quick-footed and distrustful prince. In the chapter on fear and love, Machiavelli configures the issues of love, friendship and promises touched on by the Player-King's speech:

When thow shalt deserve well of them, but have noe neede of them, then will they all be thy followers, spende their bludd in thy cause, their goodes, their lives, their famelyes, but yf extremities happen (as I have often sayde) thow shalt have them to sekke. A prince that trusteth to their promises and taketh their fayre woordes for warrantey of their good willes, shall not slyp onlie in the foote, but fall downe hedlonge, for frendshippes which are purchased by benefittes, (not vertues,) are boughte by good tournes, and yet in tyme of neede will not serve anie turne [Craig, 72].

The puns on turning and the vivid image of fall as downfall (tricks of the Elizabethan translator, not the original) suggest the wheel of Fortune as the tragic destiny of the traditionally virtuous Christian prince, not, as in the "Fall of Princes" convention, the ambitious and fraudulent king. Temperance, standard political virtue stressing self-identity over time, yields to contrary values of self-fashioning as self-revision. Borrowing the grave digger's pun on suicide, we might say that Machiavellian *virtù* defines *se defendendo* as *se offendendo*.[9] The Player-King's image of love tending on fortune recalls that strumpet Fortune of an earlier interchange:

> *Hamlet*: Then you live about her waist, or in the middle of her
>   favours?
> *Guildenstern*: Faith, her privates we.
>
> (II.ii.232–4)

The body politic becomes the grotesque and unruly woman Fortune. The modern politician, the actor, and Fortuna (fortune as allegory, but also allegory as fortune) all share the realm of contingency, duplicity, and licentious play.

The presence of politics is appropriate, since the marriage at issue is the second wedding, which the wife names "treason" and "base respects of thrift" (lines 174, 178), of a queen. The Player-King's counsel finds vivid precedent in Anna's marital advice to her sister Dido, pledged to remain faithful to a husband killed by her own brother.[10] Dido, ambiguous exemplum of chastity in widowhood, stands along with Hecuba as a foil for Gertrude. In the chapter on fear and love, Machiavelli treats Dido as a new prince who "exusthe her tiranie by the newnes of her tytle" (Craig, 72). Perhaps in anticipation of similar dangers to a vulnerable widow, including murderous brothers, the Player-King inaugurates his analysis of promising, a speech designed to enforce his predicting benediction: "and haply one as kind / For husband shalt thou—" (171). Kin, and more than kind.

The Player-King's speech addresses issues of faith and friendship current in Elizabethan Machiavellism.[11] Mutability, a scepticism masquerading as "distrust," and a problem with promises characterize the court politician as both actor and inactor. So speaks Claudius later:

> That we would do,
> We should do when we would: for this 'would' changes
> And hath abatements and delays as many
> As there are tongues, are hands, are accidents.
>
> (IV.vii.112–30)

Claudius, Hamlet and the Player-King all confront and embrace self-definition structured on discontinuity. This is, finally, a model of identity at once theatrical and political, as is the Machiavellism it finds and founds.

The presence of Machiavellism at the center of the play disables the apparent antinomies between Hyperion and satyr, Christian king and Machiavel. *The Murder of Gonzago*, by casting nephew as murderer, not only condenses Claudius and Hamlet as villains, but Claudius and the dead king as victims. The father appears on stage twice as a ghost of questionable origin, and then in the figure of the Player-King, whose Machiavellian speech aligns him as much with Claudius as with a fairer feudal order. The brothers speak the same language, the play-within-a-play rationalizing in political terms thrifty second weddings; the Player-King doth protest too much. The mirror at the center of *Hamlet*, contrary to the purpose of playing, confounds virtue and scorn, reflecting identity where there ought to be difference. The thematic overlap extends to the murder at the root of *Hamlet* and Hamlet's play, reinforcing the potentially disfiguring alliances between the drama's many princes: Claudius and the brother he murders, Hamlet prince of Denmark, and the Player-King at the center who ultimately mirrors them all.

### III.  *Schools of Abuse*

The primal scene of *Hamlet*, the episode which both triggers and inhibits its action, is the killing of the king: purpose is the slave of memory. Like a dream, King Hamlet's murder is recollected or represented, but never present: retold by his ghost, replayed twice in the course of Hamlet's "Mousetrap," and remembered by the son throughout the play. Like a dream, too, the murder distorts through pictorialization or figuration what could be called an original dream thought: theatre and politics as poison. The murder, that is, literalizes the terms framing the contemporary attack on the theatre, especially the diagnosis of drama as poison or plague, but also as both demilitarizing and unruly.[12] Interestingly, similar language marks the reception of Machiavelli, since his analysis of power raised comparable threats to political, moral, and ontological order.

Stephen Gosson's *The Schoole of Abuses* (1579), one of the most articulate early Elizabethan tracts against the theatre, established the arguments and metaphors for many of the works, both defensive and offensive, which followed in the next sixty years. Gosson develops the metaphor of poison, traditional since Plato, to conceptualize theatre as a trick or trap which slips in tettering thoughts and desires under cover of sweetness. Poisoning is not only the insidious death performed against one man, but a potentially systemic taint contaminating the body politic:

> and are not they accursed thinke you by the mouth of God, which hauing the gouernment of young Princes, with Poetical fantasies draw them to the schooles of their own abuses, bewitching the graine in the greene blade, that was sowed for the sustenance of many thousands, & poisoning the spring with their amorous layes, whence the whole common wealth should fetch water? [81].

Here, the recurrent fantasy of the Jews and the well works to frame art as poisonously poetic counsel pervading the state through its prince. Poison swiftly becomes synonymous with infectious disease: as a metaphor at once of mass contagion and insidious death, it figures the major official complaints, periodically enforced, against the theatre as occasion for disorderly assembly and spread of plague. Hamlet wittily conceptualizes the globe as theatre of infection.

> this most excellent canopy the air, look you, this brave o'erhanging firmament, this majestical roof fretted with golden fire, why it appeareth nothing to me but a foul and pestilent congregation of vapours [II.ii.299–303].

Theatre is poison run riot, a congregation of pestilent vapors: theatre is plague. Hamlet projects the City's standing grievances against the theatre, disease and sedition, onto globe and Globe.

The representation of *The Prince* as poison spread in the century following its appearance. Reginald Pole calls the book a potion that teaches madness: "tanquam potio furorem inducens in Principes" (138). Gentillet describes Machiavelli's notoriously aphoristic modes of persuasion:

> For *Machiavel* hath not handled every matter in one same place, but a little heere, and a little there, interlacing and mixing some good things amongst them, as poysoners doe, which never cast lumpes of poyson upon a heape, least it be perceived, but doe

most subtillie incorporate it as they can, with some other delicate
and daintie morsells [A iii].[13]

Richard Harvey, citing a line from Machiavelli, comments, "'A right Italian
sentence, a notable word, a fit preserve against the other venims which this
Spider gathered out of old philosophers and heathen authors.'"[14] Harvey
transforms the image of the bee gathering honey from many flowers—
classical topos for the varied sweetness of literary imitation—into the spider
distilling its poison from a sickening pagan past. The trope framing the
discourse of Machiavellism cast him as a literal poisoner. Machiavelli was
chief dispenser in Nashe's cosmopolitan Italy, "the Apothecary-shop of
poyson for all Nations" (Nashe I: 186).[15] The stock villain poisoning his
victims acts out the critical response to Machiavelli's texts.

In the same constellation of metaphors is the spectre of the poetic or
historical example that breeds: the danger implicit in both theatre and
Machiavelli was the incitement of lust and crime through representation,
even in art meant to be admonitory. The English translation of Gentillet's
famous tract against Machiavelli begins with an attack on the theatre:[16]

> Then *Solon*, (striking hard upon the earth with his staffe) replied
> thus: Yea but shortly, we that now like and embrace this play, shall
> find it practiced in our contracts and common affaires. This man
> of deepe understanding, saw that publicke discipline and
> reformation of manners affected once in sport jeast, would soone
> quaile: and corruption, at the beginning passing in play, would
> fall and end in earnest [iii].

Theatre, even when representing evil for the sake of didactic purposes, offers
models of immorality which generate further misbehavior, ill-acting.[17]
Images of proliferation proliferate in anti-theatrical discourse: "Neither
staied these abuses in the compasse of that countrey: but like unto yll weedes
in time spread so far, that they choked the good grayne in every place"
(Gosson, 85). The exemplary nature of art founds both its didactic value and
its moral threat, the staging of deeds as repeatable actions inspiring like the
plague images of spreading social disorder.

The importance of these metaphors in *Hamlet* demands little
elaboration. The primal scene of murder, and the images it generates, seem
to literalize Sidney's summary of anti-theatrical arguments in *The Defense of
Poetry*. The essay adopts and mimics the vocabulary of *The Schoole of Abuse*,
which Gosson had inappropriately dedicated to Sidney:

first, that there being many other more fruitful knowledges, man might better spend his time in them than in this; secondly, that it is the mother of lies; thirdly, that it is the nurse of abuse, infecting us with many pestilent desires, with a siren's sweetness drawing the mind to the serpent's tail of sinful fancies (and herein especially comedies give the largest field to ear, as Chaucer says); how both in other nations and in ours, before poets did soften us, we were full of courage, given to martial exercises, the pillars of man-like liberty and not lulled asleep in shady idleness with poets' pastimes; and lastly and chiefly, they cry out with open mouth (as if they had overshot Robinhood) that Plato banished them out of his republic. Truly this is much, if there be much truth in it [34].

The pun on 'ear,' the vision of art as pestilent sweetness, the allusion to the serpent, the shady idleness of sleep, the fall of martial prowess: all these figurations of art find embodiment in the murder of King Hamlet. The ghost tells Hamlet

> 'Tis given out that, sleeping in my orchard,
> A serpent stung me—so the whole ear of Denmark
> Is by a forged process of my death
> Rankly abus'd—but now, thou noble youth,
> The serpent that did sting thy father's life
> Now wears his crown.
>
> (I.v.35–40)

Sleep, serpent, poison in the ear, the death of that "fair and warlike form" (I.i.49) at the hands of a devious successor allegorize the murder as the crime of rhetoric.

King Hamlet's tale of the serpent, at once false report, poetic irony, and metaphor for language's endemic deception, allegorizes the king as victim of poor counsel—and a fatally uncritical reader. Advice was the major political role available to the nobleman in a monarchy, the "mirror for the prince" the corresponding genre of traditional European political theory, and Machiavelli its most notorious author (Gilbert; Pocock 338–41). The king's sleepy murder by wicked counsel projects the fall from feudal arms to the disarming politics of the court, a transition figured prominently both by Claudius' cunning maneuvers and Hamlet's idleness. Fittingly, the play ends with a fencing exhibition, which exhibits war as art.[18] The metaphors of poison and pestilence spread through the play, demarcating political corruption as the reign of rhetoric, theatre as the politicization of virtue: "Something is rotten in the state of Denmark" (I.v.90). Poison becomes the breeding plague of rumor and rhetoric, infesting not only the ear of the king but the porches of the multitude: Laertes "wants not buzzers to infect his ear / With pestilent speeches of his father's death" (IV.v.90–91). The poisoning of King Hamlet functions as both cause and after-image of Denmark's fraudulence: he has died an Italian death at the hands of an Italianate villain. Shakespeare underlines, even parodies, the provenance of poison by attributing *The Murder of Gonzago* to an Italian source: "The story is extant, and written in very choice Italian" (III.ii.256–57). Perhaps Hamlet's "Marry, this is miching malicho. It means mischief" after the dumb show jangles with the master mischief-maker from the south (III.ii.135).

Defenses of poetry and theatre, and even attacks upon them, stress the responsibility of the reader in correctly employing a work of art.[19] The same arguments were used by Machiavelli's few defenders. Edward Dacres, the translator of the first authorized English edition of *The Prince* (1640), apologized in a marginal animadversion:

> Poysons are not all of that malignant and noxious quality, that, as destructives of Nature, they are utterly to be abhorred; but we find many, nay most of them have their medicinnal uses. This book carryes with its poyson and malice in it; yet mee thinks the judicious peruser may honestly make use of it in the actions of his life, with advantage [cited in Raab; 98–99].

At stake for Dacres in the pairing of poison and medicine is the responsibility of the reader to use properly the text before him.[20] Dacres defends Machiavelli by recasting poison as medicine. Unfortunately, such arguments assume the reader's wholly conscious or rational receptive abilities, sidestepping the anti-theatrical critique of rhetoric as deceptive and subversive, a play of language that works by circumventing the reader's will. If one is asleep in the orchard, "full of bread," "crimes broad blown, as flush as May" (III.iii.801), surely one is less able to determine best uses of a poison, or a text. If, sick, one is already far from former state, then hearing is probably impaired. At Elsinore, the poisoning is systemic, and the pestilence predates the serpent in the garden. The mirror at the center of the play reflects an event that has already happened, and which, emblem for the generation of theatrical degeneracy, is repeated again and again in the many subterfuges and countermines of *Hamlet*.

## IV. *"A Vice of Kings"*

The Machiavellian villain bridged both generic and social lines, a double movement aptly caught in Nancy Struever's analysis of the new prince as picaresque hero. For Elizabethans, the notion of a "new prince" was an oxymoron rapidly loosing the luster of paradox.[21] On the one hand offering rich material for the representation of misgovernment as deceitful ambition, the Machiavellian machinator doomed to tragic fall assimilates the comic attributes of the late-medieval vice figure. Names of morality vices like "Nicholas New Fangle," "Hypocrisy," "Dissimulation," "Tyranny," "Avarice, alias, Policee" indicate the covalence between the witty, subversive, metatheatrical vice and the Machiavellian villain. According to David Bevington, the morality play is founded structurally and thematically on the multiple roles and limited cast of traveling troupes; the Vice, his own role a condensation of parts, figures forth doubling as a condition of popular theatre (123).[22] The Machiavel succeeds the medieval tyrant, out-Heroding him at his own blustering, popular game.

Hamlet calls Claudius "a vice of kings" and a "king of shreds and patches" (III.iv.98,103), aligning him with the theatrical tradition which Hamlet tries to exorcise in his famous critical speeches on theatre. The clowns detract from the major matter at hand: "there be of them that will themselves laugh, to set on some quantity of barren spectators to laugh too, though in the meantime some necessary question of the play be then to be considered" (III.ii.40–43). Shifting attention from necessary questions, the villainous clowns threaten the frame of illusion, at once social and theatrical, advised by Hamlet: "That's villainous, and shows a most pitiful ambition in the fool that uses it" (III.ii.43–45)—'Villain,' a variant of 'villein,' plays, like 'clown,' double duty as 'peasant.' The theatrical fool, like the new prince, is accused of ambition, leaving his place. Following Sidney in the *Defense*, Hamlet is worried about generic decorum as social decorum (Sidney, 49). Claudius' chiasmus of mirth in funeral, dirge in marriage, an inversion of feasts, notoriously recapitulates Sidney's disparagement of tragicomedy: "we shall find that they never (or very daintily) match hornpipes and funerals" (49). Villainy and clowning are together associated with mixed genre, festive misrule, inconstancy, a frame-breaking metatheatricality, an impertinent social mobility: and all this, but only apparently, in the figure of Claudius.

For Hamlet, too, exhibits attributes of the vice and villain. Hamlet more than Claudius takes on the comic, frenetically verbal functions of the vice, speaking an antic prose that belies the decorum he counsels. Like Claudius, Hamlet engages in cunning theatrics: the play-within-the-play, casting nephew as poisoner, figures forth both Hamlet's coming revenge and his present abuses of language. Even Hamlet's melancholic disposition taints him with villainy. The "Elizabethan malady" was associated with social discontent, seditiousness, atheism, Italy, and Machiavelli. The melancholic "by his contemplative faculty, by his assiduity of sad and serious meditation, is a brocher of dangerous Matchiavellisme, an inventor of stratagems, quirkes, and policies" (Walkington, cited in Babb, 585, cf. 74, 81). Hamlet's melancholy borders on Claudius' "wisest sorrow," understood at once as the cunning use of grief, and the sadness which shadows worldliness.

The discourse on villainy throughout the play variously identifies Hamlet as Machiavel. Hamlet's first soliloquy founds the initial connection between promises, memory and Machiavellism which the Player-King's speech develops. In the echo of the ghost's "Adieu, adieu, adieu. Remember me," Hamlet tries to clear his memory ("I'll wipe away all trivial fond records"), but distraction, in the form of expletives, sets in:

>     Yes, by heaven!
> O most pernicious woman!
> O villain, villain, smiling damned villain!
> My tables. Meet it as I set it down
> That one may smile, and smile, and be a villain—
> At least I am sure it may be so in Denmark.
> So, uncle, there you are. Now to my word. [Writes.]
> It is "Adieu, adieu, remember me."
> I have sworn't.                                    (104–12)

The stage direction, inserted by later editors, does not specify what Hamlet writes. Grammatically, he sets down "That one may smile, and smile, and be a villain," a line which echoes Richard of Gloucester's words in the final *Henry VI* play.[23] The sentiment, "Why I can smile, and murther whiles I smile," begins one of Shakespeare's most explicit acknowledgments of Machiavelli:

> I can add colors to the chameleon,
> Change shapes with Proteus for advantages,
> And set the murtherous Machevil to school.
>               (*3Hen6*, III.ii.191–93)

A cliché of the stage Machiavel coined from an earlier, and thoroughly political, Shakespeare play accompanies Hamlet's effort to remember the ghost's commandment. Hamlet promises not to revenge but to remember:

"my word" at the end of the soliloquy is either the full word given in oath, or an emptier mnemonic. He is an actor memorizing lines in order to repeat them, shuffling plays into a constellation of topics (promises, memory, Machiavel and Machiavelli, action as acting) replayed and displayed in the play-within-a-play. The theatre of his memory is a "distracted globe"; like the tragicomic stage, it is disrupted by villainous and pitifully ambitious clowns.

Hamlet returns to villainy shortly after when his friends drill him about the ghost: "There's never a villain dwelling in all Denmark / But he's an errant knave" (I.v.129–30). The feinting tautology locates the villain in a cluster of words (rogue, rascal, knave, beggar, truant, slave) epitomized by actor as vagabond. In *Hamlet*, historical change displaces the players, forcing them to leave the city: "their inhibition comes by the means of the late innovation" (II.ii.330–31). The actor is on the move, both a sign and instigator of social transition and an outcast from self-identity. Vagabondage defines the actor as an errant knave whose truancy threatens a social order already dismayed. An equivalency emerges between villain, actor, the new prince, and the displaced or dispossessed, all unfortunate travelers in a changing world.

Hamlet's soliloquy following the vagabonds' initial performance, contrasting the mourning skills of the player and Hamlet, curiously identifies actor and prince in class terms that bring into focus the correlation between actor, villain, peasant, and outcast, between Hamlet the dispossessed heir and Claudius, Machiavellian vice of kings. Hamlet's famous line, "O what a rogue and peasant slave am I!" connects him at once to the vagabonds who have just performed and to Claudius further on:

> I should ha' fatted all the region kites
> With this slave's offal. Bloody, bawdy villain!
> Remorseless, treacherous, lecherous, kindless villain!
>
> (II.ii.575–77)

In between Hamlet imagines a scenario in which he would be called villain, an epithet both morally and socially debasing:

> Am I a coward?
> Who calls me villain, breaks my pate across,
> Plucks off my beard and blows it in my face,
> Tweaks me by the nose, gives me the lie i'th' throat
> As deep as to the lungs—who does me this?
>
> (564–71)

Hamlet, an errant knave, gives himself the lie and calls himself villain. The soliloquy stages a flyting of *se offendendo* and failed *se defendendo* whose dialogic nature figures the crime itself: a truant disposition as the modern basis of action, inaction, and acting.[24] The soliloquy ends with the design of a "mousetrap," both drama and trial, which will mirror the same damaging equivalencies of villain and villein, actor, prince, and king.

The discourse on villainy continues throughout the play to link Claudius and Hamlet as actors and politicians, as Machiavels. Hamlet caricatures himself to Ophelia as the machinating villain which he is and is not, once more through an imagined or oblique self-accusation:

> I am myself indifferent honest, but yet I could accuse me of such things that it were better my mother had not borne me. I am very proud, revengeful, ambitious, with more offences at my beck than I have thoughts to put them in, imagination to give them shape, or time to act them in [III.i.124–27].

As before, the villain belies himself: "We are errant knaves all, believe none of us" (129–30). Hamlet, recounting to Horatio his experiences en route to England, replays the scene of his turn to politic language:

> Being thus benetted round with villainies—
> Or I could make a prologue to my brains,
> They had begun the play—I sat me down,
> Devis'd a new commission, wrote it fair—
> I once did hold it, as our statists do,
> A baseness to write fair, and labour'd much
> How to forget that learning, but sir, now
> It did me yeoman's service.
>
> (V.ii.29–36)

In this scene of recollection, Hamlet remembers, not his father's "fair and warlike form," but an earlier political education in writing fair: the metatheatrical terms conflate politics and drama as "villainies." Statecraft and writing are together contaminated by lower-class associations, "yeoman's service"; they are doubly villainous, blotted by the stigma of print and labor as well as subterfuge.

After the play-within-a-play, Hamlet refrains from killing Claudius at prayer, for fear he will send the murderer to heaven:

A villain kills my father, and for that
I, his sole son, do this same villain send
To heaven.
Why this is hire and salary, not revenge.

(III.iii.76–79)

Since the eighteenth century, critics have argued about Hamlet's motives: Is the horribly vengeful theological argument sincere, or merely a pretext for delay? Machiavellism informs both the scene and the question of intention it raises: "eternal revenge" was associated with Italy and Machiavelli, while the stage Machiavel conflates being and playing, effectively thwarting the question of motive.[25] It is the scene in which Hamlet becomes most like the man he promises to murder, in part because inaction and villainy coincide, effectively eclipsing differences between them. Critical tradition casts Hamlet either as villain or as the humanist who only plays the villain: the term is such that the alternatives are the same. The villain is always a player waiting upon occasion. Hamlet's words to his mother shuffles the various terms together:

A murderer and a villain,
A slave that is not twentieth part the tithe
Of your precedent lord, a vice of kings.

(III.iv.97–99)

The passage lists the multiple role of the stage Machiavel, juggling the masks of high and low, actor and king. Machiavelli, defining politics as a kind of theatre, was himself cast as a character in Elizabethan drama, a vice and villain constantly exposing through use and abuse the conditions of power and illusion. This infamous persona emblematized a political discourse which colored attitudes towards love and passion, politics, ethics, language, and the self. Such issues necessarily mark the structure and self-understanding of the texts which engage them. Machiavelli and his Elizabethan reception inhabit Hamlet's play, and the play *Hamlet*. Villain, murderer, vice of kings: the same terms apply to Claudius and to Hamlet, and to King Hamlet as well. As ghost, as actor, as politician, Hamlet's father is three times a player-king, an "extravagant and erring spirit" (I.i.159). At the reflective center, Machiavellian arguments disfigure moral categories and dramatic oppositions, and associate Christian king, Machiavellian brother, and antic prince.

## NOTES

1. The earlier position was first put forth by Eugene Meyer's 1895 *Machiavelli and the Elizabethan Drama*, which remains valuable for its collection of citations. Felix Raab (1964) offered the first major revisionist position, but see also Napoleone Orsini (1937, 1937–38, 1946) and George Mosse (1957). The most important recent work is J. G. A. Pocock's *The Machiavellian Moment*, which argues for the reception of Machiavelli's republicanism in England and America. On Machiavelli and Tacitism, see Schellhase. Hardin Craig's invaluable edition of the manuscripts is used in this essay. There is also a 1929 reprint of Edward Dacres' 1640 translation, although without his animadversions. See Orsini, 'Elizabethan Translations' and *Studii sul Rinascimento*, which reprints two manuscript prefaces.

2. On Machiavelli and anti-theatricality, see Barish, 96–99.

3. Citations from *Hamlet* are from the Arden edition, ed. Harold Jenkins, and other plays by Shakespeare from the Riverside Shakespeare.

4. Egidio Colonna, one medieval commentator, writes, "For not all are so good and perfect that from mere love of what is upright and of the common good, and from affection for the legislator, whose function it is to regard the common good, they cease from doing evil. Therefore it is necessary to lead some toward good and restrain them from evil by fear of punishment" (*De regimine principum*, 3.2.36, composed before 1286; cited in Gilbert, 109.)

5. Sir Philip Sidney, *The Countess of Pembrokes Arcadia*, 2.6., p. 186. Cited in Gilbert, 99–100.

6. Machiavelli's most notorious example of such delegation combines it with the effects of public punishment: Cesare Borgia executed his deputy in order "that he might the better quench the remembrance thereof, cleere himself and wynn their heartes.... Ths cruell sighte on the sodaine satisfied the Peoples hunger and amazed their myndes" (Craig, 30).

7. Pole writes of Henry VIII in one of the first responses to Machiavelli written by an Englishman: "What indeed was performed in that tragicomedy without the appearance of religion? Although he had deviated from passion to cruelty, and had created a mixed comedy out of a true tragedy with his flagrant cruelty—by which he has overcome all tyrants and impious men—he was not able to express the precepts of his master better. All this was done ... in order that he might serve his own desires and appetites under the veil of religion, in which is contained the complete doctrine of Machiavelli and Cromwell" (translation courtesy Curtis Breight; Pole, 144–45). The Duke of Milan in Beaumont's *Woman Hater* (c. 1606) delivers a Machiavellian speech which stresses the role of desire in political decisions (I, i; cited in Orsini, "'Policy,'" 129).

8. For the tradition of the Player-King's remarks on friendship and their importance in the play, see Wimsatt, who does not mention Machiavelli as a possible subtext.

9. John Higgins writes in the 1574 edition of *The First Parte of the Mirour for Magistrates* that lack of temperance is the primary cause of a prince's fall (Campbell, 37–38). Temperance, like constancy, stresses self-identity over time—precisely what Machiavelli's politics counsel against. On constancy and anti-theatricality, see Barish, 104–5.

10. "And dost thou not call to mind in whose lands thou art settled?" Anna reminds Dido. "On this side Gaetulian cities ... on that side lies a tract barren with drought.... Why speak of wars rising from Tyre, and thy brother's threats?" (*Aeneid* 4:44–49). Elizabeth had received similar advice. See also Natalie Zemon Davis's provocative remarks on *Hamlet* and festive *charivari* (123).

11. In Chapman's *All Fools*, the Machiavell Gostanzo counsels against oath keeping (III.i.69–76). Compare also Robert Greene's "Mamilia" (Grosart 2:205; cited in Meyer,

28). The Moor's Son associates promises and false friends in a Machiavellian speech in Peele's 1591 *Battle of Alcazar* (Dyce: II.iv., p. 428; cited in Meyer, 62).

12. I thank Laura Levine for sharing and discussing her fine dissertation on anti-theatricality (in progress, Johns Hopkins). See her 'Men in Women's Clothing,' *Criticism*, 28.2 (1986).

13. On the Machiavellian associations of the word group 'aphorism,' 'maxim,' 'aphorismer,' see Orsini, "'Policy.'"

14. Harvey, 'A Theological Discourse of the Lamb of God and His Enemies' (1590); Short title catalogue 12915; cited in Meyer, 53–54.

15. Meyer, listing the principal crimes attributed to Machiavelli later in the drama, comments, "Especially is ... poison to be noted; for the Florentine nowhere expressly recommends its use. It became, however, the prime factor in Elizabethan Machiavellism" (77).

16. Other conjunctions of anti-Machiavellism and anti-theatricality include *Politique Discourses, Trueth and Lying: An Instruction to Princes to Keepe Their Faith and Promise* (1586), which includes an extended attack on the theatre [Taylor]. The third English edition of Pierre de la Primaudaye's *French Academy* is prefaced by an indictment of atheism, Machiavelli, and drama. Atheism is theatre: "the pretense and shewe of religion" (cited in Meyer, 77).

17. The 1597 drama of tyranny *Selimus* represents the Machiavellian politician as public example or mirror: "Let them view in me / The perfect picture of right tyrannie" (Grosart 14: 703; cited in Meyer, 65).

18. Gosson calls fencing the "craft of Defence" and compares its present abuse to logicians' "caueling": the "abuses" of sword and pen. In his defense of theatre, Thomas Lodge argues that fencing, as preparation for war, is legitimate theatre (Kinney, 53).

19. See also Gosson, 80, 82, 86, and Sidney, 37. On Sidney as a defender of poetry using the idea of "abuse" to develop a theory of critical reading, see Margaret Ferguson, esp. the section "The Defense against 'Abuse of Power,'" 146–54. I thank Margaret Ferguson for advice and encouragement on this article.

20. In 1599, John Levitt, who produced a manuscript translation of *The Prince*, "to further my practise in the tongue," similarly appeals to the reader's judgment (Orsini, *Studii* 43–47).

21. Robert P. Adams argues that Claudius' apparent legitimacy marks a change in Elizabethan Machiavellism; the notion that a king, and not a usurer, could be tyrannical was a dawning realization in the later Elizabethan period. The term 'new prince' was not, however, a paradoxical phrase for Machiavelli, who often played on the etymological relation between *princeps* and *principium*. For Machiavelli, a prince always marks a beginning.

22. See also L. W. Cushman's still valuable *The Devil and the Vice*.

23. "It is usual to make Hamlet produce a property notebook at the end of the speech and write down that 'one may smile, and smile, and be a villain'" (Alexander, 47).

24. This passage among others links Hamlet to Claudius. Claudius tells Laertes, "You must not think / That we are made of stuff so flat and dull / That we can let our beard be shook with danger / And think it pastime" (IV.vii.30–33).

25. On the debate, see Jenkins, 513–15. Sara Dears (also Jenkins, 514) suggests that Hamlet's desire for "eternal revenge" comes from Gentillet's (tendentious) attribution of such tactics to Machiavelli. Another possible subtext is Nashe's *The Unfortunate Traveller* (Jenkins, 514) which ends with the public confession and execution of "one *Cutwolfe*" in Bologna: "With my selfe I deuised how to plague him double for his base minde: my thoughts traueled in quest of some notable newe Italionisme.... All true Italians imitate me in revenging constantly and dying valiantly" (I:325, 326).

## References

Adams, Robert. 'Opposed Tudor Myths of Power: Machiavellian Tyrants and Christian Kings.' In *Studies in the Continental Background of Renaissance English Literature; Essays Presented to John L. Lievsay.* Ed. Dale B. J. Randall and George Watson. Durham, N.C.

Alexander, Nigel. *Poison, Play and Duel: A Study in Hamlet.* London, 1971.

Babb, Lawrence. *The Elizabethan Malady: A Study of Melancholia in English Literature from 1580 to 1642.* East Lansing, Mich., 1951.

Barish, Jonas. *The Anti-Theatrical Prejudice.* Berkeley, Calif., 1983.

Bevington, David. *From 'Mankind' to Marlowe: Growth of Structure in the Popular Drama of Tudor England.* Cambridge, Mass., 1962.

Campbell, Lily B., ed. *Parts Added to 'The Mirror for Magistrates' by John Higgins and Thomas Blenerhasset.* Cambridge, 1946.

Chapman, George. *The Plays of George Chapman: The Comedies.* Ed. Allan Holaday. Urbana, Ill., 1970.

Craig, Hardin. *Machiavelli's 'The Prince': An Elizabethan Manuscript Translation.* Chapel Hill, N.C., 1944

Cushman, L. W. *The Devil and the Vice in the English Dramatic Literature before Shakespeare.* Halle a.S., 1900.

Dacres, Edward, trans. *The Prince by Niccolò Machiavelli.* London, 1929.

Davis, Natalie Zemon. 'The Reasons of Misrule.' In *Society and Culture in Early Modern Europe* (Stanford, Calif., 1975), 97–123.

Deats, Sara M. 'The Once and Future Kings: Four Studies of Kingship in *Hamlet*.' In *Essays in Literature* (Macomb, Ill., 1982), 9(1):15–30.

Dyce, Alexander, ed. *The Dramatic and Poetical Works of Robert Greene and George Peele.* London, 1961.

Ferguson, Margaret W. *Trials of Desire: Renaissance Defenses of Poetry.* New Haven, Conn., 1983.

Gentillet, Innocent. *A Discourse upon the Meanes of Wel Governing: Against Nicholas Machiavel the Florentine.* Trans. Simon Paterikce, 1577; printed 1602; rprt. New York, 1969.

Gilbert, Allan H. *Machiavelli's 'Prince' and Its Forerunners: 'The Prince' as a Typical Book de Regimine Principum.* Durham, N.C., 1938.

Gosson, Stephen. *The Schoole of Abuse* (1579). Ed. Arthur Kinney. Salzburg, 1974.

Grosart, Alexander B., ed. *The Life and Works of Robert Greene, M.A.* London, 1881–83.

Jenkins, Harold, ed. *The Arden Hamlet.* London, 1964.

Kinney, Arthur F. *Markets of Bawdrie: The Dramatic Criticism of Stephen Gosson.* Salzburg: Salzburg Studies in English Literature, 1974.

Kyd, Thomas. *The Spanish Tragedy.* Ed. J. R. Mulyrne. London, 1970.

Machiavelli, Niccolò. *The Prince and The Discourses.* Trans. Luigi Ricci. New York, 1950.

Meyer, Edward. *Machiavelli and the Elizabethan Drama* (1897). Rprt., New York, [1969].

Mosse, George. *The Holy Pretence: A Study in Christianity and Reason of State from William Perkins to John Winthrop.* Oxford, 1957.

Nashe, Thomas. *The Complete Works.* Ed. Ronald McKerrow. London, 1908.

O'Connell, Michael. 'The Idolatrous Eye: Iconoclasm, Antitheatricalism, and the Image of the Elizabethan Theatre.' *ELH* 52.2 (Summer, 1985), 279–310.

Orsini, Napoleone. 'Elizabethan Manuscript Translations of Machiavelli's *The Prince*.' *Warburg Institute Journal* 1 (1937–38), 166–69.

———. '"Policy," or the Language of Elizabethan Machiavellianism.' *Journal of the Warburg and Courtauld Institute*, 9 (1946), 122–34.

———. *Studii sul Rinascimento italiano in Inghilterra con alcuni testi inglesi inediti*. Florence, 1937.

Pocock, J. G. A. *The Machiavellian Moment: Florentine Political Thought and the Atlantic Republican Tradition*. Princeton, N.J., 1975.

Pole, Reginald. *Apologia ad Carolum Quintum*. In *Epistolarum Reginaldi Poli*. Vol. 1. (Brescia, 1744), 137–52.

Raab, Felix. *The English Face of Machiavelli*. London, 1964.

Schellhase, Kenneth C. *Tacitus in Renaissance Political Thought*. Chicago, 1976.

Shakespeare, William. *The Riverside Shakespeare*. Ed. G. Blakemore Evans. Boston, 1974.

Sidney, Sir Phillip. *The Defense of Poetry*. Ed. Lewis Soens. Lincoln, Neb., 1970.

Struever, Nancy. 'Machiavelli and the Critique of the Available Languages of Morality in the Sixteenth Century.' Unpublished paper, 1983.

Taylor, George C. 'Another Renaissance Attack on the Stage.' *Philological Quarterly*, 9 (1930), 78–81.

Virgil. *Aeneid*. In *Virgil in Two Volumes*, I. Trans. H. Rushton Fairclough. Loeb Classical Library. Cambridge, Mass., 1916.

Wimsatt, James I. 'The Player King on Friendship.' *Modern Language Review*, 65 (1979), 1–6.

BERT O. STATES

# The Melancholy Dane

I imagine the arras through which Hamlet stabs Polonius as a richly figured tapestry of scenes from Renaissance life. On it might be woven pictures of the seven ages of man, of country and city life, of the professions and sports, household affairs and public ceremonies—the kinds of things, in short, that Hephestus embossed on the shield Achilles carried into combat against Hector: the world simply going its routine way, doing, as Bright says, what "nature requireth." Nothing in the text suggests such an idea—unless it is the text taken as a whole, of which the arras is an insignificant part—and I am not urging it on readers or scene designers. I cite it as a private instance of how a fiction teaches one to fill in details that are not there at all and to do so in the style of those that are. This spilling over of a play's "known" or expressed world into what we might call its own blank spaces is one of the most intriguing dimensions of the process of metaphor, and one for which we scarcely have an adequate critical language. For example, in a slight exchange like "Have you had quiet guard? / Not a mouse stirring." there is, obviously, a very palpable mouse stirring. In that miraculous organ Hamlet calls the mind's eye one sees it scurrying along a dank wall of the imagination and disappearing into such darkness as might shroud a ghost. So the mouse—like the glow worm, the woodcock, the mole, the porpentine, the weasel, the kite, the crab, and the serpent—is a creature of some brief influence in the creation of the unique space in which *Hamlet*'s story unfolds.

From *Hamlet and the Concept of Character.* © 1992 by The Johns Hopkins University Press.

All plays, certainly all Elizabethan plays, create their visual worlds by such suggestive means. But *Hamlet's*, as we all know, is especially luxurious: it hangs in the air more densely, more variously, than other dramatic worlds. For instance, there is very little sense of a thick periphery of "things" in *Macbeth's* metaphysical spaces, though there are rooks and wood choughs enough. Somehow, everything seems critically in thrall to the central deed: even the stones prate of the murderer's whereabouts. *Hamlet's* world, by contrast, opens out far beyond the decayed garden we hear so much about in the criticism. It is a universe made up of an almost encyclopedic procession of persons, animals, objects, processes, and instances from rural, professional, and household affairs, many of them strangely self-contained and portable, all spun out by characters who, even in Shakespeare's immense gallery, have an unusual habit of getting detained in the making of word-pictures. More matter and less art, the Queen reminds Polonius, though Laertes might have said the same to her as she reports his sister's death:

> There is a willow grows askant the brook
> That shows his hoary leaves in the glassy stream.
> Therewith fantastic garlands did she make
> Of crowflowers, nettles, daisies, and long purples,
> That liberal shepherds give a grosser name,
> But our cold maids do dead men's fingers call them.
> There on the pendent boughs her crownet weeds
> Clamb'ring to hang, an envious sliver broke,
> When down her weedy trophies and herself
> Fell in the weeping brook.
>
> (4.7.165–74)

Not that this passage is in any sense overembroidered. On the contrary, it is fully and symbolically warranted by the occasion: the perfect exit for Ophelia. What is curious about it, and so much at home in this play, is the way it swerves through these liberal shepherds and cold maids who come trooping in from the country on the stems of long purples which are themselves but garlands on the event. Here, in other words, one of the central tragic events of the play is overwhelmed by "country matters," young people playing the sexual game. As Auden says in his poem about Bruegel (who uses this same technique of pitting the world against the event), "Everything turns away / Quite leisurely from the disaster." Like Christ in Bruegel's *Procession to Calvary*, Ophelia is virtually lost to the eye, which sees rather the participation of nature in her drowning. Indeed, one might say that she is drowned in scenery.[1] As the play itself is. From the other end of

the spectrum, let me cite an example that will reveal this same temptation
running away with Shakespeare and producing one of those passages
directors invariably cut. It occurs in act 4 where Claudius is plotting Hamlet's
downfall with Laertes. Although Laertes has just given every sign of being
ahead of Claudius, Claudius feels he must be made even "riper" for the
treachery, and so goes on to praise him for that special "part" which will turn
the trick:

| | |
|---|---|
| *Laer.* | What part is that, my lord? |
| *King* | A very riband in the cap of youth— |
| | Yet needful too, for youth no less becomes |
| | The light and careless livery that it wears |
| | Than settled age his sables and his weeds |
| | Importing health and graveness. Two months since |
| | Here was a gentleman of Normandy— |
| | I have seen myself, and serv'd against, the French, |
| | And they can well on horseback, but this gallant |
| | Had witchcraft in't. He grew unto his seat, |
| | And to such wondrous doing brought his horse |
| | As had he been incorps'd and demi-natur'd |
| | With the brave beast. So far he topp'd my thought, |
| | That I in forgery of shapes and tricks |
| | Come short of what he did. |
| *Laer.* | A Norman was't? |
| *King* | A Norman. |
| *Laer.* | Upon my life, Lamord. |
| *King* | The very same. |

                                        (4.7.75–91)

Of course devious devices require devious approaches. But here the
tail, so to speak, is plainly wagging the horse. From the dramatic standpoint,
Lamord is summoned on a suspiciously slim, if not altogether avoidable,
mission and allowed a full fifteen lines of "shapes and tricks" before his
function becomes evident. What induced Shakespeare to sandwich such a
portrait between "What part is that, my lord?" (l. 77) and "[Why ...] art and
exercise in your defence" (l. 98)? Was it, as one unhappy critic says, his
"unconquerable impulse to pour out poetry on the slightest provocation"?
Or is it, as some suggest, that Lamord was one of those real gentlemen at
Elizabeth's court who (like the little eyases) was simply good copy for an
audience that liked to see its own reflection in plays, even at the expense of a
thickening plot?

My point, of course, is that Lamord is a symptom of a habit which "o'erleavens" this play, to use Hamlet's word, and reaches into the very rhythm and logic of its development. So often one senses in *Hamlet* the working of an irresistible principle of growth (I would call it cancer if the word had any healthy connotations) which causes the images, examples, and proofs to resist a purely auxiliary service in the business at hand and to struggle, like Lamord and the liberal shepherds, toward a life of their own. The astonishing thing about *Hamlet* is the sheer number of lines that are devoted to an elaboration of the elsewhere, the other, the previous, or the timeless: what we might, for general purposes, call the atmospheric content. I call such passages word-pictures because so often they seem to be framed, or to stand out in a peculiar way, like scenic turn-outs on the highway of the plot. Quite often they take the form of mini-discourses on character and behavior: the expectations and inclinations of character, the abuses of conduct, the ways to behave, to grieve, to travel abroad, to act, to play, to preserve one's virtue, to "assume" virtues and dispositions; the transformations of character into madness, gloom, and ecstasy; the portraiture and prototypes, the flourishes and excesses of character; the causes of defects in, the effects of causes in, and so on. No other Shakespeare play is quite so Burtonesque, so given over to sheer portraiture of people and things. Everywhere, the play manages to get detained in matters of behavior. Even common conversation is character-prone:

| | |
|---|---|
| *Pol* | What do you think of me? |
| *King* | As of a man faithful and honourable. |
| *Pol* | I would fain prove so. |

(2.2.129–31)

But the word-pictures are not always concerned with character or landscapes. Very often they take the form of "documents," or essayistic set-speeches on natural law (for instance, Claudius's remarks above on youth and settled age). Moreover, the word-pictures themselves are only the chunkiest manifestation of the habit. The very grammatical soil from which they spring is so fecund that it induces prolixity of other kinds: over and over, we find characters falling into a seriatim rhythm in which they seem compelled to inventory a thing or process within an inch of its life before passing on to more urgent matters. Thus the structure of Hamlet's "Tis not alone my inky cloak, dear mother ..., Nor ..., Nor ..., No, nor ..., Nor ..., Together with all forms, moods, shapes of grief..." is a common one, not only to Hamlet but to the other characters as well. For example: Ophelia's survey of Hamlet's overthrown qualities; or that great talker the Ghost ("Brief let me be") taking time to "unfold" (among other things) two anatomizations of the body in a state of seizure; or Claudius on unmanly grief; or Rosencrantz, very late in his career as a silent yes-man, suddenly breaking loose for thirteen lines on "the cess of majesty"; or the Player on the rugged Pyrrhus; Polonius on the proper conduct of departing sons or the genres of drama; Hamlet cataloging the sources of corruption in particular men, or wiping the tables of his memory, or Hamlet on acting, on suicide-Hamlet, in fact, on almost anything.

I don't know how far this habit ought to be documented, or to what extent I ought to answer the obvious charge that such an embarrassment of riches was the common dividend of every Shakespeare play, and if a little more embarrassing than usual in *Hamlet* it was simply because Shakespeare had more on his mind. In any case, the question of whether these word-pictures are excessive to dramatic needs invites nothing but an excursion into personal taste. My purpose has been to set them into a somewhat exaggerated relief from the rest of *Hamlet* in order to make a certain stylistic tendency more visible to the eye. I have no idea where word-pictures begin and end, as distinct from ordinary imagery, but it is clear that Shakespeare was under some compulsion, beyond simple self-indulgence, to crowd *Hamlet* with an unusual amount of scenic and atmospheric ballast, so much so that it has a significant effect on our options for interpreting the play.

We all have our own impressions of the *Hamlet* universe. But in reading criticism of the play's imagery, one has the odd sense of getting only the gloomy and cankered part of its world. For instance, Caroline Spurgeon, at the end of her very dreary picture of Denmark, remarks that "the ugliness" of the disease imagery is "counter-acted and the whole lighted up by flashes of sheer beauty."[2] The problem here, I suspect, is that she had no "scientific" means of dealing with these "flashes," except in an offhand way, since image analysis is based on the computer principle of statistical reenforcement. Once the critic has detected a thick nest of images (say, disease), her apparatus will drop only those cards that belong in the nest or can somehow be correlated into a larger complex of cooperating nests (decay, death, disease, etc., in *Hamlet*; the "babe" and "clothing" figures in *Macbeth*). The procedure itself is adequate, as far as it goes, but in *Hamlet*'s case it seems to me that the picture-making function of the imagery is rather more complicated than simply pointing arrows at the hidden impostume. There is another whole world in these flashes of sheer beauty and it is precisely its presence that enables us to diagnose *Hamlet*'s disease as being of a different order of magnitude than the disease, say, of *Troilus and Cressida* or a virulent play like *The Duchess of Malfi*.

Take, as an example, Claudius's image of Lamord, "a very riband in the cap of youth." It is possible to put it in the cluster of youth/age images deriving from the father/son theme, though this seems remote. In any case, it hasn't the degree of "symbolic" significance of such images as "the mildewed ear" or "the fat weed that roots itself in ease on Lethe wharf." I think that the main significance of the "cap of youth" is that it is participating in something far less pointed in its effect than the "disease" group. Here we get a quick glimpse of the "light and careless" lad beneath it, straight out of Franz Hals, speeding about some mischief or other that has nothing whatever to do with the murky goings-on in "the tragedy." By himself he is insignificant and instantly lost in the flow of Claudius's words. But his *quality* is not, for it is repeated in countless portraits of "free" creatures like him who are indentured to no crisis, come betwixt no mighty opposites—in short, do no very heavy work in the plot except that of keeping the air crowded with life of a special kind. For convenience, I will call this universe of "free" images the play's counter-world, though it would be impossible to separate it cleanly from the world it is countering. But it includes all those word-pictures, however fleeting or extended, which we recognize on instinct as belonging to an independent and stable order of nature that is apparent not so much in our memory of particular things in it as in our subliminal awareness that some new manifestation of it is never long absent from the poetry. Its effect, the sense of its presence, may even be as subtle as that of a grace note in a musical composition.

Before going on, it seems necessary to put this idea into a wider perspective. The sort of "free" imagery I am talking about is quite common in the comedies and history plays. There, however, it does not compose a counter-world at all, as I am using the term, but merely a wider or more tolerant one. In fact, the whole affective movement of comedy and history (less so, perhaps, history) is toward inclusiveness, toward life-celebration, and this enables them, as genres less severely dramatic than tragedy, to mingle more varied qualities of nature without thematic confusion. To illustrate how imagery normally behaves in the tragic world, on the other hand, we might cite *King Lear*. From the standpoint of word-picturization, it is perhaps as crowded as *Hamlet*. The point about *Lear*, however, is that its profusion of life and elemental scenery is critically bound to the same overwhelming revolution of Fortune's wheel in which Lear is decivilized and "accommodated" among the beasts of the earth. In other words, in Lear we have a standard case of Ulysses's Law: that is, of a natural world being "untuned" and totally transformed into the context of the tragic qualm. When Lear is cast into the elements, nature, literally charged by cosmic lightning, loses any neutrality and qualitative range it may have possessed before the "division." Professor Clemen is right in saying that the words *atmosphere* and *background* no longer suffice in *Lear* "to designate what of nature, landscape and animal world is evoked by the imagery. This 'atmosphere' ... becomes a world in itself."[3] Very often, this sense of a qualitatively imploding universe is so powerful in Shakespeare that it becomes a distinct rhetorical feature of the tragedy. In the centers of plays like *Lear* and *Timon* action virtually ceases while "each thing" is cataloged and reassigned a place in the fallen world. As an instance in which this principle is somewhat compromised, we might cite *Antony and Cleopatra*, whose sympathetic bonds with history and romance seem to enable it to maintain a steady impression of spaciousness and sumptuous diversity—of some of nature, at least, staying in place while kingdoms topple.

It would be perverse to argue against the current of three centuries that *Hamlet* is a bright tragedy. What I do suggest is that *Hamlet*'s world, the "things" in its visualized space, describe a qualitative range which is uniquely broad, even in Shakespeare's comprehensive vision of life, and as a result, the poetry is not allowed to submit completely to the monochromatic and negative influence of the disease polarity. To go a step farther, in plays like *Lear*, *Macbeth*, and *Othello* one is hard-pressed to find anything at all that is not thoroughly attached to the immediate tragic theme. For instance, until Macbeth's one shot at summing things up ("Tomorrow, and tomorrow, and tomorrow ..."), you can scarcely imagine him making a general speech like Hamlet's "So oft it chances in particular men," though it is a better diagnosis of Macbeth's flaw than of anyone's in Denmark. It isn't because Macbeth is less perceptive than Hamlet, but because he is too busy with a set of escalating fears to be idling over behavioral recipes for the species. The thing which differentiates *Hamlet* from the other tragedies, in fact, is its incredible capacity to absorb universal knowledge in almost undigested form. The characters of *Hamlet* are abnormally axiomatic, as the twenty-one columns of quotations in Bartlett's will testify (*Lear* gets seven). They have what Prosser Frye calls an "extra-mural portion" of lifelikeness that is not precisely called for by the plot they are involved in. For instance, Claudius's injunction to Hamlet to throw to earth his unprevailing woe is obviously a strategy for wooing Hamlet back to court society where he can be watched; but it is also an eloquently expressed home truth, like so much other "advice" in the play, and its effect is to give Claudius a degree of wisdom and reliability that is, strictly speaking, in excess of the demands of his character as a villain. A more familiar example of this effect occurs in Polonius's farewell to Laertes, which is often played for laughs, as if Polonius were droning out clichés from his chapbooks. But that doesn't in the least diminish the impression it has, in the text at any rate, of putting him momentarily above his own foolishness. A similar extra-mural portion of "life" is present in Hamlet's "passion's slave" speech to Horatio, which Hamlet himself finally realizes is getting out of hand. Of course, by this time we are so used to Hamlet's lectures on natural law that we scarcely notice the plot has stopped and that character has become the expressive instrument of an almost autonomous world of moral philosophy. This is not a criticism of Shakespeare's characterization in *Hamlet* but an observation of its peculiar adaptability to almost any occasion. Image critics are reluctant to notice that Hamlet's is not the only exquisite sensibility in the play; he is simply the *primus inter pares* of a whole cry of artist-philosophers who cannot seem to move without making an aphorism that is both visually rich and morally apt, or pressing distinctions to the point of overscrupulousity.

This family characteristic of compulsive "documentation" may be encouraged, in part, by the revenge play's problem of having to flesh out what is normally a rather direct and simple act of violence. This brings us, once again, to the issue of Hamlet's delay. My interest in it here is not thematic or psychological but purely aesthetic. In any case, to lay the source of the delay on the revenge drama itself would seem to augur for a short play on the order of *Macbeth* rather than this monster in baggy trousers Shakespeare left us. Still, delay and style (as I have been discussing style here) are intimately connected in *Hamlet*. Francis Berry, among others, hints at this at the end of his section on *Hamlet* in *The Shakespeare Inset*: "All through its course," he says, "the action ... —because [it] is throttled, its straightforward frontal plotline is impeded—tends to explode into compensatory Insets. They are corridors retreating to an enigmatic but fascinating hinterland, often minatory or pathetic, and it is this hinterland, which builds up behind the imprisoned *Hamlet* exposed on the stage, that gives this play its depth."[4] While this nicely supports my argument, the "minatory and pathetic" aspects of this hinterland seem overstressed. I am not trying to whitewash *Hamlet* into a pastoral kingdom but to see the "depth" of its world as a product of pictorial range and variety. That is (to put it in the form of a planetary metaphor), the diseased center of the *Hamlet* universe, though exceedingly powerful, is succeeded by a series of spheres, or concentric planes of imagery, some caught in the gravitational pull of the "impostume," some threatening and pathetic (in the general ominousness of tragic tone itself), and still others, as we near the perimeter of the qualitative world, benign or neutral. The quality thus becomes more positive, or "healthy"—in a word, more sanguine—as one moves out and we enter a sphere of influence which might be summed up best in Schiller's observation about Homer's poetry: that it shows us "the quiet existence and operation of things in accordance with their natures." I am indebted for this remark to Erich Auerbach, to whom I turned remembering that his discussion of

Homer's style in *Mimesis* touched on these same problems. It was interesting to see that Auerbach was in fact trying to account for the "retarding element" of Homer's poetry, or the tendency of its movement to be "opposed to any tensional and suspensive striving toward a goal." In short, the respect in which Homer is an epic, not a dramatic poet. And it consists, he says, in illuminating every detail as clearly as possible, "so that a continuous rhythmic procession of phenomena passes by."[5] It would certainly be stretching the point to say that a tragedy as ponderously dramatic as *Hamlet* was engaged in any such "epic" business. But it is hard not to see a connection between a word so provocatively Hamletic as *retardation* and an artistic technique whereby imagery and visual detail become so prominent as to make the text seem "fraught with background," if I may adapt Auerbach's famous term to my own uses.

Perhaps the best example of Homeric illumination in *Hamlet* is a scene out of Troy itself, and far from a benign one. I refer to the "rugged Pyrrhus" speech, which is a highly stylized succession of word-pictures so inexorably detailed and obsessed with "getting everything in" that even the windy Polonius is soon bored. Like many of Homer's great battle pictures (for instance, Hector storming the Argive wall in chapter 12), this speech is really longer in the recitation than the action it describes; at least it seems to unfold in a time-lazy drift from detail to detail, like a camera fondly exploring the surface of a huge classical fresco—even stopping altogether at

> *For lo, his sword*
> *Which was declining on the milky head*
> *Of reverend Priam, seem'd i' th' air to stick;*
> *So, as a painted tyrant, Pyrrhus stood,*
> *And like a neutral to his will and matter,*
> *Did nothing.*
>
> (2.2.473–78)

The thematic implications of the Pyrrhus passage are well-known. What impresses one about it is that the play can afford to hire such a long-winded actor to echo its central action of vengeance at such a remove. The presence of these sixty-odd lines in *Hamlet*, for whatever reasons scholars suggest, is one of the best indications of the play's open susceptibility to metaphoric expansion. Taken as a symptom of overall style, the Pyrrhus speech perfectly illustrates the play's act–scene ratio, to come back to Burke's pentad. That is, any act (or, thinking more here in terms of retardation, *non*-act) becomes credible by virtue of occurring in an appropriate setting, or one that implicitly contains the qualities the act is to make explicit. Following the idea of retardation into the play's language, in other words, the proper rhetorical scene for *Hamlet* might be one that was continually jamming the circuits leading to action, or more correctly, jamming the audience's expectations regarding action—which is to say vengeance—as *the true subject* of the play. Like the Player here, the poet would throw the attention of his audience onto a careful elaboration of the moral and emotional conditions which give the act its significance. To put this another way, the poet would give the play-world a character that mirrored the character of its principal agent, duplicating in its very construction the dialectical tension that is not so much on the hero's mind as somewhere inside it beneath the threshold of expression. In such a world, which has such encyclopedic diversity in it, the question of vengeance becomes relativized—not negated but displayed in the context of its partiality. Vengeance must be emptied before it can be fulfilled; and this, I suggest, is the infra-logic behind the anatomical craving of the play.

It is time to fold Hamlet into the picture. And as a way of relating Hamlet's character to that of the binary world I have outlined, I will return to the question of the humors. In her book on the four major tragedies, Lily B. Campbell (writing over a decade before O. J. Campbell) disputes the then accepted idea that Hamlet was a man of "natural melancholy humour." Rather, she says, he is "quite clearly ... of the sanguine humour" and she proceeds to cite contemporary descriptions of the sanguine temperament that are "applicable to Hamlet in all essential details."[6] The specific sanguine characteristics are those we associate with social adjustment: wit, affability, and "gracious faculty" of speech, tolerance, level-headedness, "constant loving affection," congeniality, loyalty to friend and country, bravery of spirit and action—those characteristics we might sum up generally in Shakespeare's words *generous* and *noble*. Only through "excessive grief" has Hamlet become melancholy; it is "unnatural melancholy [of] sanguine adust, induced by passion" (p. 113). In spirit, I find this a perceptive observation, but of course, as Louise Turner Forest has said, it is a strictly medical, or physiological, explanation of Hamlet's behavior and it bypasses the question of how a mistaken medical theory could have produced a characterization as rich as Hamlet's. My interest here, of course, is not in diagnosing the cause of the change in Hamlet from the sanguine to the melancholy but in the textual evidence for assuming that there was a change. How does one get from the melancholy Hamlet, with his choleric fits and his phlegmatic gloom, to the former man?

In the essay I have already mentioned, Amelie Rorty writes: "To know what sort of character a person is, is to know what sort of life is best suited to bring out his potentialities and functions."[7] Let us follow the possibilities of this notion by asking what sort of person Hamlet would be if there were no need for vengeance, no wrong to be redressed in the world. Such a question might seem to belong in the vein of Mrs. Jameson's curiosity about the girlhood of Shakespeare's heroines. But a careful study of character requires a full attention to everything involved in the *illusion* of character: its duration and continuance offstage, its implied past, its openness to other possible experience—in a word, its suggestiveness. It is out of just such attentions that the actor derives an impression of character when he takes the character home with him or splices relevant aspects of his own experience and history into the motivational gaps in the role he must play. Like all forms of connotation, such suggestiveness is traceable to images in the text—or, again, to the something in Hamlet that is larger than Hamlet; I suggest that much of our affective interest in Hamlet arises from the tension between the Hamlet who is plagued by melancholy, by anger and lethargy, and the Hamlet who speaks of these afflictions of mind and soul from a point of view to some degree outside of and prior to them. Thus Hamlet's behavior is complicated by a certain bitemporality: Hamlet is and is not Hamlet, as Wylie Sypher puts it, though a better way to put it might be to say that there is a capacity in Hamlet—as there is not in Lear, Macbeth, and Othello—to undergo passion and yet not be psychically coincident with it, somewhat as a physician might chronicle the progress of his disease as though it belonged to someone else. This is a tendency we observe immediately in Hamlet's first substantial speech in the play:

> Seems, madam? Nay, it is. I know not "seems".
> 'Tis not alone my inky cloak, good mother,
> Nor customary suits of solemn black,
> Nor windy suspiration of forc'd breath,
> No, nor the fruitful river in the eye,
> Nor the dejected haviour of the visage,
> Together with all forms, moods, shapes of grief,
> That can denote me truly. These indeed seem,
> For they are actions that a man might play;
> But I have that within which passes show,
> These but the trappings and the suits of woe.
>
> (1.2.76–86)

This is a perfect example of anatomy and you will find its comic mate in Jaques's anatomy of his own melancholy in act 4 of *As You Like It*,[8] where the melancholic begins by defining all the things he is not and ends by escaping through a psychic side-door ("that within") through which there is no entry for others. Indeed, "that within" is spoken from the outside: it is a *there* and not a *here*, another departure, not an arrival. This rhetorical self-division is the model of Hamlet's public deportment: he is impenetrable, not equivalent to the signs that depict him, and poised between irony and self-confession. An actor could take it in either direction, depending on his conception of the role, because as we discover elsewhere it is Hamlet's habit to mix truth—or self-truth—and strategy in the same sentiment. One may say that Hamlet tells the truth while lying.

Yet how is it possible to suffer deeply, as Hamlet certainly does, and to be, as it were, the anatomist and raconteur of your own suffering? The answer is that one must be an actor—or be like an actor. But let us not confuse this with a cheap self-theatricality or an art of "feigning," or even with the commonplace that melancholics play roles in order to avoid detection. I speak rather of that virtue Diderot places at the heart of acting: the actor "must have in himself an unmoved and disinterested onlooker."[9] There is no implication here that Hamlet is imitating passions: he has them, all right. Yet we have always known that there is a confusion in Hamlet, that the antic disposition is both put on and not put on, at once a device and an outlet. And if one were asked why Hamlet should have adopted such a strategy, one would point first to his abundant sympathy with the actor—not, however, as one who weeps for Hecuba or moves others to weep, but as one who is the natural student of passion, one who knows—by disposition—the palpability, the woe and wonder, of emotion, and as a consequence, like my physician, or like the "melancholizing" Burton, can be outside emotion and inside it at the same time. For the actor is preeminently one who capitalizes on his own emotions, and there are tales about actors (Talma, for example) standing in tears at the funerals of friends and cataloging the symptoms of grief for future use. If you think this is shabby, consider what it may be like to be trained in the business of making your living on emotions and living beyond them while you are having them. In any case, the image of the actor that dogs the history of Hamlet and, I suspect, drives the great actors to "play" him is a symptom of something within the characterization that has the quality of what today we call the out-of-body experience, or the sensation of having within oneself an unmoved and disinterested onlooker.[10]

We can see this more clearly in Hamlet's advice to the players in mid-play. To put aside all the things that might be said about this scene's relevance to Elizabethan or Shakespearean acting theory, the central point is that it is a discourse on the control of passion as a means of rendering "the modesty of nature," and we should note that nature, for Hamlet, is modest, not extravagant, despite the corruption in it. What Hamlet is preaching, in effect, is Bright's definition of sanguinity: the actor's "spirits" should be "in their just temper in respect of qualitie, and of such plenty as nature requireth, not mixed or defiled, by any straunge spirit or vapor ..., all the members so qualified by mixture of elementes, as all conspire together in due proportion, [to] breedeth an indifferencie to all passions."[11] The main connection I would make is that Hamlet's master-class on acting does not simply represent a Renaissance theory of acting, in the same sense that Ulysses's disquisition on "degree" is a Renaissance theory of cosmological order; it is a contribution to Hamlet's character. For this interval Hamlet and sanguinity are identical. Hamlet is here being reasonable. That the scene is immediately preceded by Hamlet's atrociously choleric abuse of Ophelia produces the still more complex impression of there being, once again, "two" Hamlets: the Hamlet who himself "o'erdoes Termagant" in the sphere of present personal affairs—the Hamlet who would make a ghost of anyone who stands in his path—and the Hamlet of old, of "that noble and most soverign reason," now quite quite down.

But, as we see here, not "down" where the discrimination of value is concerned. For Hamlet is not defined by what Hamlet does. And this is mainly what I mean by the metaphor of the out-of-body experience. There are two dimensions in which a character behaves and exists before us: as body, as acter, doer and speaker of things, as entity in physical space; and as "spirit," as judgment, sensibility, thought, and imagination—in short, as actor in Hamlet's sense of the "unmoved" mover whose degree of "temperance" and "discretion" will direct the quality of the portrait of "humanity," in the theater as in life. This mind/body distinction is an artificial one, but only in the biological sense. For the power of art is that it has a thousand ways of allowing the spirit to soar above the body. For example, Cleopatra, in saying "I am fire and air; my other elements I give to baser life," is really becoming ethereal, or self-transcendent, before our eyes, going out of body on the energy of the image. Indeed, what is Cleopatra if not an image?

The obvious link between Hamlet's view of the actor and Hamlet's view of humanity is found in his relationship to Horatio. The connection is most visible in the virtually diametric parallel between the advice to the players and the "passion's slave" speech addressed to Horatio directly following it. Clearly Horatio is here being played off against Rosencrantz and Guildenstern, who are repeatedly linked to Fortune and fortune-hunting, whereas Horatio, the true friend, is not. This speech seals the parallel by rounding out a dialectic of friendship based on the common denominator of the friend's relation to Fortune. And of course the speech is a return, in thin disguise, of the very advice Hamlet has been giving the players. That is, it translates the theory of acting into the sphere of human conduct. Horatio is to the perfect actor as Rosencrantz and Guildenstern are to the ambitious clowns who pad their roles to steal laughs. In other words, we could consider the first ninety-one lines of 3.2 as the centerpiece of the play, a kind of "cloverleaf" for all thematic traffic respecting the crucial opposition of blood and judgment, Fortune and *virtu*. And this, I take it, is the point of having Polonius and Rosencrantz and Guildenstern pop in between its two key discourses with nothing better to do than show their faces and then rush off to tell the players what Hamlet has already told them. Altogether, one has the intimate sense of being in Shakespeare's workshop here, looking over his shoulder as he shuts down the machinery of the plot to make a critical point about his hero's character. For it is not simply that Shakespeare has had Hamlet speak, ex cathedra, about the art of the theater; he has gone on to back it up with a "proof" of the same artistic principle at work in his characterization of Hamlet's close friend, Horatio—whom we may consider, I suggest, as Hamlet's spiritual double.

From one standpoint, you might wonder if having Hamlet praise Horatio for equanimity of soul isn't a little abstract—like having Lear praise Kent for observing degree or loyalty to state, as opposed to going through hell for him. But if one considers Horatio's service to the play, Hamlet pays him exactly the right compliment. What counts is not his loyalty and love for Hamlet but his almost emblematic value as the play's symbol of "just proportion."[12] But the case might be better put the other way around: it is Hamlet's loyalty to Horatio, or to the Horatio principle, that emerges as the operative value of the speech. For it is through this compliment to Horatio that Shakespeare completes the retuning of his hero's "jangled" music that was begun in the scene with the players. If the speech does nothing else, it gratifies our hope that Hamlet will pause somewhere in his busy career of mayhem and self-involvement to acknowledge the services of this dear friend who, as I have suggested, is the dramatic embodiment of our own intimacy with Hamlet.

But to come at the speech from the standpoint of character: the virtue Hamlet speaks of here—the happy marriage of blood and judgment—is the very virtue Hamlet manifestly lacks. At least I am unable to agree with J. K. Walton, who feels that in referring to Horatio's commeddlement here Hamlet "is telling us about these qualities in himself."[13] It is true that something *like* this gets reflected to Hamlet but by a much subtler route. The value of the speech seems to me to lie not in its identification of Hamlet's commeddlement but in the display of a capacity of judgment that has survived its loss. By putting this compliment in the "air" of the play Shakespeare achieves for his splenetic hero the even greater virtue of being able to recognize virtue when he sees it. It is one order of man to be naturally commedled in blood and judgment, quite another to have a "dear soul" that can see through the absurd pomp of the world to the heart of honesty's heart and "of men distinguish her election." Such a man may commit all sorts of injustices, he may even "sometimes stab"; but if we see that his values are "spiritually" intact, his transgressions (which are, after all, what he owes us as a tragic hero) are bearable. A man, you might say, is truly known by the company he keeps. Hamlet's choice of Horatio is, in a dramatic sense, a metaphorical act of self-extension whereby Horatio becomes a "shadow" Hamlet, the visible sign of Hamlet's sanguine self.

The obvious objection to all this is that Horatio is such a bland figure and that if he is Hamlet's spiritual double we are better off with the body alone. However, I am not referring to Horatio's liveliness and interest as a personality but to a certain visible immunity he carries with(in) him to the perturbation and disease that rage in Elsinore. Horatio's thematic weight and value derive primarily from two qualities: his simplicity and his silence. As Hamlet puts it, he is like one who in suffering all, suffers nothing, and therefore there is an element of *the outside* in his presence, a kind of otherness that sets him apart from all others in the play. Moreover, in a world dominated by speech and the runaway principle of the anatomy, Horatio is conspicuously not garrulous. Bakhtin offers the interesting observation that "irony is a special kind of substitute for silence."[14] What, then, is the dramaturgic logic of coupling a supreme ironist and a man of "few words"? Simply that Horatio's silence, like Alyosha's kiss, is an understanding of Hamlet's irony and therefore its perfect audience and companion. I do not refer to the "kin/kind" or "sun/son" kind of irony, but to the irony lodged in the unspeakable depth of Hamlet's "failure" to act. This is the non-conversation of true intimates. I am not saying that all of this is "textually" in Horatio, only that the Horatio/Hamlet intimacy, the complementarity of the relationship, invites such a reading.

To return to my original question, "what sort of life would be best suited to bring out Hamlet's potentialities and functions?" we can say unequivocally that it is not the challenge of doing a murder to settle the family honor. Yet it is in the nature of Hamlet's role as a tragic figure in such a drama that we cannot imagine him in a better world doing other things, like gaming, or running a country, or (as sanguine people do) making love. You cannot put Hamlet into a situation that is not, in some sense, structured like his own, any more than you can imagine Macbeth cracking a joke or Othello wondering how long a corpse will lie in the earth ere it rots. Hamlet will always play the same role, something not of his making that brings on his unmaking due to the peculiar "mixture" of these things we have been calling blood and judgment. Professor Campbell feels that the eteology of his melancholy can be explained as the burning of the sanguine humor (blood), which provokes a form of melancholy that is simply an unnatural extension of his natural disposition. But this is simply a medical way of saying that a sanguine man will go berserk in a sanguine way and that melancholy is, after all, simply a universal "port" of perturbation. All we are probably saying is that there is strong evidence for saying that Hamlet is, or was, a reasonable man (if a little passionate) who finds himself in an extremely unreasonable situation, and that he trails into it his natural sensitivity to the just proportion of nature, or what he calls its modesty. So it is not important to know what Hamlet was in the other life, only that a good part of his stage-life consists in defining the sanguinity of the nature around him against the deep loss of his permanent exile from it.

Another way to express this division might be to think of it, to come back to Schiller, as a tension of the naive and the sentimental. On one hand, there is the naive world of nature living in a harmony and a modesty of which it is unconscious; this is a world perhaps more hypothetical than actual, one that is necessarily observed sentimentally from the outside, and to be outside it encourages one to idealize it, to credit it with attributes that may be projections of an innate wish for perfection, or at least for something better than one has. Given a choice, man, on the whole (as W. C. Fields might put it) would rather be in Philadelphia than in a world plagued by death and mutability. On the other hand, there is the real world one lives in, the world complicated by desire that leads inevitably to the infinite forms of "corruption," in Hamlet's word. Between the two worlds, then, stands "sentimental" Hamlet, a citizen of the real world, an onlooker at the other.

Late in the writing of this book, I received a considerable boost in reading Devon Hodges's excellent study of *Renaissance Fictions of Anatomy* (1985), being also pleased, as I read, that she had chosen *King Lear* as her Shakespearean example of tragic anatomy, rather than *Hamlet*. For much of what I have been advancing here about the sanguine/melancholy polarity is supported by her discussion of anatomy as a paradoxical strategy "for revealing order" that actually "decays" order in the process, and I can imagine what she might have to say about *Hamlet* in this connection. In any event, the following quotations from her chapter on Robert Burton are irresistible in their resonances with my notion of *Hamlet* as an anatomy-prone play:

> An anatomy will reduce a body to order by turning it into a heap of fragments. The strength of the *Anatomy* lies in this paradox. Animated by a struggle between reason and madness, order and fragmentation, Burton's text demonstrates its power not by

imposing order, but by escaping all efforts to have an order imposed on it. *Anatomy of Melancholy* is located on the boundary that lies between reason and madness. It is a scientific and theological treatise—and a mirror of the madness that is the book's subject.[15]

In essence, this is what I mean in saying that the phenomenon of character extends into the world of *Hamlet*. *Hamlet* is a "mirror" or an extension of Hamlet in a way that *Othello* is not an extension of Othello (or Iago). It is not simply that they are different plays in having different subjects but that they abide by altogether different scene–agent ratios. *Hamlet* is Shakespeare's anatomical play par excellence, or the play in which he gives us a "rigorous anatomical analysis" (p. 109) of the boundary between reason and madness by making them, in effect, the "two antagonists ... [of] the same text" (p. 108). This antagonism is reflected both in the binary nature of the *Hamlet* world (the diseased and the healthy worlds) and in the binary character of the play's hero and his reflection in the other characters. Like Burton, Hamlet is a melancholy anatomist "animated by a struggle of reason and madness, order and fragmentation"—driven, on one hand, to define and to "set down" in his tablets "all the uses of this world" and on the other to chaos-that is to say, to the fate of Ophelia, or suicide, a possibility Burton himself takes up in the face of his enduring melancholy. So it is that Hamlet feeds on the air of his own play. A second quotation will make the point more clearly:

> Anatomy and melancholy have an affinity; they are both an effect of loss—the loss of meaning, the loss of any clear path to the truth, the loss of power to master an uncertain world..... Something is lost that cannot be restored: constancy, coherence, the essences of love and of truth ("a true model of the world"). A melancholy sense that something is lost propels a desire to conduct an anatomy—and anatomy itself creates loss. Anatomy, then, is a cure for melancholy that creates the conditions that produce it. No wonder that Burton endlessly writes his *Anatomy of Melancholy*. (p. 121)

Thus it falls out that the melancholiac anatomistically searches the world for what has departed from it, the probe of "order" being analogous to the fury with which one might reorganize everything in the house while looking for the car keys. (Here would be the mundane version of reason chasing madness, and vice versa!) The appetite for *ordering* (as opposed to *finding* order) grows by what it feeds on, a procedural as opposed to an executive motivation. And it is certainly safe to say that Hamlet's is a procedural personality: that is, he is detained by material and formal causes rather than speeded on by final ones. (To put it another way, as a philosopher Hamlet would have been a phenomenologist rather than an ethicist.)[16]

But the problems of the anatomist run even deeper. He for whom the world is a vast anatomy finally achieves a kind of flatness of existence—not by any means the flatness of boredom, or the torpor of the phlegmatic, but one that comes with knowing nothing but a life of intense experience—the flatness, if you will, of the lives of Don Juan, Odysseus, or James Bond, those great collectors of experience who are able to live only on the knife edge of adventure. So too, the anatomist gradually comes to live in an infinity of the finite, and before infinity, as Jean Paul Richter says, "everything is equal and nothing."[17] Indeed, the anatomist is like Borges's character Funes the Memorious, who has no choice—so perfect is his memory—but to live each instant of his life as an intolerably precise and lucid present unattached to past or future, continuity forever swallowed in repetition, time endlessly out of joint. Nothing—no instant, no leaf or limb of tree, no glance, no cloud on the farthest horizon—escapes Funes's undivided attention. "In the teeming world of Funes," the narrator tells us, "there were only details, almost immediate in their presence."[18] Inevitably, the madness of the anatomist would lead even to the meaninglessness of the categories into which things are being sorted, since they themselves would become as profuse and hierarchically undifferentiated as the things each of them contains (a point that has often been made about Burton's book).

Hamlet's plight is not Funes's, but it springs from a similar affinity of lucidity and immediacy, the overwhelming sense of the world's variety and sameness, and the absence of a transcendent category that might enable a decision, a doldrum in concentration, or a self-completion of one's story. It is not simply that Hamlet goes about making lists of things (which he does) but that, like Funes, he is unable to advance, in thought or deed, to a stage where he is not repeating himself—which is to say, repeating the dilemma of lucid immediacy. Hence the melancholy wisdom of "the readiness is all": "it"—which, as James Calderwood notes, is repeated seven times in five lines[19]—will come to you in any case and it will pass through the needle-eye of an all-consuming "now"; everything is bent toward the *now*, be it the matter of memory or the matter of expectation—ergo, "let be." No wonder that Hamlet ends, as Dr. Johnson puts it, "by an incident which Hamlet has no part in producing."[20] Left to his own devices, Hamlet (like Burton) would go on writing his book forever.

●　●　●

The reader may ask of all this what a book written in 1621 can profitably tell us about a play written two decades earlier. My point in concentrating on Burton is simply to suggest some respects in which melancholy, in implying a certain relationship between self and world, also provokes (or can provoke) a behavioral tendency toward the activity best represented by the anatomy. This is not to say that all anatomists are melancholiacs, or vice versa (witness Marlowe's or Jonson's great anatomists). There is, let us say, an affinity that offers ample ground for speculation. As Stanley Fish says, Burton—an apparent melancholiac writing about melancholy in order "to avoid" melancholy—plays a "double game": "the impulse to anatomize and the impulse to assimilate."[21] Or, as Ruth A. Fox puts essentially the same point, in Burton "we see simultaneous dissection and unification, cutting and joining, as the essential artistic act."[22] But we must ask what the condition may be that genetically binds these two obsessive needs together and makes them aspects of a single theme. It is surely not only a question of a rhetorical strategy of author-concealment or reader-frustration (Fish's primary concern) but of a psychosis of which the strategy is a symptom. There is apparently no better word for this condition than *melancholy* and it is not something we find only in Burton or in other Renaissance anatomists. For example, we have the same phenomenon in the endless "irresponsible" sentences of Proust, a true modern melancholiac, and not by accident the modern artist who most attracted Samuel Beckett (even more, I suspect, than that other great anatomist who wrote *Ulysses* and *Finnegans Wake*). All three are melancholics in Burton's sense of melancholy as being "the character of mortality,"[23] or the psychosis brought on by an interminable awareness of loss. Indeed, in Proust the impulse to anatomize and the impulse to assimilate, or to "go home again" by mnemonic proxy, reaches a point where (in Fish's words) "a total unreliability and a total subjectivity" (p. 330) are fused, as they are in Burton, and (I am suggesting) in a very different way in Hamlet.

To sum up: we may see the four key terms circulating in this discussion—*melancholy*, *anatomy*, *delay*, and *decay*—as forming an associational cluster, like the structure of a disease. If *melancholy* is the mode of mourning the world's passing, *decay* may be said to be the causal agent that brings it on—at least it is so in Shakespeare's Denmark. The quintessential line is pronounced by the Queen: "All that lives must die, passing through nature to eternity." And when she asks Hamlet why this "common" truth seems so particular with him, he responds (speaking for all melancholy men) with an anatomy of mourning ("Seems, madam? Nay, it is ... etc."), meaning that he "dissects" the condition, rather than explaining its origin or clarifying his own grief. The interchange, in short, lacks advancement and thus the momentum of *delay* is re-established. Indeed, there is literally only an "l" of a difference between decay and delay; for delay asserts itself (as usual) in the enumeration of the forms of world-decay.

There is a provoking essay on Burton by Maurice Natanson that approaches this same aspect of melancholy as a form of *thesaurism*. A thesaurus, for Natanson, "is not the expected movement of word to word but the linguistically arhythmic shift from meaning to being."[24] My understanding of this idea—only roughly sketched out by Natanson—is that melancholy, or thesaurism, would be a way of using language, as a "rhetoric of listings," to carry oneself out of the field of signs into the presence of the world's "decadence and decay," which are "ultimate moments of melancholy" (p. 131). It is at once a kind of piling up and sloughing off of despair. Melancholy is "less a disease than an atmosphere of the self" (p. 135), and, I would add, an atmosphere in which the self can be immersed in a form of being that may begin in language but finally aspires to swallow the world itself, rather like a Shakespeare play. Thus, in "the being" of melancholy "despair is less the sickness unto death than the unavailing recognition by the individual that *this* is where he is, that *this* is the place of his being, and that ... *this* will not retreat or give up its hold on the self" (pp. 137–38).

To move from theory to example, a perfect modern instance of this principle of melancholic thesaurism might be the great pell-mell speech of Lucky in Beckett's *Waiting for Godot*, a play that belongs centrally in the tradition of *Hamlet*. Commanded to "think," the silent phlegmatik unleashes a torrent of "stored" melancholy in an anatomy of Burtonesque proportions. It begins "reasonably" as a syllogism ("Given the existence ... of a personal God ... who ... loves us dearly"), but soon proliferates into a catalog that reduces the world "to order by turning it into a heap of fragments" ("skating tennis of all kinds dying flying sports of all sorts autumn summer winter winter tennis of all kinds"), and it ends in an inversion of Christ's final words on the cross ("unfinished"), which is to say that even at the edge of the "firmament" we are no closer to a stopping place. As the play's philosopher, one may say that Lucky, speaking for its interests at large, is in the position of Burton and Hamlet: he has lost "any clear path to the truth," yet he must compulsively pursue the truth, having—as Beckett would say, no choice but to "go on"—and as a consequence of this plight his anatomical analysis falls, as Hodges would say, "on the boundary that lies between reason and madness." And this is the prevailing psychosis in Beckett's work at large, especially the novels, all of which might be subtitled anatomies of melancholy.[25]

There is one speech in *Hamlet* that virtually anticipates Lucky's monologue and embodies this agonistic relation between anatomy and melancholy, reason and madness, delay and decay, as they may be perceived in tension in Hamlet's character. It is Hamlet's incomparable response to his two adder-fanged friends who ask—or rather, he tells them—what is wrong with him:

> I will tell you why; so shall my anticipation prevent your discovery, and your secrecy to the King and Queen moult no feather. I have of late, but wherefore I know not, lost all my mirth, forgone all custom of exercises; and indeed it goes so heavily with my disposition that this goodly frame the earth seems to me a sterile promontory, this most excellent canopy the air, look you, this brave o'erhanging firmament, this majestical roof fretted with golden fire, why, it appeareth nothing to me but a foul and pestilent congregation of vapours. What a piece of work is a man, how noble in reason, how infinite in faculties, in form and moving how express and admirable, in action how like an angel, in apprehension how like a god: the beauty of the world, the paragon of animals—and yet, to me, what is this quintessence of dust? Man delights not men—or woman neither, though by your smiling you seem to say so. (2.2.293–310)

Here, indeed, the affinities of anatomy and melancholy are perfectly expressed: a discourse on melancholy in the form of an anatomy of the cosmos—infinity in a nutshell or, as Hodges would put it, a true melancholic model of the world. Here, one might say, the lost is found—and immediately lost and found again. For the "technique" of the anatomy rises from the psychology of repetition and the rhythm of the synonym, as if rhetoric could somehow encompass the plenitude of the experience by rendering it again and again, each time in a different image, a sort of cubism that might go on forever: "this goodly frame ..., this most excellent canopy of air ..., this brave o'erhanging firmament ..., this majestical roof" and so on, through the anatomy of "a man." "True repetition," Kierkegaard says, "is eternity,"[26] meaning, in this case at least, that repetition (like character itself) is a means of standing vividly still while seeming to go further. It is at once a form of deferral and a way of being—there in the thick of *things*: the fury and the calm at the heart of delay.

Editors point out that it is a commonplace of melancholiacs to draw such comparisons (between self and universe) and that Hamlet was offering a conventional diagnosis of his problem designed to confuse his enemies. But the speech is simply too intense to be taken as a deliberate disguise. It takes a dull ear to miss the urgency in the expression and the sense that if Hamlet is lying, by way of omitting something, he is also telling the truth; for there is nothing in the speech that does not coincide with all that the private Hamlet has told us. Moreover, the speech is a perfect example of Hamlet's habit of getting outside of himself to talk about himself and the world from a superior point of view. Moving by turns from plaint to hymn of praise, and back again, he here regards the universe in a "sentimental" state of mind we might describe as nostalgia for the present, which is to say nostalgia for a valued world from which he has, of late, been estranged. Nowhere else in the play are the diseased and the counter-worlds brought into such a sharp conjunction. Here is the full circumference of the *Hamlet* world, extending from the sterile promontory of Elsinore to the brave o'er-hanging firmament, and man, within it, is both the quintessence of dust and the paragon of animals, depending on how thinking makes it so. Thinking has made it very undelightful for Hamlet, but the essential feature of the speech is that Hamlet never once hints that the universe itself has been altered by the vapors of the mind; it is altered only in the mind, and outside, as Hamlet knows and can still eloquently report, it remains what it has always been, man's tragedies notwithstanding. It is this capacity to be self-immersed, bound in his nutshell, and yet to see the kingdom of infinite space, and all value and beauty in it, that distinguishes Hamlet from the other tragic heroes. It is also what distinguishes the play, which has, in its compulsive anatomical fashion, set before us, in minute detail, the world Hamlet sees in this speech.

In a recent reading of the speech William Beatty Warner notices a similar "strangely remote" quality in it:

> Apparently, this speech is an illustration of Hamlet's disposition, through a performance at one remove.... But this casts suspicion upon both Hamlet's "disposition" and his expressed opinions. For how genuine are feelings that can be repeated at one remove from their original locus, and how genuine are the ideas enunciated in this stage performance ...? Here language is not a medium of communication ...; nor is [it] simply nonsense. Instead Hamlet has begun to use language as a way to rupture the social world, with which he no longer wants to communicate."[27]

To a point, this supports my own reading and I admire Warner's observations that Hamlet speaks much of the time "as if in half-soliloquy" and that his use of theatrical language functions as a "compromise formation" that permits him to express "ideas and feelings incompatible with [the] social world" he is forced to inhabit (p. 240): a fine insight. The difference between our readings is that I have no problem with the sincerity of the feelings, nor with the honesty of the "disposition" Hamlet is exhibiting here—if one can get past the communicational factor of language. And I would do so along these lines: There is a certain zone of speech that enables one to speak to oneself of oneself only by speaking to others who could not possibly understand (for example, when people "share" their private problems with animals). Speech is not so much duplicitous as self-cathartic, if not self-ironical. In such cases one is effectively speaking a half-soliloquy that depends for its effect on a double audience, as Iago *half* lets the cat out of the bag when he tells the truth about himself before people who could not possibly get his drift.

Such speech is certainly a "stage performance," but it is also something of a *performative utterance* in J. L. Austin's sense that *the saying* itself ("I will tell you why ...") accomplishes an action (self-divorce). In Hamlet's case, the psychic need behind his "compromise formation" is that it acts out his distance from the world and, more importantly, from his own social self, or the part of his identity that he can never inhabit again—what we might sum up as the sanguine side of his disposition. It is a way of putting one's dying social body at mind's length. And here is another aspect of the affinity of anatomy, melancholy and thesaurizing: To itemize anything is an act of exteriorization, or a dramatization of its otherness, as when Tamburlaine, at the end of his life, itemizes the events of his history-in-time by symbolically striding over a huge map of Asia. This is also the respect in which the great summing-up speeches of tragedy ("Soft you, a word or two ...") and the final "pan" shots of many films (for example, *Citizen Kane*) may be said to be melancholy: they are itemizations of the foregoing history viewed from the standpoint of an extra-temporal "moment." What makes them melancholy is their durational paradox: everything is all over but at the same time right there at the height of its intensity, a kind of joyous grief, as the Player King would have it. Or, as still another Shakespeare character says, it is also a way of becoming absolute for death—and, in the bargain, of preparing an audience for the demise of the work in which it has been caught up.

•   •   •

We may describe *Hamlet*, then, as a play about a man who is informed from without: he is summoned from grief to the platform where he discovers a truth he expresses thereafter in countless ironies and puns—that anything in nature, from clouds to kings, may also be something else in disguise, and more centrally, something on its way to another form via the process of decay. This truth, so bitter in its local implications, is what isolates Hamlet from the company of men, but is also what activates his sympathy for all things in nature which are behaving naturally.

The spiritual dynamic of *Hamlet* is thus the very opposite of that of *Othello*, a play about a man who is informed from within—if one thinks of Iago as an extension of Othello's overactive imagination; and more importantly, of Othello's intense habit of equating the All with his One, putting the whole cosmological weight of the world on Desdemona's virtue (as Lear does on his daughter's love and Macbeth on his murder). From the outset, our impressions of the universe of value at stake in the play are controlled by Othello's misapprehension of reality, and we observe the inevitable collapse of the "Othello system" because at its center—for this reason—it is dangerously open to contrivance.

In *Hamlet*, we have a very different, far more ambiguous and complex, sense of the relationship between the world of value and the heroic company in which we experience it. Hamlet may be an even bigger egoist than Othello, but he is no solipsist; he sees the world pluralistically, or, as Claudius would say, with one dropping and one auspicious eye. His very difficulty, if I may quote something I have said elsewhere, is that he confronts the entire range of value and can, until the end, find no clear place in it for himself. He hovers, strangely alone, above the spectrum of excellence and flaw we observe in the play, and in his generosity and cruelty is himself a paradoxical manifestation of both poles.[28] Certainly his motives can be explained on other grounds than these. What I have tried to express here, however, is not a new explanation of Hamlet but the sense of something infinite in him, and in the play, that finally makes the question of what the play means less interesting than the question of how it is able to mean such different things to every new reader.

## NOTES

1. In fact, Coleridge was so taken by the passage that he saw Ophelia as scenery: "Who does not see her, like a little projection of land into a lake or stream, covered with spring flowers, lying quietly reflected in the great waters, but at length being undermined and loosened, becomes a floating faery isle, and after a brief vagrancy sinks almost without an eddy!" Quoted from *Coleridge's Writings on Shakespeare*, ed. Terence Hawkes (New York: Capricorn Books, 1959), p. 155.

2. Caroline F. E. Spurgeon, *Shakespeare's Imagery and What It Tells Us* (Cambridge: Cambridge University Press, 1935), p. 319.

3. Wolfgang H. Clemen, *The Development of Shakespeare's Imagery* (New York: Hill & Wang, n.d.), p. 137.

4. Francis Berry, *The Shakespeare Inset: Word and Picture* (Carbondale: Southern Illinois University Press, 1971), p. 143.

5. Erich Auerbach, *Mimesis: The Representation of Reality in Western Literature*, trans. Willard R. Trask (Princeton: Princeton University Press, 1974), p. 6.

6. Lily B. Campbell, *Shakespeare's Tragic Heroes: Slaves of Passion* (New York: Barnes & Noble, 1930), pp. 112–13.

7. Amelie Oksenberg Rorty, *The Identities of Persons* (Berkeley & Los Angeles: University of California Press, 1976), p. 305.

8. The speech goes: "I have neither the scholar's melancholy, which is emulation; nor the musician's, which is fantastical; nor the courtier's, which is proud; nor the soldier's, which is ambitious; nor the lawyer's, which is politic; nor the lady's, which is nice; nor the lover's, which is all these: but it is a melancholy of mine own, compounded of many simples, extracted from many objects; and indeed the sundry contemplation of my travels, in which [my] often rumination wraps me in a most humorous sadness ..." (4.1.10–20).

9. Denis Diderot, *The Paradox of Acting*, and William Archer, *Masks or Faces?* (New York: Hill & Wang, 1967), p. 14. Or, to put the point a somewhat different way, this observation by James Calderwood: "In Hamlet, Shakespeare seems to have created a character who is, though it seems odd to say so, conscious of his dual identity and able to express both sides of himself, almost as though he were an actor at a rehearsal. He puzzles over the fact that as a character he is fully equipped for revenge but that as an actor, or instrument of the plot, he is not allowed to proceed with it" (*To Be and Not To Be: Negation and Metadrama in "Hamlet"* [New York: Columbia University Press, 1983], pp. 31–32).

10. Obviously, I am thinking of out-of-body experience as a metaphor and one that has certain analogies, appropriate in Hamlet's case, to the experience of lucid dreaming wherein the dreamer is, to a degree, able to detach himself from the world of the dream while, so to speak, remaining in it as one of its citizens. I see such a view being validated in *Hamlet* by the very nature of Hamlet's situation: his body, one might say, inhabits, moves in, the alien dream-world of the court where he is regarded with suspicion by virtually everyone he meets; but he carries within himself a secret that "decenters" him, putting him outside the tenor of life around him (somewhat like the "alienated" Brechtian actor who does not altogether *coincide* with his character). To this extent, he may be said to be outside the Hamlet that others perceive. Again, here we have overtones of Iago ("I am not what I am."), the Elizabethan villain in general, and the clown who takes pleasure in living in two worlds at once. The wages of living thus, at least in Hamlet's tragic case, is that of a deep self-division, the unstable ground on which melancholy grows.

   Or, to put the case in still different terms, we may cite Kierkegaard's commentary on the ironist, for whom the "given actuality [the irony of the world itself] has only poetic validity.... The ironist is the eternal ego for whom no actuality is adequate.... Life is for him a drama, and what engrosses him is the ingenious unfolding of this drama. He is himself a spectator even when performing some act. He renders his ego infinite, volatizes it metaphysically and aesthetically, and should it sometimes contract as egotistically and shallowly as possible, at other times it unfurls so loosely and dissolutely that the whole world may be accommodated within it.... Because the ironist poetically produces himself as well as his environment with the greatest possible poetic licence, because he lives completely hypothetically and subjunctively, his life finally loses all continuity. With this he wholly lapses under the sway of his moods and feelings. His life is sheer emotion" (*The Concept of Irony, With Constant Reference to Socrates*, trans. Lee M. Capel [Bloomington: University of Indiana Press, 1965], pp. 300–301).

11. Timothy Bright, *A Treatise of Melancholie* (New York: Columbia University Press, 1940), p. 97.

12. This point is also made by John W. Draper in *The Humors and Shakespeare's Characters* (Durham: Duke University Press, 1945), pp. 84–86.

13. J. K. Walton, "The Structure of *Hamlet*," *Hamlet*, Stratford-upon-Avon Studies 5 (1965), p. 68.

14. M. M. Bakhtin, *Speech Genres and Other Late Essays*, trans. Vern W. McGee (Austin: University of Texas Press, 1986), p. 148.

15. Devon L. Hodges, *Renaissance Fictions of Anatomy* (Amherst: University of Massachusetts Press, 1985), p. 108. From the standpoint of a "reading experience" of Burton, Stanley Fish offers a similar discussion in *Self-Consuming Artifacts: The Experience of Seventeenth-Century Literature* (Berkeley & Los Angeles: University of California Press, 1972): "Nothing stands out in Burton's universe, because nothing—no person, place, object, idea—can maintain its integrity in the context of an all-embracing madness. Even syntactical and rhetorical forms—sentences, paragraphs, sections—lose their firmness in this most powerful of all solvents.... What we have, then, is a total unity of unreliability, in the author, in his materials, in his readers, and in his structure, a total unreliability and a total subjectivity" (pp. 329–30). Much of what Fish has to say about Burton corroborates Hodges's later argument, but Fish is not really concerned with the question of melancholy as a sickness, or with anatomy as an operation of mental ordering that might have more enduring implications for the nature of melancholy.

16. The phenomenological aspect of melancholy is briefly treated in a recent essay by Anselm Havercamp: "The phenomenology of melancholy, one could say, is caught within the melancholy of phenomenology, as Burton already knew. Thus, the origin of melancholy marks the origin of phenomenology" ("Mourning Becomes Melancholia—A Muse Deconstructed: Keats's 'Ode on Melancholy,'" *New Literary History* 21 [Spring 1990], 701). Truncated as I must offer it here, this idea may sound like postmodern double-talk. But it is at least a melancholy form of it, for it comes near to what Burton meant in saying that he *avoided* melancholy by melancholizing ("I would ... make an Antidote out of that which was the prime cause of my disease," p. 22). So too phenomenology, in its obsession with consciousness, with "transcendental subjectivity," with the self as the origin of all possible meaning, is in the position of melancholy Hamlet who on the occasion of his father's death puts the world in brackets and enumerates its discontents. Hamlet's "ethics," I am suggesting, are overweighed by his concern for what the phenomenologist might call "pure experience," or what happens at the intersection of self and world.

17. Jean Paul Richter, *Horn of Oberon: Jean Paul Richter's "School for Aesthetics,"* trans. Margaret R. Hale (Detroit: Wayne State University Press, 1977), p. 88.

18. Jorge Luis Borges, *Labyrinths: Selected Stories and Other Writings*, ed. Donald A. Yates and James E. Irby (n.p.: Penguin, 1974), p. 94. Something of the Funes raptness in the immediate moment is suggested by Maurice Charney: "Hamlet's vengeful thoughts are an object of contemplation in themselves. They more than gratify his inflamed desire for revenge, whereas murder at this point would only be unsatisfying and anticlimactic" (*Hamlet's Fictions* [New York: Routledge, 1988], p. 66). My own point of view would be slightly different. I think murder itself would be quite satisfying and climactic to Hamlet at almost any point, as we see on the platform in act 1, in the arras scene of act 3, and in the great burst of Hamlet energy that wipes out the court at the end. The problem is that contemplation of revenge and the act of revenge do not stand in a hierarchical order, or in a means-to-end relationship: Hamlet, like Funes, takes each instant as it comes. This openness and *availability* to all experience, come what may, is seen throughout the play in what we might call Hamlet's receptive/reactive mode of behavior: with the exception of his strange visit to Ophelia's chamber, he never initiates contact with others. The rule of thumb might be: if Hamlet has a chance to think, or retreat into irony, he will; if provocation occurs "on the hip" he will oblige in kind.

19. James L. Calderwood, *Shakespeare and the Denial of Death* (Amherst: University of

Massachusetts Press, 1987), p. 70. Moreover, Hamlet is still up to his iterative tricks in killing Claudius *twice*, which is, as Calderwood says, "pragmatically superfluous ... [though] the fit fulfillment of Hamlet's vow to avenge his father's death" (p. 86). To which I would add, it is the final touch of the anatomist in him ("How can I kill thee? Let me count the ways!").

20. *Selections from Johnson on Shakespeare*, ed. Bertrand H. Bronson with Jean M. O'Meara (New Haven: Yale University Press, 1986), p. 345.

21. *Self-Consuming Artifacts*, p. 322.

22. Ruth A. Fox, *The Tangled Chain: The Structure of Disorder in the "Anatomy of Melancholy"* (Berkeley & Los Angeles: University of California Press, 1976), p. 12.

23. *Anatomy of Melancholy*, p. 16.

24. Maurice Natanson, "From Apprehension to Decay: Robert Burton's 'Equivocations of Melancholy'," *Gettysburg Review* 2 (Winter 1989), p. 131.

25. A word or so on the anatomy as a form of dramatic speech: An anatomy is not only a symptom of theme but a display of virtuosity (of author or character, or both). What is so compelling in Hamlet's response to his mother's question, "Why seems it so particular with thee?" ("Seems madame, nay it is ... etc.") or his "I have of late" speech to Rosencrantz and Guildenstern if not the deluge itself? Thus the anatomy is a structure that overwhelms in its performance of a certain rhetorical and imaginative power. Indeed, this is evident in real life as well; for the fascination of the list—when it is well contrived—is that the mind could have "ready to hand" such an inventory of discrete items belonging to a single category and that it could disgorge its contents with such consummate skill.

There are, of course, degrees in which anatomy is noticeable (at what point does a list become an anatomy?). Works with a great deal of repetition or serial or pattern formation may be said to be anatomical. Epics are normally more anatomical than tragedies or comedies. In Jonson and Marlowe the anatomistic tendency is quite strong in that both were drawn to personalities who are addicted to the quantification and storage of the world's "goods." There is the example of Faustus, who was not so much given to making verbal lists as to exhausting the possibilities of human freedom in action. (Like Burton, Faust wants to get *everything* in.) On the other hand, one has the impression that Tamburlaine not only conquered the world in order to own it but to recite retrospective summaries of his holdings to anyone who would listen. Jonson, of course, is the arch-anatomist of the Renaissance, if not of all drama, and a great deal has been written about the hoarding instinct that animates the speech of his characters. Jonson offers the unique example of the play whose cast of characters is already an anatomy (or a bestiary) in itself, which is to say, a set of variations on a single addiction, with each addict getting the chance to perform anatomistic arias on the themes of acquisition, opulence, hatred, or flattery.

The anatomy shades off on one side into the lyric and the lament and on the other into the harangue and tirade. All of these may be considered as strategies for expressing humoristic states of mind, in Jonson's sense of drawing the spirits and powers "all to run one way," as opposed to strategies for argument, narrative, or confession in which we begin with one kind of thing and end with another. There may be a good reason for putting things into some sort of order in an anatomy, but it has nothing to do with a hierarchy or priority of meaning. Indeed, anatomy is the great "leveler." If anything governs the conduct of anatomy, it is balance, rhythm, sound, and crescendo, the same means by which music contrives to overwhelm us. It is not by accident that Beckett's great run-on anatomists, and Pinter's and Shepard's as well, are in the habit of "revelling" in the sound of words. Indeed, words, for the anatomist, are the building blocks of the world, and something can get on a list by virtue of its sound and texture.

26. Soren Kierkegaard, *Repetition: An Essay in Experimental Psychology*, trans. Walter Lowrie (New York: Harper, 1964), p. 18.

27. William Beatty Warner, *Chance and the Text of Experience: Freud, Nietzsche, and Shakespeare's "Hamlet"* (Ithaca: Cornell University Press, 1986), p. 239.

28. I have taken this sentence from my *Irony and Drama: A Poetics* (Ithaca: Cornell University Press, 1971), p. 47.

ANTHONY LOW

# Hamlet *and the Ghost of Purgatory:*
# *Intimations of Killing the Father*

Once an angry man dragged his father along the ground through his own orchard. "Stop!" cried the groaning old man at last, "Stop! I did not drag my father beyond this tree."[1]

Shakespeare's Hamlet and Milton's Satan are two pivotal figures born out of the imaginative stirrings in early-modern culture that led to the rise of Enlightenment, Romantic, modernist, and post modernist individualism—all arguably beads in the chain of a single, sinuous, long-wave development toward liberal autonomy. Great literary inventions, Hamlet and Satan are also grand portents of subsequent cultural change. Moreover, buried deep in the tragedy of *Hamlet*, as I shall argue in this essay, are intimations of what may be called the transformative event that led to still another essential paradigm of modernity, a necessary adjunct to autonomous individualism, for which the brutally appropriate name is *killing the father*. With the rise of postmodernism (and as emphasis has shifted further from generations to genders), it is even more evident than it was earlier in this century that the Reformation, Enlightenment, Romantic, modernist, and postmodernist projects (all of which I shall include under the umbrella term of modernism) require an attack on patriarchal tradition. As Freud's writings often suggest, killing the father is not a new idea. But unlike earlier generations, the modernists did not stop at the customary tree.

From *English Literary Renaissance* 29, no. 3 (Autumn 1999). © 1999 by *English Literary Renaissance*.

In one of a number of similar passages, Gertrude Stein writes, "I have been much interested in watching several families here in Belley that have lost their fathers and it is interesting to me because I was not grown when we lost our father. As I say fathers are depressing any father who is a father or any one who is a father and there are far too many fathers now existing. The periods of the world's history that have always been most dismal are the ones where fathers were looming and filling up everything. I had a father, I have told lots about him in *Making of Americans* but I did not tell about the difference before and after having him.... Then our life with out a father began a very pleasant one."[2] Similarly, Virginia Woolf writes in her diary for November 28, 1928: "Father's birthday. He would have been ... 96, yes, today; & could have been 96, like other people one has known; but mercifully was not. His life would have entirely ended mine. What would have happened? No writing, no books;—inconceivable."[3] To bring us into postmodernism, we may quote J. Hillis Miller's deliberate provocation: "a deconstructionist is not a parasite but a parricide. He is a bad son demolishing beyond hope of repair the machine of Western metaphysics."[4]

The transformative event I have mentioned, which made it possible to repudiate tradition and kill the father in early-modern English and European culture—an event successfully obliterated from modern memory by early, deliberate acts of forgetting and by the decision of Renaissance politicians and gentry to rewrite history—was the abolition of Purgatory. If modernism is largely a process of desecularization (an analysis which discomfits both secularists and Christians, yet which is virtually unavoidable),[5] then crucial, irreversible steps in that direction were taken by the Chantries Act and Royal Injunctions of 1547 and by the Church of England's declaration, in the Edwardian Prayerbook of 1549, that Purgatory did not exist and consequently that Christians should not mourn or pray for their dead. The issue is far too large to be proven in a single essay or even a book, but I put it forward here as a hypothesis, and as a way of making better sense of certain speeches and events in *Hamlet*.

Before the modern autonomous individual can step forth in all his glory, he must first free himself—and increasingly herself—from the past, from tradition, from ancestral piety, and especially from the father and the paternal lineage. We find exactly this gesture of repudiation in several of Shakespeare's heroes and villains. Coriolanus most explicitly embodies the modernist desire for total autonomy. In the pivotal scene in which Shakespeare has him deny his family and his country in the face of three generations of that family—mother, wife, and son—who beg him not to destroy Rome, he utters these ominous words:

I'll never
Be such a gosling to obey instinct, but stand
As if a man were author of himself
And knew no other kin. (5.334–37)[6]

Since the nineteenth century the word "instinct" has had a particular scientific meaning, but for Coriolanus it means to be bound by an un-selfconscious inward stain or tincture to the obligations of family, culture, citizenship, and tradition. Now Coriolanus will throw off all these instinctive restraints. He will become the "author of himself," forget all other ties, and act from unnameable internal principles, which we now recognize as the underlying axioms of autonomous individualism. Even at this tragic stage of extreme of hubris, since he is a man of his own time or rather of Shakespeare's, Coriolanus implicitly recognizes that he cannot actually *be* the "author of himself"; yet he is determined to act "*as if*" he were the "author of himself." The arc of the action reveals this gesture to be an act of hubris, for which he will be tragically punished. Yet we know that such acts of self-fashioning, although they begin as role-playing, can issue in authentic change, first in the individual, then in the culture.

Similarly Shakespeare's Edmund, that enterprising bastard whom most modern readers and playgoers instinctively admire—because they are themselves the children of modernist egalitarianism and self-assertion—repudiates what he calls "the plague of custom" (*Lear*, 1.2.3), which in its context is much the same thing as Coriolanus' "instinct," in favor of a proto-Darwinian version of "Nature"—a Nature virtually "red in tooth and claw," according to whose laws it is every man and every beast for himself. After he comes to this resolve, Edmund determines to displace his brother and betray his natural father, Gloucester, as well as his feudal father, King Lear. Above all, he is determined to stand on his own, to deny the influence of stars, gods, custom, or natural law (Nature in its older sense), and to be the arbiter of his own free will. Here again the first prerequisite of self-conscious autonomy is killing the father. The self-declared iron law of Edmund's brave new world is: "The younger rises when the old doth fall" (3.3.26). In the old natural order sons replaced fathers in the ripeness of time, but in *King Lear* sons and daughters, who have become "monsters of the deep" (4.2.50), devour their fathers before their time.

As Ulysses tells Agamemnon, in his ironically placed speech on order and degree in *Troilus and Cressida*, "Take but degree away, untune that string ... / And the rude son should strike his father dead" (1.3.109, 115). In recent years, E. M. W. Tillyard has been much pilloried for interpreting this seminal speech at face value. Yet, however much we enclose it in nesting boxes of subversion and containment, recognize the irony of speech and speaker, and understand that the words should be read in a cultural as well as a literary framework, Ulysses' speech still tells us much about how the Elizabethans feared such subversive notions.[7] After all the political deconstructions Ulysses' troubling question still remains: what can possibly prevent the son from striking his father dead—literally, psychologically, or culturally—once the civilizing achievements of the past—what Ulysses calls "degree," Milton and Chapman "discipline," others tradition, custom, ancestry, patrimony—once those achievements, the lineage that bears them, and the culture that provides their matrix, have been destroyed and forgotten?

Buried deeply in *Hamlet*, in the relationship between the prince and his father, is a source tale, an unspoken acknowledgment that the modernist project of achieving complete autonomy from the past rested (at least for the great majority of Shakespeare's contemporaries who were still Christian) on the denial and forgetting of Purgatory. Before pursuing this disturbing topic any further, however, we should first remember that Shakespeare's personal religious beliefs are notoriously difficult to pin down. For every place in the plays that a critic has identified an outpouring of Protestant nationalism, another has found covert Catholicism, and a third has found skeptical agnosticism. Not coincidentally, these findings tend to chime with the critics' own beliefs. What we know, however, is that whatever Shakespeare personally believed about religious matters, whether his deepest allegiances were national or universal, Protestant or Catholic, nostalgic or progressive, spiritual or agnostic (all positions for which critics have found at least some evidence), he knew his audience and knew how to play on their expectations. Given the difficulty of extracting "Shakespeare" from his plays, I shall not consider the question of whether he personally believed in the existence of Purgatory or regretted its disappearance from English life not long before he was born. But there is ample, only partly covert, evidence in the play that he understood very well that the abrupt and, to a large degree, forcible dismantling of Purgatory at mid-century, together with its deep psychic resonances among the common people, its elaborate cultural associations, and its extensive institutional supports, had drastic consequences for society and for the individuals who formed and were formed by society. Before the Reformation, few countries had a deeper investment (financial, cultural, and spiritual) in Purgatory and in commemoration of the dead than England. After the Reformation, few countries turned their backs more abruptly on Purgatory and, with it, on their own dead.

II

The early history of the development of the doctrine of Purgatory is too long and complicated to outline here.[8] Most modern readers, if they think about Purgatory at all, are likely to think of it in terms of its notorious abuses, publicized and disparaged by Luther and the first Reformers (and by loyal Catholics such as Chaucer as well). But Purgatory was not just a hierarchical imposition on the laity, a means of social control, or a way to raise money for the popes' building projects and art collections. In England at the eve of the Reformation it was a thriving and popular institution, whose social and material framework was likelier to well up spontaneously from the laity than to be imposed calculatingly downward by the bishops. The chief interest that most people had in Purgatory was concern for their souls and those of their ancestors, together with a strong sense of communal solidarity between the living and the dead. Praying for the dead and provision for one's own soul after death were central to late medieval religion. Commemoration might be accomplished by individuals: paying for special masses, giving alms to the poor, or praying at shrines. But satisfactory commemoration could more safely and efficiently be accomplished through a variety of institutions, foundations, and voluntary fraternities. A king, a queen, or a rich noble might insure sufficient prayers for him- or herself and family after death by founding a monastery, whose grateful monks would return the gift by chanting perpetual masses and offices for their souls, or a religious hospital, which might combine prayers, charity, and almsgiving on their behalf.

People of the middling and poorer sort could band together in voluntary fraternities, confraternities, guilds, burial societies, and the like. Far from taking their instructions from priests, these lay groups customarily hired priests to say masses on their behalf and for their dead, presumptively in Purgatory. Through most of the later middle ages in England there was a surplus of clerics, which in effect created a buyer's market when lay trustees sought to staff a chantry or a chapel.[9] Thus, for example, "the guild of the Virgin in the church of St Giles Cripplegate (later Milton's parish church) had, by 1388, acquired sufficient lands to employ a perpetual fraternity chaplain to celebrate mass every day. The chaplain was to be chosen by the vicar of the church (if he were a member of the guild), the two wardens and twelve of the best men of the guild. The chaplain was to be provided with a house, he was to be attentive to all brothers and sisters, poor as well as rich, sick and healthy."[10] Although the chaplain could not be dismissed except for cause and with consent of the directors, the guild was financed and controlled by its lay members, gathered in voluntary association. Thus the priest had the faculties provided by ordination to say mass, hear confessions, and absolve from sins, but the laity took the initiative and controlled the funds. In this regard the system was closer to Congregationalism than anything available to ordinary people in the Church of England after the Reformation. Nor could such a dispersal of authority and initiative among the laity flourish in the same way under the Catholic Counter-reformation, which in its struggle against Protestantism likewise tightened clerical and hierarchical control.

Corpus Christi fraternities were founded by the laity for the purpose of honoring the Real Presence of Christ in the Eucharist. Nevertheless, as Miri Rubin remarks, these fraternities too were routinely preoccupied with proper burials and regular prayers for the dead. "Thus, all Corpus Christi fraternities made provisions for commemoration, 32 out of 42 employed a chaplain for regular daily or annual celebration of masses for the dead, and half of the fraternities provided for burial of their poorer members at the gild's expense."[11] As J. J. Scarisbrick puts it, "What was a fraternity? It was an association of layfolk who, under the patronage of a particular saint, the Trinity, Blessed Virgin Mary, Corpus Christi or similar, undertook to provide the individual member of the brotherhood with a good funeral—as solemn and well-attended a 'send-off' as possible—together with regular prayer and mass-saying thereafter for the repose of the dead person's soul.... In their most modest form, therefore, fraternities were simply poor men's chantries. They were inseparably connected with the doctrine of Purgatory.... The humblest village fraternity might aspire to no more than the individual funeral mass for every deceased member, for which all the living members had to subscribe a 'mass penny,' plus an annual mass and audit.... Many guilds undertook to bring back for decent burial a brother's body from wherever he happened to die."[12]

Wealthier founders of chantries and other institutions connected with Purgatory by no means acted only from self-interest. (The question of self-interest is somewhat anachronistic, since only after Kierkegaard has anyone imagined motivations so altruistic that one's own salvation was not primary.) The usual formula was to offer prayers "for n. and n., and for all who suffer the pains of Purgatory."[13] Colin Richmond describes the elaborate and (to the modern sensibility) amazing benefactions that Geoffrey Downes specified in his Last Will and Testament of 1492. Together with Joan Ingoldsthorpe, Downes founded and endowed a chapel in Cheshire, with two priests to say daily masses. In addition, he established a trust for the purchase of a hundred cows, to be "individually rented to the poor of Pott Shrigley," the rent being "'oonly to pray for the sowle of Jane and Geffrey and for all the sowlles in the paynes of purgatory.'" Downes appointed lay trustees to hire and (if necessary) fire the priests, who are to live devoutly and "not to keep horses, hawks or hounds." They are "to burn candles before the Images of Mary and Jesus on their feast days." In addition, they are to teach local children, tell their beads, say their offices, and run a small lending-library of devotional books, which may be borrowed "for the space of 13 weeks" by members of the fraternity "or any other Gentleman."[14] Downes's device of endowing a herd of cows to be lent to the poor in return for their prayers is especially ingenious, thus neatly combining as it does almsgiving and prayers, to most efficiently benefit the living and the dead. In the coming age of Reformation, and later of Capital, such ingenuity will be turned in other directions.

Many things were repudiated at the English Reformation, including Transubstantiation, Confession as a sacrament, the monasteries, and the primacy of Peter. But the Church of England retained the Lord's Supper, claimed apostolic succession for its bishops, and permitted (although it did not encourage) auricular confession. Few things were ended so absolutely as Purgatory. In the Book of Common Prayer as published under Elizabeth, article 22 reads: "The Romish Doctrine concerning Purgatory, Pardons, Worshipping and Adoration, as well of Images as of Relics, and also Invocation of Saints, is a fond thing, vainly invented, and grounded upon no warranty of Scripture, but rather repugnant to the Word of God." Also relevant is part of Article 19: "As the Church of Jerusalem, Alexandria, and Antioch have erred, so also the Church of Rome hath erred, not only in their living and manner of Ceremonies, but also in matters of Faith." In his fascinating study of the psychic and social effects of the abolition of Purgatory, Theo Brown suggests that when the Anglican Church promulgated its repudiation of "The Romish Doctrine concerning Purgatory" in the first Book of Common Prayer (1549), the bishops did not intend to dispose of Purgatory altogether, but only to correct well-known abuses.[15] I find this interpretation of the historical event unpersuasively sanguine. Just as the English government used particular abuses in some monasteries as excuses to do away with the monastic life, root and branch, and to sell off or confiscate the monastic properties, so it used abuses in the administration of Indulgences to do away with Purgatory, root and branch, and to loot and sell off the chantries, free chapels, and other properties by which that doctrine and associated practices were supported. Even the colleges at Oxford and Cambridge barely escaped, by distancing themselves from the terms of their foundation. Both abolitions took place in the earliest phases of the English Reformation. Moreover, the abolition of Purgatory occurred for most of the same combination of reasons as the abolition of monasteries. Reformist mistrust of Rome and her institutions and zealous indignation against real abuses combined with weariness at paying old spiritual debts inherited from the past, but, above all, with greed to confiscate wealth, which pious ancestral donors had given over the preceding centuries to chantries, free chapels, fraternal endowments, guilds, poorhouses, hospitals, dependent colleges, and many other institutions.

The effect of these events may be read in the wills of ordinary people. In the late middle ages last wills and testaments were as concerned with insuring proper prayers for the deceased as for insuring proper disposal of their goods. Indeed, the obligation to pray for the deceased was legally attached to accepting or inheriting property. Beginning in the late 1530s, however, wills began to change. "[M]oney for prayers, masses and anniversaries was entrusted to families or executors in preference to public bodies such as gild or parish, presumably due to fear of confiscation." By the mid-1540s, "*testators requested elaborate funerals and commemoration only 'if it be lawful.'*" By 1547, under Edward VII, "all this was absent from the will and the testator's personal tastes were marked by opaque phrases 'at the discretion of myne executors', 'according to the laudable custome of the realm.'"[16] Presumably the writers of these wills did not fear political retribution after death. Rather, they did not venture to ask their heirs to pray for their souls explicitly, because they feared confiscation of any goods associated with memorial purposes, even within the family. Thus, in marked contrast to earlier wills, after 1647 children inherited goods and estates from their parents but inherited no explicit, legal obligation to pray for them. Insofar as these heirs were in tune with the times, they felt no moral obligation either. This does not necessarily imply that children loved their parents less than formerly; but as attitudes changed they no longer thought it useful to pray for them.

Not only dispossessed Catholic layfolk of the common sort, but some of the more conscientious reformers such as Latimer (see his "Sermon of the Plow"),[17] Crowley, and Hutchinson agreed that the peculiar path taken in England by the Reformation "turned the English into a nation of looters."[18] In the course of a generation the gentry who ran the Church and the state simply decided that it would be convenient to cease remembering their dead. Instead, they took the money that their ancestors had left and spent it on themselves. Funds used to endow fraternities and other practices of popular piety, which the Crown had once been content to license and tax, now were confiscated altogether. Those sweeping alterations, in which Reformist zeal competed with greed and guilt, must have had on their perpetrators some of the same combination of effects that Satan mentions in his first soliloquy in *Paradise Lost*. By ceasing to pray for the dead, to borrow Satan's words, the first generation of English Protestants "in a moment quit / The debt immense of endless gratitude, / So burthensome still paying, still to ow" (4.51–53).[19] Yet like Satan, one of the original arch-individualists, they were left with a question. What does one do when the past has been erased and forgotten, and with it one's very origins? Satan's is the defiant modernist response: "We know no time when we were not as now; / Know none before us, self-begot, self-rais'd" (5.859–60). With this utterance, Satan shares with Coriolanus the novel illusion that the creature can create himself, beget himself, and shape himself as he will, illusions from which Prince Hamlet, although less designedly, is not altogether free.

### III

Much has been written concerning who the Ghost is and where he comes from. Although they recognize that, as Hamlet's friends warn him (1.5.69–78), he must be cautious not to be lured to destruction by a demon in disguise, most critics have nonetheless concluded by taking the Ghost at his word. He is the Ghost of Hamlet's father, come from the next world to tell his son the story of a brother's treacherous murder and to demand vengeance. Where, then, does he come from? Let the Ghost tell his own story:

> I am thy father's spirit
> Doom'd for a certain term to walk the night,
> And for the day confin'd to fast in fires,
> Till the foul crimes done in my days of nature
> Are burnt and purg'd away. But that I am forbid
> To tell the secrets of my prison-house,
> I could a tale unfold whose lightest word
> Would harrow up thy soul, freeze thy young blood,
> Make thy two eyes like stars start from their spheres (1.5.9–17)[20]

Clearly this Ghost has not come from Heaven. Nor can he have come from Hell, since he has been "doomed" to remain in his "prison-house" only for a "certain term," after which he will be released from confinement. In Shakespeare's day, as earlier, all major churches and denominations agreed that damnation was eternal, and that there was no escape from Hell. The only remaining alternative, as most Shakespeare critics agree, is Purgatory.[21] Also consistent with Purgatory is the Ghost's mention of "foul crimes" or "imperfections" committed while he was still alive (in his "days of nature"), which are in the process of being "burnt and purg'd away." As Harold Jenkins remarks, "We need not suppose that 'crimes' implies offences of great gravity."[22] Since the Ghost has not been condemned to Hell, we may safely conclude that they are venial rather than mortal sins.

No distinctively Catholic bishops or priests appear in *Hamlet* (as in many of Shakespeare's other plays), only the nondescript "Doctor [of Divinity]" who supervises Ophelia's burial rites.[23] Still it is evident that King Hamlet was a Catholic. The religion of Prince Hamlet and of Denmark at the present time is, as we shall see, much more ambiguous and diminished. Unlike France and Italy, where Shakespeare set other contemporary or near-contemporary plays, Denmark in his time was Lutheran. But Shakespeare obscures the time, so we cannot be sure whether the action of *Hamlet* takes place before or after the Reformation. The Ghost informs us that he, King Hamlet, was Catholic, but his son's religion remains indeterminate. In Shakespeare's sources, Saxo Grammaticus and Belleforest, the events take place much earlier. Claudius' reference to English tribute also would put us somewhere before the Conquest. But an early dating is sharply contradicted by the noise of cannons, instruments of modernity. In any case, Shakespeare often engages with contemporary events and controversies even when, as in the Roman plays, his chosen period is distant and distinct.

Further to establish King Hamlet's religion, the Ghost tells his son that, when Claudius murdered him in his sleep, he gave him no chance to prepare himself as a Catholic should for death:

> Cut off even in the blossoms of my sin,
> Unhousel'd, disappointed, unanel'd,
> No reck'ning made, but sent to my account
> With all my imperfections on my head.
> O horrible! O horrible! most horrible! (1.5.77–80)

In other words, the Ghost was deprived of his chance to receive three of the Sacraments that would have prepared him to face death and individual judgment. The Ghost's "housel" is an old-fashioned word that suggests the Catholic Eucharist. Becon contrasts Anglican celebration of "the Lordes Supper" with, "as the Papistes terme it, ... their Hushel."[24] "[U]nanel'd" refers to oil of Extreme Unction (no longer in use among Anglicans) and "disappointed" refers to missed preparations for Confession and Absolution.[25]. We may further speculate that Hamlet Senior would have made use of the Sacraments of Penance and Communion at least once yearly at Eastertide prior to his unexpected death, since that was the accepted late-medieval practice. That would help explain his not having been in a state of mortal sin. Although the King must have died in a state of grace, with unconfessed venial rather than mortal sins "on his head"—otherwise he would not be in Purgatory—Claudius had no way of knowing that when he killed him, nor did he evidently care. According to the indignant Ghost, this callousness to a brother's eternal fate in the next world more than anything else—including fratricide, regicide, possible adultery, and incest—renders his deed triply and superlatively "horrible." Through most of the middle ages, marriage to a brother's wife was technically incestuous, as Hamlet repeatedly complains. In the Renaissance, dispensation was possible and presumably granted to Claudius and Gertrude. The issue was made familiar by Henry VIII's "great matter." He had a papal dispensation to marry his dead brother's wife, Katherine of Aragon. After failing to produce a male heir and wishing to marry Anne Boleyn, he claimed that his conscience told him his marriage was incestuous after all, and sought annulment. The king's ministers solicited favorable opinions from canon lawyers all over Europe.[26]

Before the Reformation it was common belief among everyone from theologians to peasants that if ghosts appeared to the living they came from Purgatory, not from Heaven or Hell. In his magisterial book *The Birth of Purgatory*, Jacques Le Goff (not given to overstatement) puts the general case clearly: "Purgatory would become the prison in which ghosts were normally incarcerated, though they might be allowed to escape now and then to briefly haunt those of the living whose zeal in their behalf was insufficient."[27] That, of course, is precisely what happens in *Hamlet*. After the English Reformers dispensed with Purgatory, however, it was no longer clear to anyone where ghosts came from.[28] Educated people were inclined to doubt their existence, or to think that they were demons in disguise. There was, nevertheless, a great popular outburst of superstitious ghost lore among the common people beginning at mid-century. Theo Brown amply documents this outbreak and associates it with the sudden abolition of Purgatory. Instead of doing away with ghosts, the abolition caused them to flourish, at the same time that they became theologically inexplicable, vaguer, more sinister, more demonic and menacing. The result is not altogether surprising, since, as Norman Cohn has argued in another connection, the weakening of institutional religion by changes, doubts, and internecine conflicts often results in an increase in superstition, as it did about the same time in the better-known case of witchcraft.[29] Thus a reader or a playgoer familiar with Purgatory would recognize at once where King Hamlet's Ghost comes from; but Horatio, Marcellus, the guards, and Prince Hamlet have all forgotten, or prefer not to acknowledge, that once-common lore belonging to their fathers' generation. Horatio, a modern skeptic, has heard tales about ghosts, and does in part believe them—he must believe them on the pragmatic evidence of his own eyes. But for him and his friends ghost lore lingers on obscurely as remembered folktales and superstitions rather than present and authoritative knowledge.

The Ghost calls on Hamlet to avenge him against Claudius for his foul murder. But his last command to Hamlet is significantly broader. It is: "Adieu, adieu, adieu. Remember me" (1.5.91). These words touch Hamlet most deeply and linger longest in his memory:

> Remember thee?
> Ay, thou poor ghost, whiles memory holds a seat
> In this distracted globe. Remember thee?
> Yea, from the table of my memory
> I'll wipe away all trivial fond records,
> All saws of books, all forms, all pressures past
> That youth and observation copied there,
> And thy commandment all alone shall live
> Within the book and volume of my brain,
> Unmix'd with baser matter....
>     Now to my word.
> It is 'Adieu, adieu, remember me.'
> I have sworn't. (1.5.95–112)

But Hamlet takes his oath to "remember" with reference only to vengeance. He never remarks that to remember the dead in Purgatory means chiefly to pray for them, especially by offering masses for their souls. The last of his words when the Ghost has departed and Hamlet's friends approach opens a cryptic possibility: "For every man hath business and desire, / Such as it is— and for my own poor part, / I will go pray" (1.5.136–38). But, as Horatio says, these are "wild and whirling words." Their import is far from clear, perhaps even to their speaker. Jenkins speculates on "pray": "Perhaps for strength to carry out his task. But perhaps because 'it behoveth them which are vexed with spirits, to pray especially.'"[30] If we consider Hamlet's behavior in this scene and after, the least likely reading of his words is that he firmly intends to pray for his father's soul. He loves his father, but he recognizes no special obligation to pray for him.

## IV

Among the first of the Church Fathers to write more than briefly concerning this obligation was St. Augustine. In the *Confessions* he remembers his mother Monica, whose last request to her son was that he should remember her in his prayers:

All she wanted was that we should remember her at your altar, where she had been your servant day after day, without fail....
[I]nspire those of them who read this book to remember Monica, your servant, at your altar and with her Patricius, her husband, who died before her, by whose bodies you brought me into this life, though how it was I do not know. With pious hearts let them remember those who were not only my parents in this light that fails, but were also my brother and sister, subject to you, our Father, in our Catholic mother the Church, and will be my fellow citizens in the eternal Jerusalem for which your people sigh throughout their pilgrimage, from the time when they set out until the time when they return to you. So it shall be that the last request that my mother made to me shall be granted in the prayers of the many who read my confessions more fully than in mine alone.[31]

Remembering his mother and father with love and affection, yet regarding them as his sister and brother in religion, Augustine incidentally renders them less threatening than if he had "killed" or "forgotten" them. A dead father can be much more burdensome than a living one, as Donald Barthelme suggests in *The Dead Father*. And we need not limit the case to fathers. A dead mother is likewise more oppressive than a living one, as D. H. Lawrence finds in *Sons and Lovers* (not to forget that Paul Morel kills his mother with sedatives). So too Stephen Dedalus' neglected mother troubles his conscience after death in *Ulysses* as she never did while she lived. The efflorescence of ghost stories at the abolition of Purgatory manifests similar connections.

Although (as Le Goff shows) the doctrine of Purgatory unfolded gradually and was not fully formed until the high middle ages, Augustine already distinguished in many of his works between *poenae purgatoriae*, *tormenta purgatoria*, *ignis purgatories*, or *poenae temporariae* (purgatorial punishments, purgatorial torments, purgatorial fires, or temporary punishments) and *poenae sempiternae* (eternal punishments, that is, the fires of Hell).[32] Much earlier than Augustine, however, "at a very early date," possibly in Apostolic times, Christians were already remembering and praying for their dead. Indeed, to pray for the dead was a distinctively Christian custom from the beginning. According to Le Goff: "This was an innovation, as Solomon Reinach nicely observes: 'Pagans prayed to the dead, Christians prayed for the dead.'"[33] To represent the contrasting pagan view, we may recall the Sibyl's stern rebuke of Palinurus, when he begs permission to cross over the Styx: "unde haec, o Palinure, tibi tam dira cupido? ... desine fata deum flecti sperare precando" (Whence, O Palinurus, this dire longing of yours? ... Cease to dream that prayer can turn aside the decrees of Fate).[34]

As we are reminded by Augustine's reaction to the death of his mother, it was especially the duty of family members—husbands, wives, sons, daughters, servants, clients—to remember and to pray for their dead. A son might, like Augustine, also ask others, friends and fellow parishioners, to pray for his dead parents, since he assures us that in the light of eternity all Christians, living and dead, are brothers and sisters "in our one Catholic mother the Church," and that one day they will all be "fellow citizens in the eternal Jerusalem." Like receiving the Eucharist and the Sacrament of Penance, to which the Ghost of Hamlet's father specifically refers, prayers for the dead were, until the Reformation, related to a sense of family and of the community between the living and the dead. The ancient creedal phrase is "the Communion of Saints."

Notably, when Hamlet's father asks his son to "remember" him, he asks for something more than vengeance, but couches his request in terms less explicit than to ask him to lighten his burdens through prayer. It is perilous to argue from absence, but the ambiguity in the Ghost's solemn request may be explained, at least in part, by two considerations. First, Shakespeare may have judged that his mostly Protestant audience would take it amiss if the Ghost were to ask Hamlet explicitly for prayers and masses. It is all very well for a dead king from out of the past to express belief in what most of the audience would take to be Catholic superstitions—confession, absolution, "housel"—but it would be another matter altogether, much more likely to offend, if Prince Hamlet were to be implicated in those superstitions, which are now safely relegated to the dead past, for most of the audience and perhaps for Hamlet as well. Conversely, if Hamlet were to deny an explicit request by the Ghost to pray for him, that would strike a false note too. Second, throughout the play it appears that Hamlet and his friends, as members of the younger generation, simply are not prepared to hear such a request. The Ghost can only ask what Hamlet is ready, psychologically, culturally, and perhaps also politically, to hear and respond to. As we have seen, after 1547 English fathers who wished their sons to inherit safely put aside old ritual formulas and prudently evoked no more than the "discretion" of the executors or "the laudable custome of the realm." If the heirs were prepared to understand these hints, so much the better; if not, no harm was done. In the nature of the case, these explanations are speculative. What we can say with greater certainty is that even though the Ghost plainly comes from Purgatory, and says so in terms as explicit as may be, short of an open declaration, neither Hamlet nor any of the younger Danes ever openly reveals that he has heard of such a place as Purgatory. As was the case in England, so in Hamlet's Denmark. Purgatory is not just abolished but effectively forgotten, as if it never were.

## V

Nowhere in the play does anyone mention Purgatory or pray for the dead. Although the word "pray" occurs often, it appears mainly as a fossilized part of polite clichés: "I pray you now receive them" (3.1.95), for example. But if there is no mention of Purgatory, in several places there are significant absences, where the word would seem to be appropriate. In one of the play's most memorable sayings, for example, Hamlet declares: "There are more things in heaven and earth, Horatio, / Than are dreamed of in your philosophy" (1.5.74–75). Heaven can be taken as synecdochic for everything otherworldly, as in one part of the creedal phrase "visible and invisible." Still the words fall aslant when speaking about a Ghost who brings news from Purgatory. It is still odder when Hamlet says that he is "Prompted to my revenge by heaven and hell" (2.2.580), as if he is repressing the real source of his prompting. Similarly, when he refrains from killing Claudius at his prayer (which is not a prayer), he seems not to remember why his father three times condemned his uncle's deed as "horrible," since he vows to imitate that deed and, worse, deliberately do to his uncle what his outraged father accuses his brother of nearly doing to him by accident, namely, to "trip him that his heels may kick at heaven / And that his soul may be as damn'd and black / As hell, whereto it goes" (3.3.93–95). Hamlet takes no thought of Purgatory; he conceives of two states or places, with nothing in between. Nor does he consider the third place when he answers Claudius's question, "Where is Polonius?" Hamlet mockingly replies: "In heaven, send thither to see. If your messenger find him not there, seek him i' th' other place yourself" (4.3.32–35). There is no doubt where that "other place" is, or that he thinks Claudius properly belongs there. The best evidence of omission, however, may be Hamlet's outcry immediately after the ghost vanishes: "O all you host of heaven! O earth! *What else?* / And shall I couple Hell? O fie! Hold, hold my heart" (1.5.92–93; italics added). As Dover Wilson acutely remarks: "Heaven, earth—and what? Purgatory? He knows nothing of Purgatory." Wilson also notices Hamlet's oath, "by Saint Patrick" (1.5.142), which, he conjectures, is spoken in a low voice to Horatio.[35] St. Patrick was traditionally associated with Purgatory. According to a thirteenth-century account by an English Cistercian who visited Ireland, "St. Patrick's Purgatory" was an opening to that realm. Le Goff reports that the ancient account was reprinted in 1624, but a printed source need not be hypothesized since the place and tale were still notorious.[36] If his oath indicates that Hamlet's thoughts stray momentarily into territories forbidden by Elizabethan official culture, he does not follow them up.

In the same way, the closest anyone in the play comes to suggesting that it would be good to pray for the dead is negatively, when the Doctor of Divinity declares that there must be no official prayers or rites for Ophelia. "We should profane the service of the dead / To sing sage requiem and such rest to her / As to peace-parted souls" (5.1.229–30). This can be read as a Catholic's statement that no Requiem Mass may be offered for the soul of a presumed suicide, but a Protestant clergyman would say much the same thing about the service for "The Burial of the Dead." Scholarly opinion has leaned toward identifying the Doctor of Divinity as a Protestant cleric. Martin Holmes, recognizing that the Ghost is "unquestionably in Purgatory" and therefore that Catholicism is in the air, proposes that a "copyist" or "type-setter" might have inserted the Protestant title, so there is no need to play him as "an aggressively post-Reformation Doctor of Divinity."[37] Another explanation is that King Hamlet and Prince Hamlet belong to different generations and possibly different religions. "Requiem" is not an exclusively Catholic term, as witnessed by Spenser's complaint that no one offers a "*Requiem*" for the Earl of Leicester.[38] Shakespeare neglects an opportunity to make a Catholic priest look villainous to a Protestant audience sympathetic to Ophelia. Instead, he leaves the present state of religion in Denmark ambiguous, as he does everywhere else.

Laertes naturally takes violent exception to the Doctor's words. So does Hamlet, as soon as he hears the name "Ophelia" and understands who is being buried. Both leap into her grave together, wrestle and choke each other as they trample on the corpse. (Although Shakespeare is reticent, we may guess from the bones thrown up earlier by the grave diggers that Ophelia is buried in a winding-sheet, not a coffin, and that in due course her bones will likewise go to the charnel-house.)[39] The rival mourners seek to outboast each other as to what they would do for their beloved Ophelia. It never occurs to either of them for an instant to do the one thing needful: pray for her soul. Hamlet shouts at Laertes, whose hand is at his throat, words of extreme irony: "Thou pray'st not well." In fact, neither of them prays at all, unless we count Laertes' curse, "The devil take thy soul!" or Hamlet's rejoinder, "I *prithee* take thy fingers from my throat" (5.1.251–53; italics added). It is hard to think that this cluster of mock prayers appears here accidentally; this is as close as they get to praying. Whatever Laertes offers to do for Ophelia, Hamlet boasts he can do better: "Woo't weep, woo't fight, woo't fast, woo't tear thyself? / Woo't drink up eisel, eat a crocodile?"

(5.1.270 71). An impatient reader might wonder, what about praying for her? The Doctor of Divinity has provoked their struggle in the first place by forbidding their prayers for the wretched Ophelia. His grim stricture is scarcely needed, however, since praying for her soul is the last thing to occur to anyone attending the funeral.

## VI

"Remember me," the Ghost pleads. Toward the beginning of the play, Hamlet is the only person at the Court of Denmark who remembers his dead father. His "inky cloak" and "customary suits of solemn black" (1.2.77–78) cause him to stand out dramatically against the colorful costumes worn by everyone else on stage. They have put off black according to the times, to celebrate the royal wedding. If it seems odd that everyone in Denmark has forgotten or cannot speak about Purgatory in just the six months which have passed since the old King's death, it is surely no odder than that they have forgotten the King, too. At this juncture, at the sight of Hamlet's visual stubbornness, King Claudius gives him good Reformist advice, such as was often heard in sermons preached in England in the latter part of the sixteenth century:[40]

> But to persever
> In obstinate condolement is a course
> Of impious stubbornness, 'tis unmanly grief,
> It shows a will most incorrect to heaven,
> A heart unfortified, a mind impatient ...
>     Fie, 'tis a fault to nature,
> To reason most absurd, whose common theme
> Is death of fathers (1.2.92–104)

Claudius' words sound heartless and self-serving to us, but they may have sounded all the more ironic to Shakespeare's auditors because they parody the rigorist language of sixteenth-century sermons. For example, at the funeral of Martin Bucer in 1551, Matthew Parker, future Archbishop of Canterbury, forbids all mourning: "Moreover, it agreeth not with the rules of faith, for a christian man to bewayle the dead. For, who can deny that to be against faith, which is flatly forbidden by the scriptures? And how can that be sayed to agree with the rule of fayth, whiche the scriptures most evidentlye proove to be done by those that have no hope?"[41] When Claudius scolds Hamlet for displaying excessive and therefore impious grief, implying that further persistence would be a mark of reprobation, he says no more than

Parker does. Only "those that have no hope" are guilty of such conduct. At bottom, of course, it is the absence of Purgatory that renders grief and prayers inadmissible. As Augustine recognized, although one may pray for the most wicked of sinners while they are still in life, hoping for their conversion, there is no point in praying for those already in heaven or hell. "And likewise there is the same reason for praying at this time for human beings who are infidel and irreligious, and yet refusing to pray for them when they are departed. For the prayer of the Church itself, or even the prayer of devout individuals, is heard and answered on behalf of some of the departed, but only on behalf of those who have been reborn in Christ and whose life in the body has not been so evil that they are judged unworthy of such mercy, and yet not so good that they are seen to have no need of it."[42] By this logic, once Purgatory is excluded, commemoration has no purpose.

Yet if Hamlet loves and remembers his father while everyone else forgets him in their eagerness to get on with their lives and to pursue the devouring business of preferment, Hamlet does not really remember *why* or *how* he should remember his father. He cannot swallow Claudius' advice not to mourn the dead, except by concealing his discontent and outwardly deferring to him. Yet like most English of the late sixteenth century, he has forgotten the old way to pray for the dead, that is, how to "remember" them: *memorare* and *commemorare*. The ancient liturgical formula, from the canon of the Mass, is *Memento, Domine, famulorum famularumque tuaram [nn.] qui nos praecesserunt cum signo fidei, et dormiunt in somno pacis* (Remember, O Lord, thy servants [names] who have gone before us with the sign of faith and sleep in the sleep of peace). In his *Comparison of the Lord's Supper and Mass*, Thomas Becon mocks the practice: "for Philip and Cheny, more than a good meany, for the souls of your great grand Sir and of your old beldam Hurre, for the souls of father Princhard and of mother Puddingwright, for the souls of goodman Rinsepitcher and goodwife Pintpot, for the souls of Sir John Husslegoose and Sir Simon Sweetlips, for the souls of your benefactors, founders, patrons, friends and well-willers, which have given you either dirge-groats, confessional-pence, trentals, year-services, dinner or supper, or anything else that may maintain you."[43] Becon allows Sir John Husslegoose much the same contemptuous godspeed that Prince Hal gives old Sir John Falstaff.

When Hamlet's mother as well as his uncle accuses him of unusual excess in his grief, and therefore of dangerous impiety, he cannot grapple with the theological questions implied. Instead, he is driven inward, into the most famous of all early-modern gestures of radical individualist subjectivity: "But I have that within which passes show, / These but the trappings and the suits of woe" (1.2.85–86). His assertion would not really be to the point, if

Hamlet did not so forcefully make it so, turning the discussion momentarily away from Protestant suspicion of excessive mourning to the question of where true authenticity lies. What his plangent words reveal is that his deepest concern is not only for his lost father but for himself and for his innermost identity. So it is hardly surprising that, as the play progresses, the only way that he—and in response Laertes—can conceive of to "remember" his father is by resorting to vengeance instead of intercessory prayers. Although he cannot respond to his father's implicit plea to pray for him, he can respond to his call for vengeance and kill for him. As the play ends, Hamlet and Laertes repent and generously forgive each other. That is as close as they come to formal confession and absolution. Nor does Hamlet die asking his friends to pray for his soul, as he follows his father into the next world—perhaps into Purgatory. Rather, his penultimate words reveal his dutiful anxiety to settle the royal succession. His last words preserve, and take to a higher level, Shakespeare's refusal to define Hamlet's religion and Hamlet's earlier uncertainty about what lies beyond death: "the rest is silence" (5.2.363).

In spite of Hamlet's notable last omissions, the skeptical Horatio, left to do the private honors as Fortinbras enters to make the public arrangements, is prompted to spontaneous words of prayer: "Good night, sweet prince, / And flights of angels sing thee to thy rest" (5.2.341–42). Horatio's prayer is all the more moving in that it is so clearly spontaneous and heartfelt. As is everywhere the case with the younger generation of Prince Hamlet's friends, it is also theologically naive. It could be nothing else, if we imagine the alternatives. If Horatio had said, "And may the Lord have mercy on your soul," he would have stepped out of character. His oxymoronic combination of "flights of angels"—a flight of fancy which rises to the occasion—with the religiously neutral yet deeply satisfying "rest" (satisfying to Catholics, Protestants, and doubters alike) is precisely right. If he had been still more specific, and said, "And may your stay in Purgat'ry be short," he would probably have provoked a riot, both in Elsinore and at the Globe, followed by an official inquiry.

## VII

As becomes more and more apparent, Hamlet and Horatio live in, but are not the makers of, their particular "time" and culture. Circumstances force them to recognize that their "time is out of joint," but they are incapable of knowing how to "set it right." Audiences have always responded strongly to the moment of Horatio's prayer. Well they might, since it is the first and last time in the play that anyone finally breaks through into even a short, nondenominational prayer, unless it be Hamlet's notably displaced prayer to Ophelia: "Nymph, in thy orisons / Be all my sins remember'd" (3.1.89–90). In his notorious closet scene, Claudius suffers from a blocked psyche and consequent inability to pray. But all of Denmark—perhaps by implication all of England—suffers from a similar affliction. At least it seems similar, but it is not the same. Because he belongs to the older generation of King Hamlet, Claudius understands that if only he were to consent to give up his ill-gotten gains—his Queen and his kingdom—he could repent, confess his sins, and receive absolution. Restitution is the necessary prior condition, and he will not make restitution. In contrast, Hamlet and Horatio, although their spiritual state is not depraved like Claudius', have forgotten what even the self-damned Claudius knows but cannot put to use. Perhaps Shakespeare alludes to this strange forgetting in Hamlet's extreme decision to wipe the slate of his mind clean of everything but vengeance: "all trivial fond records, / All saws of books, all forms, all pressures past / That youth and observation copied there" (1.5.99–101). Alastair Fowler comments, "This must have been deeply shocking to a generation for whom the book was a symbol of devout Protestantism."[44] Perhaps Hamlet wiped away or repressed an underlayer of Catholic lore too. Unlike Hamlet, Claudius belongs to the older generation, which threw the times out of joint by committing an unnameable deed, involving more than a single act of murder and usurpation. Prince Hamlet belongs to the next generation. He and his friends have forgotten (or dare not name) what went wrong, because their predecessors have taken that knowledge and thrown it down Orwell's "memory hole."

Hamlet does not kill his father, he avenges him. He does not forget his father, he remembers him—insofar as he is capable. But there are different sorts of memory. The abolished rite was: *Memento, Domine, famulorum famularumque tuaram.* Unwittingly Hamlet implicates himself, as all the younger generation are unwittingly implicated, in the hidden crime committed by the fathers. That crime, paradoxically, was to kill the fathers: "Sir John Husslegoose and Sir Simon Sweetlips ... your benefactors, founders, patrons, friends and well-willers, which have given you either dirge-groats, confessional-pence, trentals, year-services, dinner or supper, or anything else that may maintain you," as Becon mocks them (Bossy, p. 43). Presumably, the persons responsible were Claudius and his chief ministers—including Polonius. If so, it is the greater irony that his daughter Ophelia is denied "sage requiem," a peaceful departure, and prayers for her soul.

Probably some of Shakespeare's audience would have noticed that Claudius has it in common with Henry VIII that he married his dead brother's wife—as we have remarked, it was a very famous case—although he far exceeds Henry by murdering his brother first. Moreover, an overwhelming burden of restitution lies on both kings' consciences. It would not be unprecedented to find covert political reference in these resemblances, but one cannot press the point too far. Whatever he thought, Shakespeare could not afford to risk drawing an explicit connection. A Catholic in his audience might have imagined that Claudius combines elements of several kings. Henry VII usurped the throne, Henry VIII had marriage troubles and, by confiscating the monasteries and passing the Chantries Act of 1545, showed the way for the stewards of Edward VI to abolish Purgatory altogether, in the Chantries Act of 1547 and the Prayerbook of 1549.[45]

As a crowning irony, Henry VIII's last will and testament, which took effect at his death in 1547, left over £1,200 for masses to be said for his soul.[46] He was one of the last important men in England who dared risk confiscation by providing for memorial masses in his will. Having made it impossible for anyone else to do so, however, by setting in motion the abolition of the chantries, the monastic orders, the religious guilds, and purgatory itself—and having enriched himself by confiscating the funds that had been left in connection with these institutions—his deeds rebounded on his head. There was no longer any will or way among his successors to honor his last intentions. Thus was "the enginer / Hoist with his own petard" (3.4.208–09).

The abolition of Purgatory was only one change among many, but it was perhaps the most sweeping and uncompromising of all those changes. It was deeply traumatic at the time, and its effects have lingered long after the event itself has been forgotten. As Virginia Bainbridge sums up these large cultural transformations: "The tearing apart of death and charity, the reciprocity between the living and the dead, and the poor, their substitutes, struck a blow at the very core of medieval concepts of community."[47] The focus turned from community and solidarity, with the dead and the poor, toward self-concern and individual self-sufficiency. If, as Hamlet fears, "the time is out of joint," and according to his lineage he is "born to set it right," unfortunately he cannot know how to do so, because he cannot or will not remember what went wrong in the first place. Instead, his ironic legacy is to add to the original, unspoken crime the powerful seal of his own fall into the depths of interior subjectivity, thus completing, by driving further inward, that earlier self-regarding assertion of progressive, autonomous individualism by his predecessors, who in a moment struck out ruthlessly against the communal past and against the generous benefactions and the crying needs of the dead.

## Notes

1. Gertrude Stein, *The Making of Americans* (New York, 1926; rpt. Normal, Ill., 1995), p. 3. Research contributing to this essay was generously supported by a Pew Evangelical Fellowship and sabbatical leave from New York University.

2. Stein, *Everybody's Autobiography* (New York, 1971), pp. 133. 142; see also pp. 132, 138–39.

3. *The Diary of Virginia Woolf*, ed. Anne Olivier Bell assisted by Andrew McNellie, 5 vols. (New York, 1977–1984), III, 208. See Vara S. Neverow, "The Diacritics of Desire: Virginia Woolf and the Rhetoric of Modernism and Feminism," diss. New York Univ. (Univ. Microfilms International, 1989), which brought this passage to my attention.

4. J. Hillis Miller, "The Critic As Host," *Deconstruction and Criticism* (New York, 1979), p. 251.

5. The secular-minded object because it makes modernism seem inversely parasitic on religion, Christians because it seems to deny the continuing vitality of their religion. Christianity thrives, but at the margins where it has been put by political leaders and cultural arbiters. If secularization is the weakening of bonds between religion and the dominant culture, not the weakening of religion itself, its existence is difficult to avoid.

6. All Shakespeare's works except *Hamlet* are cited from *The Complete Poems and Plays of William Shakespeare*, ed. William Allan Neilson and Charles Jarvis Hill (Cambridge, Mass., 1942).

7. To Tillyard one may add Arthur O. Lovejoy, *The Great Chain of Being: A Study of the History of an Idea* (Cambridge, Mass., 1936).

8. For a detailed study with no axe to grind (except occasional overeagerness to debunk pious accounts), see Jacques Le Goff, *The Birth of Purgatory*, trans. Arthur Goldhammer (Chicago, 1984).

9. See, e.g., R. N. Swanson, *Church and Society in Late Medieval England* (Oxford, 1989). The Crown's chief interest in fraternities, as with other religious activities, was to license them for stiff fees, leading historians to suspect that many went unrecorded.

10. Caroline M. Barron, "The Parish Fraternities of Medieval London," *The Church in Pre-Reformation Society*, ed. Barron and Christopher Harper-Bill (Woodbridge, Eng., 1985), p. 33.

11. Miri Rubin, "Corpus Christi Fraternities and Late Medieval Piety," *Voluntary Religion*: Papers Read at the ... Ecclesiastical History Society, ed. W. J. Sheils and Diana Wood (Oxford, 1986), pp. 103–04.

12. J. J. Scarisbrick, *The Reformation and the English People* (Oxford, 1984), pp. 19–20.

13. See John Bossy, "The Mass as a Social Institution 1200–1700," *Past and Present* 100 (1983), 39.

14. Colin Richmond, "The English Gentry and Religion, c. 1500," *Religious Beliefs and Ecclesiastical Careers in Late Medieval England*, ed. Christopher Harper-Bill (Woodbridge, Eng., 1991), pp. 121–25.

15. Theo Brown, *The Fate of the Dead: A Study in Folk Eschatology in the West Country after the Reformation*, The Folklore Society (London, 1979), p. 15.

16. Virginia R. Bainbridge, *Gilds in the Medieval Countryside: Social and Religious Change in Cambridgeshire c. 1350–1558* (Woodbridge, Eng., 1997), pp. 96–97.

17. *A notable Sermon of the reverende father Moister Hughe Latemer, whiche he preached at the Shrouds at paules churche in London, on the xviii. daye of January* (1548).

18. Scarisbrick, pp. 92–93.

19. *The Works of John Milton*, ed. Frank Allen Patterson, et al. (New York, 1931–40), II.

20. All quotations from *Hamlet* are from The Arden Shakespeare, second series, ed. Harold Jenkins (London, 1982; rpt. 1989).

21. Purgatory is usually mentioned, but briefly, with the notable exception of John Dover Wilson, *What Happens in Hamlet* (Cambridge, Eng., 1964), pp. 60–86. Eleanor Prosser discusses the issue at length in *Hamlet and Revenge*, 2nd ed. (Stanford, 1971), pp. 97–143, but concludes that the Ghost's identity is ambiguous. In the Arden Shakespeare Jenkins alludes to Purgatory when he cites More's *Supplication of Souls* to gloss "fast," but his remark that "hell, after all, was physical, and its torments often included hunger" (1.5.11n.) implies that we are dealing with Hell, not Purgatory.

22. *Hamlet* 1.5.12n.

23. The Q1 stage direction includes "Priest" among those who enter with Ophelia's corpse at 5.1.211; Q2 omits this. F has "*Priest*" as speech-head at 5.1.219 and 228; Q2 has "*Doct.*" The early editions do not list the *Dramatis Personae*.

24. Thomas Becon, *Comparison of the Lord's Supper and Mass* (1564), cited in the OED, which says that "housel" went out of use in the sixteenth century.

25. *Hamlet*, ed. Jenkins, 1.5.77n.

26. See Guy Bedouelle, "The Consultations of the Universities and Scholars Concerning the 'Great Matter' of King Henry VIII," in *The Bible in the Sixteenth Century*, ed. David C. Steinmetz (Durham, N.C., 1990), pp. 21–36, 200–02.

27. Le Goff, p. 82.

28. Dover Wilson, pp. 60–86.

29. Brown, *The Fate of the Dead*; Norman Cohn, *The Pursuit of the Millennium*, 2nd ed. (New York, 1961).

30. *Hamlet*, 1.5.138n. Jenkins quotes a prominent Protestant authority, Lewes Lavater, *Of Ghosts and Spirits Walking by Night*, tr. R. H. (1572), 3.6.

31. Saint Augustine, *Confessions* (9.13.36–37), as cited in Le Goff, p. 65. Goldhammer credits K. S. Pine-Coffin as translator, possibly from the Penguin edition. On the efficacy of masses for the dead, see Bossy, "The Mass as a Social Institution."

32. See Le Goff, pp. 63ff.

33. Le Goff, p. 45, quoting from Salomon Reinach, "De l'origine des prières pour les morts," *Revue des Etudes juives* 41 (1900), 164.

34. Vergil, *Aeneid* 6.373, 376. In *Virgil*, tr. H. Rushton Fairclough, Loeb Classical Library (Cambridge, Mass., 1953), I.532; my translation.

35. Dover Wilson, p. 72.

36. Le Goff, pp. 193–201.

37. Martin Holmes, *The Guns of Elsinore: A New Approach to 'Hamlet'* (London, 1964), p. 156.

38. "The Ruines of Time" (line 196), in *The Works of Edmund Spenser* (Baltimore, 1947), VIII, 42.

39. The stage direction at 5.1.211 reads "*corse*" in Q2, "*Coffin*" in Q1 and F. All read "The corse they follow" in the text (5.1.213).

40. See G. W. Pigman, III, *Grief and English Renaissance Elegy* (Cambridge, Eng., 1985), pp. 16–39.

41. Matthew Parker, *A Funeral Sermon ... Preached at S. Maries in Cambridge, Anno 1551, at the buriall of ... Martin Bucer*, trans. Thomas Newton (1587), sig. A4, cited by Pigman, p. 29. I have regularized *u* and *v*.

42. Augustine, *City of God* (21.24), as cited by Le Goff, p. 67.

43. Cited by Bossy, p. 43.

44. Alastair Fowler, "The Case Against Hamlet," *Times Literary Supplement* (December 22, 1995), p. 7.

45. For vivid details, see Eamon Duffy, *The Stripping of the Altars: Traditional Religion in England, c. 1400–c. 1580* (New Haven, 1992), pp. 454–58.

46. George William Butler, *A Crisis of Saints: Essays on People and Principles* (San Francisco: Ignatius Press, 1995), pp. 118–19.

47. Bainbridge, p. 97.

JOHN LEE

# A King of Infinite Space

*King.* But now my Cosin Hamlet, and my Sonne?

(1.2.64)

Shakespeare's Prince Hamlet has a self which is both apart of, and important to, his sense of identity. The last chapter put forward two complementary ways of describing and following this self. 'That Within' the Prince was seen to be an area discrete, though not separate, from his society, and that discreteness was seen to have been self-created; the Prince was seen to possess a self-constituting, as opposed to a self-fashioning, agency. Such an argument refutes the basic thrusts of the arguments of Cultural Materialists and New Historicists concerning English Renaissance literary subjectivity. It also concentrates on the similarities between the Prince's senses of self and more modern senses of self. However, at the heart of the descriptive approaches to self put forward in Chapter 6 is an insistence on the non-essentialist nature of self; Prince Hamlet's senses of self must be historically sited, distinct in various ways from our contemporary senses of self. Prince Hamlet must have aspects of his sense of self that make him of his time; to a point, he must acknowledge Claudius' claim of kinship in this, as in familial matters—no matter how distasteful that kinship may be to him. This chapter focuses on one aspect of this kinship, and so on one difference between the senses of self within *Hamlet* and modern senses of self. During the Elizabethan and Jacobean periods, it is argued, there is a rhetorical sense

From *Shakespeare's* Hamlet *and the Controversies of Self.* © 2000 by John Lee.

of self. Such a rhetorical sense of self is examined as it can be seen within some of Shakespeare's plays, and is placed in relation to Prince Hamlet's senses of self.

The meaning of 'rhetorical', as used above, may need explanation. 'Rhetoric' is used here in the sense broached by C. S. Lewis in the introductory chapter to his *English Literature in the Sixteenth Century Excluding Drama*: 'Rhetoric', Lewis noted, 'is the greatest barrier between us and our ancestors.'[1] This is a rather grand statement, according 'rhetoric' a great and wide-ranging importance in all aspects of culture. Lewis leaves this assertion of importance rather unsubstantiated. On the one hand, he gives as example the sixteenth century's (to his mind) deplorable enjoyment of rhetorical figures for their own sake, and on the other he speaks (very positively) of a different, rhetorical, way of thinking, evidenced by the sixteenth century's ability to talk about the humdrum and the profound in the same breath. Each example is given baldly, as might be expected in the introduction to a literary guide.

Lewis's use of 'rhetoric' has the virtue of making immediately plain what 'rhetoric' does not mean; 'rhetoric', as Lewis used it and as it is here used, does not have its currently dominant sense of an ornamental patterning added to language, which is often seen as marking out that language as deceptive and specious.[2] 'Rhetoric' is something far larger, far more important, and far more positive than that. What that was in the English Renaissance[3] has been the subject of a large body of critical work, carried out over the last forty-five years, and on which the following discussion relies. Central to nearly all of this work is the recognition that 'rhetoric' is not a simple or single activity, but a system. What follows is an outline of the manner in which that recognition came about, and of the critical implications of that recognition.

The recognition that rhetoric was a system emerged first with the piecing-together of the sixteenth-century pedagogy of rhetoric.[4] This did not stop at the teaching of *elocutio*, that is the teaching of the use of figures and tropes. Also taught were *inventio* and *dispositio*, the means of discovering and organizing arguments respectively, as well as *memoria*, the art of memory, and *pronunciatio*—the art of delivering speeches.[5] To refer to 'rhetoric', then, was to refer to all of these categories of activity. They could all be yoked together, as together they dealt with every aspect of communication. But each also represented and generated its own field of knowledge. *Inventio*, as the means of discovering arguments, considered questions of the nature of thought and methods of thinking, and so of origin and originality, and authority and authorship.[6] *Dispositio*, as the means of arranging arguments, considered questions of logic, on the one hand, and audience on the other; and of what types of logic appealed to what audiences. Decorum was a central concept to most of the five categories of rhetoric. *Elocutio*, as well as being the occasion for long lists of figures and tropes, generated many debates concerning the nature of language;[7] was it given by God, or made by man? Were words intimately or arbitrarily related to things?[8] What gave words their power? What was a trope? *Memoria* not only offered methods for facilitating memory, but considered the nature of the mind and the way in which thought is preserved within it.[9] *Pronunciatio* investigated the physical and visual nature of expression: the impacts of tones of speech, of the speaker's appearance, and the importance of gesture.[10] Yet these concerns were only the beginning of rhetoric's field of interest. For if rhetoric had one defining aim, it was to produce language that was persuasive and so offered power in a civic context.[11] As such, rhetoric insisted on the importance of those trained in it being able to analyse social context, whether that involved a person, a group, or a social institution.[12] For only then could one discover the best means to influence one's audience.

All these various concerns can be seen in two kinds of publication which flourished in the sixteenth century, and which are most obviously representative and constitutive of rhetoric's fields of knowledge; these are the manuals of rhetoric and the genre of courtesy literature.[13] The difference between these two kinds is their relative emphases. The manuals are mainly concerned with propounding the categories of rhetoric, and dealing with the questions raised by those categories. Courtesy literature focused mainly on analysing the two-way relationship between the person and his (and less frequently her) social context. Yet both are related. This relationship is clear at the level of stated concern. On the one hand, manuals of rhetoric argue— typically in an introductory overview—about rhetoric's power and usefulness in a civic context.[14] On the other, works of courtesy literature constantly refer to the importance of eloquence and a literary education.[15] But more important is an unstated relationship; both kinds of literature argue for a tactical presentation of oneself and one's arguments, a presentation which must be tailored to one's context.

This relationship is glimpsed succinctly in George Puttenham's description of allegory as 'the Courtly figure' in his *The Arte of English Poesie* (1589).[16] Allegory is courtly for Puttenham in that it disguises what it presents in order to win its ends. In that sense, this trope is the literary device that represents the courtier's role, which role 'is in plaine termes', Puttenham says in his conclusion, 'cunningly to be able to dissemble ... whereby the better to winne his purposes and good aduantages' (pp. 250–1). Allegory becomes for Puttenham not only one of the most important and widely used tropes, but also a symbol of the nature of rule:

the vse of [allegory] is so large, and his vertue of so great efficacie
as it is supposed no man can pleasantly vtter and perswade
without it, but in effect is sure neuer or very seldome to thriue
and prosper in the world, that cannot skilfully put in vse, in
somuch as not onely euery common Courtier, but also the
grauest Counsellour, yea and the most noble and wisest Prince of
them all are many times enforced to vse it ... Qui nescit
dissimulare nescit regnare. [Who refuses to dissemble refuses to
rule] (p. 155)

What is becoming clear, here, is that to refer to 'rhetoric' is not only to refer
to the practices that map out a field of knowledge which, composed of many
other fields, sought to analyse the world in order to gain power over it.
Rhetoric's field of knowledge, and so its analyses, are also constitutive of that
world, and the persons within it. It is in this sense that one may refer to a
rhetorical world, and a rhetorical person. One might think of 'rhetoric', in
fact, as the equivalent of contemporary science, and so as a 'technology of
power' in the Foucauldian sense.[17] 'Rhetoric' understood as such a field of
knowledge makes sense of Lewis's statement of its being 'the greatest barrier
between us and our ancestors'. The meaning of 'rhetoric' is not amenable to
the formulated definitions of the dictionary; 'rhetoric' is another of those
words, as Wittgenstein said, 'used something like a gesture, accompanying a
complicated activity'.

    One would expect the rhetorical nature of persons within such a
rhetorical world to be of import to the controversies of self, and previous
literary-critical work has recognized connections between the two topics.
Michael McCanles, in his *The Text of Sidney's Arcadian World* (1989), puts
forward an argument which he sees as complementary to Greenblatt's
argument concerning self-fashioning, as that is given in *Renaissance Self-
Fashioning*. Where Greenblatt examines the role of social and political codes
in constituting identity, McCanles looks at the shaping influence of 'rhetorical
figuration' on identity. McCanles, invoking the strong Whorf-Sapir thesis
once more, argues that human reality 'is constituted from the linguistic codes
made available by culture itself', and that these codes are at this time the
figures of rhetoric.[18] McCanles's concept of identity, like Greenblatt's, has no
place for self-constituting agency, nor any sense of degrees of innerness.[19]

    McCanles's approach, in its concentration on language and most
especially on figures, that is on *elocutio*, represents a development of the most
common form of critical attempt to understand the rhetorical nature of
literature. For, rather disappointingly, when single literary texts are
examined, the attempt to recover and examine the systemic nature of

rhetoric tends to be abandoned. Thus, concerning *Hamlet*, George T. Wright argues that the use of hendiadys is particularly expressive of the play's fascination with false unions;[20] while Georgio Melchiori finds the key figure to be oxymoron, and Patricia Parker puts forward a more general concern with figures of copula and sequitur reflecting the play's concern with political succession.[21] Neil Rhodes, however, in *The Power of Eloquence and English Renaissance Literature* (1992), insists on a wider sense of rhetoric as an approach to the world (if not as a field of knowledge) and does so as a corrective to Greenblatt's arguments, again in *Renaissance Self-Fashioning*, concerning the person's lack of agency. Rhodes argues that there was a rhetorical identity which he terms 'the bravery of the self'. ('Self' rather blurs into 'identity' in Rhodes's account.) By 'bravery', Rhodes invokes that word's Renaissance senses of boasting and swaggering. For this concept of identity is one 'which stresses the demonstrative personality rather than the integrity of the inner self, and which recognizes the central importance of eloquence in creating such a personality'.[22] Rhodes insists, then, on the sense, ever-present in Renaissance manuals of rhetoric and courtesy literature, as well as in such famous texts as Pico della Mirandola's *Oration*, that the person fashions himself through acting. He reasserts the claims of a large body of Renaissance literature and of literary criticism which Greenblatt set himself against when he failed to find self-fashioning in the Renaissance.

Yet Rhodes still examines rhetoric's impact on identity only in external terms; he leaves aside the possibility of an inner self altogether, and so does not consider what might be the rhetorical nature of that self. This is neither necessary nor logical. For, whether or not one accepts the existence of a self, rhetoric, as a field of knowledge, is bound to structure the way in which Renaissance persons think; it is bound, that is, to structure them internally. Walter J. Ong makes clear the logic of this relationship in his *Rhetoric, Romance and Technology* (1971):

> Human thought structures are tied in with verbalization and must fit available media of communication; there is no way for persons with no experience of writing to put their minds through the continuous linear sequence of thought such as goes, for example, into an encyclopedia article.[23]

Ong's conception of rhetoric as a system of communication parallels the sense of rhetoric, advanced here, as a field of knowledge. Both conceptions of rhetoric see it as shaping thought, and so shaping the person's constitution of the world, and of him- or herself. This, then, is the logical argument for the existence of a rhetorical sense of self.

However, our sense of what that rhetorical sense of self might be, how it might appear in a play, is still undefined. 'Rhetoric' has so far been examined in rather abstract terms, in order to insist on its systemic nature. It is time to turn to the effects produced by this field of knowledge, to ask what might identify a sense of self as being rhetorical. Erasmus' *De Copia* (1512) was the most influential manual of rhetoric in the sixteenth century. It opens with an image of what rhetoric could both produce and be: 'The speech of man is a magnificent and impressive thing when it surges along like a golden river.'[24] Erasmus does not attempt a description of the various parts and aspects of rhetoric, but rather uses an image as a model of rhetoric's effects. That is, to recall the discussion of the use of metaphor in Chapter 6, Erasmus uses the simile of speech as a surging golden river to schematize a certain area of the activity that constitutes rhetoric's field of knowledge. (The difference between simile and metaphor in this respect is that simile has no catachretic function.)

Erasmus' model is primarily an expression of his understanding of one aspect of rhetoric's effect. The image of speech as a surging river captures the sense of the smooth and yet irresistibly powerful force that one's arguments, when properly produced, may attain. Such a river would carry away the objections of others. At the same time, the image suggests the beauty and awe that such speech may generate in its hearers; it is a 'golden' river. That 'golden' also suggests the value of such speech, holding the promise of personal success and power in the secular world. However, Erasmus' image, as such a model, may allow further understandings of rhetoric to be developed; such models, if they are profitable, allow one to think through the domain they describe.[25] For instance, the image of speech as a 'surging' river has suggestions of inhuman volume, of elemental power, and destructive force. If rhetoric produces such powerful speech, what is to stop it being used destructively and not magnificently? To argue through Erasmus' image in this way is to exploit the dramatic potential of his model of rhetoric and so of his manual of rhetoric. Most manuals denied this potential, by insisting on a link between morality and eloquence. This link derived its authority from the manuals of the classical teachers of rhetoric. Quintilian's *Institutio Oratoria*, the most influential of these, put this link thus: 'bene dicere non possit nisi bonus' ('no man can speak well who is not good himself').[26] Yet Shakespeare (and other dramatists) quite ignored this undramatic proposition. Within his plays, those who use speech powerfully often use it destructively; Iago and Richard III are obvious examples. Shakespeare, then, is no academic user of a manual of rhetoric, following its rules and employing its figures (though he does of course also do this). Rather he argues about and explores rhetoric, exploiting the manuals, as he exploited every other source-book, for their dramatic potential.

How, then, does this relate to a rhetorical sense of self? The chapter began with the aim of identifying what might make an Elizabethan sense of self of its own period and different from later senses of self. One of the largest differences between that world and our own was bound up with the rhetorical nature of the Elizabethan world. Rhetoric, it was argued, is a complicated activity which constitutes a field of knowledge; logically, such a field of knowledge ought to structure the persons within it. The external impact of rhetoric on persons was seen already to have been the focus of literary criticism. However, as a field of knowledge it was argued that rhetoric should have an internal impact as well—it should structure the self, as well as other aspects of identity. Given that rhetoric is such a complicated and wide-ranging domain of activity, only a particular aspect of its impact can here be explored—only one aspect, that is, of what might make a sense of self rhetorical and so historically sited. In the search for such an aspect, Erasmus' use of water imagery to model the impact of rhetoric as speech was examined. This, it was suggested, although not the only model used to schematize rhetoric's impact, could be used to explore that impact. Moreover, Erasmus' choice of water imagery is typical; the impact of rhetoric, as Ong noted, is usually expressed through such imagery: 'Rhetoric is typically an overwhelming phenomenon, implemented by what the classical world and the Renaissance called *copia*, abundance, plenty, unstinted flow.... Its world is commonly and aptly described in ... water symbolism.'[27] Rhetoric's world, it seems, is somehow liquid. If that is true, it seems possible that a rhetorical sense of self should share this liquidity.

In Chapter 6, metaphor was argued to offer an expressive resource for a person's sense of self, even a self which lacked a modern vocabulary of interiority. It would seem likely that a rhetorical sense of self would express and explore itself through the same complex of imagery which is used to express and explore the nature of rhetoric. If this is so, one might expect to find images of a person's self, within Shakespeare's plays, as images of water. This line of thought can be developed through Erasmus' image. If speech is a river, what then is the speaker? Some form of reservoir whose interior is also made up of the same water that composes its world. Such a liquid sense of self might strike us as unlikely; but then one might expect to find particularly unfamiliar a sense of self different from our own.

> *Ant.* I to the world am like a drop of water,
>    That in the Ocean seekes another drop,
>    Who falling there to finde his fellow forth,
>    (Vnseene, inquisitiue) confounds himselfe.

> So I, to finde a Mother and a Brother,
> In quest of them (vnhappie a) loose my selfe.
>
> (1.2.34–40)

These lines with their unfamiliar image come from Act 1 scene 2 of *The Comedie of Errors*. Antipholus of Syracuse, having just arrived at Ephesus in search of his mother and long-lost identical twin brother, pauses before entering the city. For a moment before the play's confusions of identity begins he is alone, and in that moment he suddenly tells the audience of his fears that he is losing his personal identity. He compares himself to a drop of water. This image does not match exactly the argument developed from Erasmus' image of speech as a river, but it is close. Antipholus pictures himself and his world as made up from water; both, that is, are constituted of the same element (which element, as Ong points out, is typically used to express the rhetorical nature of the world). The difference between himself and his world, a discreteness that Antipholus values highly, is expressed through the physical shape of the water-drop. The water-drop is discrete from the ocean not because of any act of 'bravery'—to invoke Rhodes's term for the external impact of rhetoric—but because it is centred on itself. The image contains no suggestions of acting or audience.

The image of a water-drop, in fact, well expresses aspects of self as those were previously defined. Like a water-drop, self depends not on any essential quality, but is constructed from the world which surrounds it. Like the forces that produce a water-drop, self orientates and shapes identity. Most important and dramatic, however, is the intense fragility conferred upon identity by picturing it as a construct of water, as the world as ocean threatens to submerge, or render it indistinct. Antipholus' fear that he is losing his identity is the fear, now unfamiliar, of the dissolution of self. 'One', as Ong notes, 'may drown in rhetoric.'[28] To us, such drowning and dissolution may be unfamiliar, but such fears were not unfamiliar to that time. Similar water imagery recurs at other moments of personal crisis. So, for example, a little later within Shakespeare's plays, when Richard II, having been taken prisoner by Bolingbroke, is brought to answer the articles against him—a scene located by the Arden edition in Westminster Hall—Richard wishes that he were 'a Mockerie, King of Snow' so that, 'Standing before the Sunne of Bullingbrooke', he might 'melt my selfe away in Water-drops' (*The life & death of King Richard the Second*, 4.1.250–2). The image's concern with matters of identity is made sharper by the passages that precede and follow it. In the lines immediately before Richard expresses his desire to melt, he bemoans the fact that he has 'worn so many Winters out' but knows 'not now, what Name to call my selfe' (4.1.248–9). In the lines immediately after, he calls for a mirror, 'That it may shewe me what a Face I haue, Since it is Bankrupt of his Maiestie' (4.1.256–7). When the mirror arrives, Richard cannot reconcile the face he still sees in it with his nameless, dissolved sense of himself. So he smashes the mirror, producing a more representative image of a face 'in an hundred shiuers' (4.1.279). Richard's wish for dissolution can be paralleled with that of Faustus in Marlowe's and his collaborator's *The Tragicall History of D. Faustus* (1588–9). At the end of the play, when the devils are about to enter to take his soul down to hell, he cries: 'O soul, be changed to little water drops / And fall into the ocean, ne'er be found!' (5.7.118–19).[29] Faustus's desire for dissolution is associated particularly with his desire that his soul escape; in the preceding lines he begged the stars to 'draw up Faustus like a foggy mist / Into the entrails of yon labouring cloud', where his body might be consumed by lightening, allowing his soul to 'ascend to heaven' (5.7.91–5). A soul is not a self, as has been seen, but Marlowe is using water imagery to express an inner aspect of identity.[30]

Richard and Faustus wish for a dissolution they cannot achieve, where Antipholus fears a dissolution that seems all too possible. This is not to suggest that one attitude predominates over the other. Antipholus' fears are also shared by others outside Shakespeare's plays. For instance, Morose, the lover of silence in Ben Jonson's *Epicoene, Or the Silent Woman* (1609–10), describes the arrival of his relatives as threatening to drown him:

> Oh, the sea breaks in upon me! Another flood! An inundation! I
> shall be o'erwhelm'd with noise. It beats already at my shores.
>
> (3.6.2–4)

These are two quite different attitudes to drowning, but both become possible as fears or hopes within a rhetorical world. That world itself seems, at times, threatened by inundation. So, for instance, the opening of 'An Homelie of Whoredome and Unclenness' deplores a situation where, 'Above other vices the outragious seas of adultery, whoredome, fornicacion and unclennesse have not onleye braste in, but also overflowed almoste the whoole worlde.'[31]

This rhetorical sense of self, expressed through water imagery, is neither constantly present nor constantly constituted within Shakespeare's plays. Antipholus' sense of dissolution is simple and his fear of it mild. This is partly due to the impersonal, overtly poetic nature of his image and partly due to the comic nature of the play. Antipholus may fear dissolution, but it is unlikely, as this is comedy, that he would drown. Antony's sense of dissolution in *The Tragedie of Anthonie, and Cleopatra* is, by contrast, complicated and immensely painful. After his final defeat at Alexandria, Antony drowns.

*Enter Anthony, and Eros*

*Ant.*    Eros, thou yet behold'st me?

*Eros.*                                    I Noble Lord.

*Ant.*    Sometime we see a cloud that's Dragonish,
          A vapour sometime, like a Bear, or Lyon,
          A toward Cittadell, a pendant Rocke,
          A forked Mountaine, or blew Promontorie
          With Trees vpon't, that nodde vnto the world,
          And mocke our eyes with Ayre.
          Thou hast seene these Signes,
          They are blacke Vespers Pageants.

*Eros.*                                    I my lord.

*Ant.*    That which is now a Horse, euen with a thoght
          the Racke dislimes, and makes it indistinct
          As water is in water.

*Eros.*                    It does my Lord.

*Ant.*    My good Knaue *Eros*, now thy Captaine is
          Euen such a body: here I am *Anthony*,
          Yet cannot hold this visible shape (my Knaue).

                                             (4.15.1–14)

Antony's drowning, his sense that he 'cannot hold this visible shape' is painful. This is registered particularly in the embarrassment of seeing the once magnificent Antony flounder in public: his question, '*Eros*, thou yet behold'st me?' is on one level absurd. Eros and the audience can quite plainly see Antony. However, Antony's 'me' refers to more than his physical presence; it refers also to his sense of his self, a sense so important to Antony that it is dominant over his sense of his own corporeality. Thus when Antony loses this sense, when his picture of his self becomes as 'indistinct / As water is in water', he cannot believe his 'visible shape' remains.

The image with which Antony represents his sense of his dissolution is layered. To begin with, Antony pictures himself as a particularly shaped cloud, whose shape is in a moment 'dislimed', that is 'dislimned', and rendered indistinct in the mass of clouds. There is a degree of corporeality to this part of the image, particularly if the pun of dislimns/dislimbs is allowed, which expresses the violence that Antony feels has been done his identity. (The reason why one might not allow this pun is the *OED*'s date of first recorded usage for 'dislimbs' as 1662.) This cloudy Antony was torn apart on a rack, rent limb from limb to his constituent parts. However, this corporeality is itself fluid, made up as it is from clouds. (Clouds were related, in Elizabethan thought—as in our meteorology—to the ocean. So, for example, Richard III laments, at the beginning of *The Tragedy of Richard the Third*, that 'all the clouds that lowr'd vpon our House' are 'In the deepe bosome of the Ocean buried' (1.1.3–4).) This fluidity is reinforced first by Antony's varying his first image of himself as a cloud with a parallel image of himself as a 'vapour'. The discrimination between the two is a fine one. However, 'vapour', in its senses of 'mist' and 'fog', as well as its scientific sense of an evaporated substance, focuses attention more closely on the liquid nature of the substance.[32] This sense of the liquid nature of the image is reinforced further when Antony expands his image by exampling the loss of distinction it portrays as the indistinctness of 'water ... in water'.

Each layer of the image pictures inner identity as constituted out of an external element, as something given a transient self-definition by its shape, a shape which is at any moment capable of flowing away. This sense of outlines, and of the self-constituted nature of these, emerges most clearly in the use of 'dislimns' (a word which also demonstrates the immense precision and effort of Antony's use of language here). According to the *OED*, the word is a neologism, not used again until used imitatively in the nineteenth century. The *OED* gives its meaning as 'to obliterate the outlines of (anything limned)'. Clearly, as a neologism, one would expect the word's meaning to suit the context, for the compiler of the dictionary's entry will have this as their aim. However, the word's precision is also seen in its invocation of the positive sense of 'limn'. To 'limn' here carries two areas of relevant meaning. 'Limning', in its older sense, referred particularly to the art of illuminating manuscripts; that is, to a form of illustration based around the use of water-colours. At around the turn of the sixteenth and seventeenth centuries it came to refer specifically to painting in water-colours.[33] The idea of water-colour painting suits Antony's image, and does so in several ways. Water-colours are, in a sense, paintings in clouds, or of water in water. Typically they make much of the fragility of their form. 'To limn the water, limn (something) on water' became, by 1620 according to the *OED*, a proverbial expression said of something transient or futile. Antony's use of 'dislimns' might here be thought to invoke it (and also the sense of vapour as 'something unsubstantial' (*OED* 2c)).

Also, in the sixteenth and seventeenth centuries, limning had come to refer particularly to the art of miniature painting. Recently, much emphasis has been placed on Henry VIII's and Elizabeth I's use of miniatures as political icons; as public representations of an ideal image of the ruler. Yet they could also be intensely personal paintings, intended for the closet as well as the box of display on a courtier's arm. Intimacy was the key to their style, and they attempted to generate such intimacy by capturing transient moments particularly expressive of personality. So, for instance, Nicholas

Hilliard, the most famous English proponent of the miniaturist's art, writes in his *A Treatise Concerning the Arte of Limning* that miniatures should attempt to capture the, 'louely graces wittye smilings, and thosse stolne glances wch sudainely like lighting passe and another Countenance taketh place'.[34] Both senses of miniature as icon and glimpse of intimacy are, perhaps, invoked by Antony's use of 'dislimnd'. Antony's sense of self is represented for a moment as a miniature (which being oval or round has the same shape as a drop of water[35]) which becomes 'unpainted'—a peculiar, quasi-magical and mysterious process in its un-creative aspect. One could imagine the effect of bleach on a water-colour, dissolving away the artist's work to the continuous texture of the canvas. Antony is thus un-painted. He loses sight of the precious picture of himself that he has valued and created through his life. He merges with his surroundings, losing his sense of his 'visible shape'. He has flowed back into the element from which he was created.

Such fluidity of form is suggestive of the figure of Proteus, who might be called the Shakespearian god, in the light of literary critics' use of Proteus to attempt to define Shakespeare's ability to create character (seen in Part II). Proteus, as has been noted, achieved especial prominence during the Renaissance: in classical myth, Proteus had been a minor sea-god who served Poseidon and had, according to Homer, both the power to change his shape and a vast knowledge; in the Renaissance, Proteus gained in importance as he came to be seen as a symbol of a defining aspect of man's nature. This aspect of Proteus was formulated strikingly by Juan Luis Vives in his *Fabula de homine* (after 1518), which itself draws on Giovanni Pico della Mirandola's more influential and innovative *De dignitate hominis* (written 1486). In Vives's fable, the world is created as a theatre and play for the gods, and by Jupiter as an after-dinner surprise for the guests at Juno's birthday party. The gods, when they have finished eating, take their seats for the performance, and soon begin discussing who is the best actor on the planet before them. Soon it becomes clear that man deserves the title; he acts different parts with each of his entrances. He can live as insensibly as a plant; or as cunningly as the fox, or as lustfully as a sow; or he can live justly and prudently with others, in the society of a city. What really impresses the gods is man's next entrance as a god; they declare man 'to be that multiform Proteus, the son of the Ocean', and they call for him to join them.[36] When he does he is acting the part of Jupiter himself, and so well that some of the gods think he is Jupiter.

Vives's fable casts man as Proteus to recognize the power of his free choice; he may choose what he wishes to be. It is this near-divine ability to form and transform himself that distinguishes man from every other creature on earth. In casting man as Proteus, Vives, following Pico, argues that man's dignity rests not in his place at the centre of creation or in his nature as the microcosm of the macrocosm, but in his being without a given nature and capable of moving through the hierarchies of creation. Man's unfixity, his 'indeterminate nature' as Pico phrases it, is his greatness; in this lies his worth.[37] This nature also gives him his goal; on the one hand, he must attempt to ascend to the nature of a god, and on the other he must beware that he does not become a beast.

Viewed in this way, the image of man as Proteus, as a shape-changer, is overwhelmingly positive; its negative aspects are minor, though dangerous. The figure of man as Proteus neatly captures the rhetorical sense of self. Proteus' element is the water, and his nature partakes of the ocean's fluidity. Proteus' element is also language, for language, as has been seen, is often pictured in water-based images. Proteus is the figure that links water, language, and human nature together, celebrating the divinity of change and the power of language. Such a positive sense of a Protean or rhetorical sense of self, however, has not been seen within Shakespeare's plays. Shakespeare, just as he dismissed the undramatic insistence of the manuals of rhetoric that only the good may speak persuasively, dramatizes the troubling aspects of the Protean sense of self. In doing so he draws on another tradition of interpreting Proteus, a darker tradition distrustful of the ability to change.[38] A. Bartlett Giamatti, in *Exile and Change in Renaissance Literature* (1984), describes these two different traditions as the difference between those who saw Proteus as a symbol of the one truth lying behind the many, and those who saw Proteus as a symbol of the many that are to be found in the one. Giamatti cites Montaigne as an example of the latter.[39]

Montaigne's descriptions of man and himself, quoted in Chapter 6, were full of oceanic imagery. So, for instance, Montaigne described man as a 'wonderfull, vaine, divers and wavering subject', and noted that within this subject 'all is but changing, motion, and inconstancy ... We float and waver between divers opinions: we will nothing freely, nothing absolutely'. As Thomas Greene points out, the variation within personality that Montaigne found was negative in the respect that it precluded transformation, whether that was a transformation, in Pico's terms, up to the godhead or down to the beast.[40] In Montaigne's *Essays* there is a horizontal multiplicity of expression, a variation which, though it spurs and shapes the formal expression of the *Essays*, can become fatiguing and wearisome. Shakespeare exploits this more negative tradition of interpretation of Protean identity more dramatically. The terror that lies within Pico's 'indeterminate nature' is staged; dramatic persons struggle constantly to be determinate, and occasionally fail, losing hold on their fluid selves, flowing into the invisibility of indeterminacy.

Shakespeare's Prince Hamlet draws on this Protean, rhetorical sense of self. Hamlet begins, one might say, where Faustus left off. The opening lines of his first soliloquy are a wish for dissolution (here of the flesh) as a means to escape his present predicament: 'Oh that this too too solid Flesh, would melt, / Thaw, and resolue it selfe into a Dew' (1.2.129–30). Hamlet desires the watery nature of a rhetorical self which the solidity of his flesh denies him. His predicament is less pressing than Faustus's; no bell is immediately to sound twelve, and no devils wait to drag the Prince down to hell—though a ghost (after the bell has sounded twelve unheard) will soon come to him, and make the Prince wonder whether he is being tempted to his own damnation. This sense of his over-solid nature is paralleled by Hamlet's sense of a lack of words; the soliloquy which begins with the desire to melt ends with his recognition that, because of the situation he finds himself in, he cannot say what he would wish to, but must keep his words contained: 'But breake my heart, for I must hold my tongue' (1.2.159).

     This initial desire for words is soon contradicted. In Act 2, when he is alone after having heard and seen the players' recital of the death of Priam, the Prince upbraids himself at some length for his inaction. Then he turns on himself for giving his feelings verbal expression:

> I sure, this is most braue,
> That I, the Sonne of the Deere murthered,
> Prompted to my Reuenge by Heauen, and Hell,
> Must (like a Whore) vnpacke my heart with words.
>
>                                   (2.2.584–7)

There is a sense here that the Prince is disillusioned with words themselves, as in his reply, earlier in the same scene, to Polonius' question as to what he reads—'Words, words, words' (2.2.194). Indeed, the Prince, as Lawrence Danson argues in *Tragic Alphabet*, might be said to be disillusioned with language itself, and is certainly keenly aware of its limitations.[41]

     This is not to say that language, in *Hamlet*, is seen as in any sense impotent, or dominated by the expressive resources of the unsaid. Nor is it to say that Hamlet's use of language, and that of other dramatic persons, is ineffective. The reverse is truer; as Inga-Stina Ewbank argues, words and the dramatic persons' use of words are prime movers within the play. Again and again words are seen to persuade, and Ewbank suggests the play be seen as 'a complex study of people trying to control each other by words'.[42] Though Ewbank never mentions 'rhetoric', her description of the dramatic persons' use of language shows them to be good rhetoricians, in the sense that they follow the manuals' advice in paying attention to their audiences:

The characters of the play, then, are on the whole very self-
conscious speakers, in a way which involves consciousness of
others: they believe in the word and its powers, but they are also
aware of the necessity so to translate intentions and experiences
into words as to make them meaningful to the interlocutor.

Prince Hamlet uses a wider range of language more effectively than anyone
else within the play, and yet he is, at the same time, disillusioned and actively
scornful of language. Aware of rhetoric's powers, he is also aware of its
deceits and tricks, that 'marriage vowes' may be 'Dicers Oathes', and 'sweete
Religion ... / A rapsidie of words' (3.4.43–7). Prince Hamlet, in fact, has
become dissatisfied with rhetoric.

   To understand this dissatisfaction and its implications, Hamlet's first
meeting with the Ghost must be returned to again. After the Ghost has left,
as the glow-worms fade in the beginnings of the day, Hamlet says:

> Remember thee?
> Yea, from the Table of my Memory,
> Ile wipe away all triuiall fond Records,
> All sawes of Bookes, all formes, all presures past,
> That youth and obseruation coppied there;
> And thy Commandment all alone shall liue
> Within the Booke and Volume of my Braine
>
> (1.5.95–103)

As has been said, the Ghost's return forces the Prince to abandon his
memories of the past by proving them (as the Prince thinks) false. The
Ghost's return also causes the Prince to try to abandon rhetoric, by
abandoning one of the founding techniques of its system of knowledge—the
commonplace book. For it is as a commonplace book, here, that the Prince
conceptualizes his mind. Commonplace books tend now to be thought of as
random collections of commonplace literary extracts collected as a matter of
personal choice. However, in the sixteenth century they were an essential
part of a rhetorical education.[43] The books took their name from the way in
which they were divided up into common-places, that is into common
subject-headings or topics. These 'topics' derived from the categories of
classification as set out by Aristotle, 'place' being the English translation of
the Greek 'topos'. A commonplace book, then, was not so called to designate
its contents, but rather to designate its particular form of structural division.

   Into the appropriate section the student would note particularly
brilliant aphorisms—the 'sawes of Bookes' as Hamlet refers to them—and

well-expressed arguments that he (or she) came across in her reading or 'observation'.[44] Commonplace books provided storehouses of knowledge; they were intended, to use a more modern image, as memory-banks. They provided a way of anatomizing literature: they provided a means of breaking down the information contained within a literary work into constituent parts and then of storing it, with the purpose of facilitating its retrieval and later use within one's own arguments or thoughts. As that suggests, the commonplace book was influential in sixteenth-century strategies of reading, writing, and thinking. Ann Moss argues that the commonplace book 'might be considered a paradigm of Renaissance literature', for, 'Renaissance literature of the imagination is at its most typical when accumulating variations round a commonplace theme and playing textual allusions against each other.'[45] The habits of thought of Renaissance literature, that is, are the habits or techniques of the commonplace book. The commonplace book is central to the discursive practices which constitute the field of knowledge that is rhetoric.

Within *Hamlet*, Polonius, as Alan Fisher has argued, exemplifies the strengths and limitations of such a system, particularly in his farewell to his son.[46] Though Polonius' thinking, as it is seen in the play, is neither perceptive nor very wise, the precepts that he gives as a parting gift, though perhaps too many, are impressive. The commonplace system preserves acknowledged wisdom well (while at the same time tending to mould new experience into old categories).[47] It explains the contradiction between Polonius' thoughts and the wisdom of his general advice, 'the seeming inconsistency' as Johnson put it, 'of so much wisdom with so much folly'.[48] Twentieth-century critics have hardly remarked on the disparity between Polonius' thoughts and his precepts, often seeing the two as complementary; the wise-saws are the clichés of the foolish counsellor. This change of critical attitude reflects the impact of mass printing and, more recently, of the electronic storage of information. As Ong points out, only a culture which is assured that it is able to preserve its knowledge deprecates sententiae and cliché.[49]

The commonplace book, then, was not only an image for the mind, as Hamlet uses it, but an image of the sixteenth-century rhetorical mind. It is that rhetorical system and body of knowledge that the Prince declares that he will 'wipe away'. Abandoning the received authorities of his childhood, and the learning gleaned from his studies, is a possible, if tragic course. Yet to step outside the system through which he has in some measure constructed himself is barely conceivable. However dissatisfied the Prince may be with rhetoric, he cannot simply replace that, or any, self-structuring system of thought in one go. Instead, the Ghost's command to revenge will be copied 'all alone' into 'the Booke and Volume' of his brain; the book itself will not itself be abandoned.

Disillusioned with rhetoric, then, and yet unable to escape its constitutive field, Hamlet is dissatisfied in many ways with his sense of self. The previous chapter touched on that dissatisfaction as it traced the Prince's loss of his narrative of self. This chapter has examined one aspect of the sources of self available to the Prince—the Protean rhetorical sense of self. Shakespeare's Prince, however, goes beyond dissatisfaction with a rhetorical sense of self; though he cannot abandon the 'Booke' of his brain, he introduces a new metaphor, and so begins to develop a new understanding, of self. It is with this beginning that this chapter closes.

When Hamlet first meets Rosencrantz and Guildenstern, he welcomes them to a Denmark he describes as a prison. His former friends argue with this description of the kingdom, and Rosencrantz maintains that Denmark only seems a prison to the Prince because of his ambition—the kingdom, ''tis / too narrow for your minde' (2.2.253–4). Rosencrantz sets up a Tamburlaine-like sense of the Prince, whose ambitious thoughts encompass far greater kingdoms of the earth than Denmark. Hamlet reverses this, and in doing so puts forward an image for the self which is not based on water, but on a more modern sense of self as area or extension. Hamlet replies to Rosencrantz:

> O God, I could be bounded in a nutshell, and
> count my selfe a King of infinite space; were it not that
> I haue bad dreames.
>
> (2.2.255–7)

The kingdom that Hamlet desires to rule is that of his sense of self; his sense of self is the 'I' that could be bounded in a nutshell. That kingdom is both impossibly small and infinitely large, containing all possible kingdoms. This sense of self is no longer constituted from water, nor is its constructed identity pictured in terms of shape; rather it is being pictured as a paradox of extension. Moreover, it is an area which has become mysterious and ungovernable; the 'I' has 'bad dreams', and yet the 'I' cannot control those dreams. Hamlet's sense of himself as a mysterious paradox of extension is not offered as cause for celebration, but as a reason for his grief. The metaphor parallels his sense of his unintelligibility to himself, and his lack of coherent narrative for his life. His loss of narrative is a loss of his ability to trace himself in time. Cut off from the past, unable to gain control over his future, his present moment extends infinitely. His sense of self becomes spatialized, offering him the opportunity of becoming king of infinite space; and yet 'bad dreams' mock this king with the memory of memories.

## NOTES

1. C. S. Lewis, *English Literature in the Sixteenth Century Excluding Drama* (Oxford: Clarendon Press, 1954), 61.

2. Such a negative sense was also current during the English Renaissance, and became more pronounced at the end of the 16th c., with the rise of satire and the plain anti-courtly style, now particularly associated with John Donne. So, to choose an example at random, the Princess Agripyne, in Thomas Dekker's *Old Fortunatus*, can talk of a soldier's wooing as 'home-spun stuff' because 'there's no outlandish thread in it, no rhetoric. A soldier casts no figures to get his mistress' heart.' (In *Thomas Dekker*, ed. Ernest Rhys (London: Vizetelly & Co., 1887), 3.1, p. 339.) However, in Dekker, as in Shakespeare, the use of a copious style of rhetoric does not in general mark the speaker out as untrustworthy, as it begins to do in the plays of Ben Jonson and others. For a discussion of this see Neil Rhodes, *The Power of Eloquence and English Renaissance Literature* (Hemel Hempstead: Harvester Wheatsheaf, 1992).

3. For an account of the relationship between Renaissance, medieval and classical rhetorics, see Kristeller, *Renaissance Thought*, esp. ch. 5.

4. The initiator of this line of research was T. W. Baldwin. His *William Shakespeare's Small Latine and Lesse Greeke*, 2 vols. (Urbana, Ill.: University of Illinois Press, 1944) carried out the monumental task of piecing together rhetoric's central place within the curriculum of Elizabethan schools. W. S. Howell's *Logic and Rhetoric in England: 1500–1700* (Princeton: Princeton University Press, 1956) looked at the competing systems of rhetoric in the period, with more emphasis on the practice of rhetoric in universities. Hugh Kearney examined the social role that such an education played within the university curriculum of England, Scotland, and Ireland in his *Scholars and Gentlemen: Universities and Society in Pre-Industrial Britain 1500–1700* (London: Faber and Faber, 1970). Brian Vickers, *In Defense of Rhetoric* (Oxford: Clarendon Press, 1988), surveys the practice and intellectual dominance of rhetoric within the English Renaissance (noting, for instance, that one of the few changes to the Statutes of Cambridge University at the beginning of Elizabeth I's reign was to replace the study of mathematics with rhetoric (p. 182)).

5. For the Ramistic reforms which challenged this approach, see Howell and Vickers, n. 4 above. The reforms' impacts were felt after Shakespeare had completed his schooling.

6. David Quint discusses the later debates as constituent moments in the emergence during the Renaissance of the sense of historical relativism necessary for the appreciation of the concept of originality. See his *Origin and Originality in Renaissance Literature: Versions of the Source* (New Haven: Yale University Press, 1983).

7. Jane Donawerth provides a general survey and source-book of these debates. See the first three chapters of her *Shakespeare and the Sixteenth-Century Study of Language* (Urbana, Ill. and Chicago: University of Illinois Press, 1984). Marion Trousdale traces the different pleasures of language fostered by a rhetoric, and so the different textual expectations of Renaissance readers and auditors. See her *Shakespeare and the Rhetoricians* (Chapel Hill, NC: University of North Carolina Press, 1982).

8. Richard Waswo argues that there was a semantic shift in the 16th c., similar to that seen at the beginning of the 20th c. This shift involved a move from a conception of words as signs, to a conception that words created meaning by virtue of their relationship to each other; that is to a constitutive view of the relationship between language and meaning. See his *Language and Meaning in the Renaissance* (Princeton: Princeton University Press, 1987).

9. See Yates, *The Art of Memory*.

10. See David Bevington, *Action is Eloquence* (Cambridge, Mass.: Harvard University Press, 1984).

11. See Frank Whigham, *Ambition and Privilege: The Social Tropes of Elizabethan Courtesy Theory* (Berkeley: University of California Press, 1984).

12. This aspect of rhetoric's activity is represented most clearly in works of 'institution literature' such as Niccolò Machiavelli's *The Prince* (1513), Sir Thomas More's *Utopia* (1516), Baldassare Castiglione's *Il Libro del Cortegiano* (1528), Sir Thomas Elyot's *Boke named the Governour* (1531), Roger Ascham's *The Scholemaster* (1570), and Henry Peacham's *The Compleat Gentleman* (1622). The term 'institution literature' is useful in focusing attention on the importance of social context within these works. It is taken from Thomas Greene, 'The Flexibility of the Self in Renaissance Literature' in Peter Demetz, Thomas Greene, and Lowry Nelson, Jr. (eds.), *The Disciplines of Criticism: Essays in Literary Theory, Interpretation, and History* (New Haven: Yale University Press, 1968), 241–64.

13. The term 'courtesy literature' is a competitor of 'institution literature' as both cover many of the same texts. So, of the texts listed in n. 12, only *Utopia* is unlikely to be considered as courtesy literature. See Whigham, *Ambition and Privilege*, ch. 1, for a productive use of the term. 'Courtesy literature', though perhaps not so helpful a term as 'institution literature', is by far the most commonly used.

14. So, to take as example the most popular manual of rhetoric in English (by reprints), Thomas Wilson in the Epistle to his *Art of Rhetorique* (1553) asks: 'If the worthinesse of Eloquence maie moove vs, what worthier thing can there bee, then with a word to winne Cities and whole Countries?' Thomas Wilson, *Arte of Rhetorique*, ed. G. H. Mair (Oxford: Clarendon Press, 1909; first pub. 1560), A.ii.b. Lazarus Pyott's *The Orator* of 1596 provides another example: 'The use [of rhetoric] whereof in every member in our commonweale is as necessary, as the abuse or wilfull ignorance is odius ... In reasoning of private debates, here maiest thou find apt metaphors, in incouraging thy souldiers fit motives ... briefly every private man may be in this partaker of a general profit.' Quoted in Baldwin, *William Shakespeare's Small Latine*, ii. 45.

15. See e.g. Baldassare Castiglione, *The Book of the Courtier*, trans. Sir Thomas Hoby (London: Dent, 1928; first pub. 1561), 56–74.

16. Puttenham, *English Poesie*, 155. Further references to this book are given after quotations in the text.

17. The Foucault, that is, of *Discipline and Punish*. Rhetoric could be well described by Foucault's genealogical approach, for it is clearly a discipline which fashioned its subjects through a microphysics of power. This, however, is not the place for such an analysis. It is also tempting to describe 'rhetoric' by an earlier term of Foucault's, that is as an 'episteme'. An episteme is 'the total set of relations that unite, at a given period, the discursive practices that give rise to epistemological figures, sciences, and possibly formalize systems' (*The Archaeology of Knowledge*, trans. A. M. Sheridan Smith (London: Tavistock, 1972; first pub. as *L'Archeologie du Savoir*, Paris: Editions Gallimard, 1969), 191). This captures nicely the importance of rhetoric as a system of thought. However, Foucault uses episteme precisely and problematically in *The Order of Things*; he divides up the period from the Renaissance into four remarkably (and unconvincingly) discontinuous epistemes. It would thus be contradictory in Foucault's terms to talk of a rhetorical episteme in the Renaissance period. Also, the rigidity and discontinuity suggested by 'episteme' does not suit the remarkable power and presence of rhetoric as a field of knowledge or 'technology' throughout history, descending from Aristotle (and earlier) to the middle of the 18th c.

18. Michael McCanles, *The Text of Sidney's Arcadian World* (Durham: Duke University Press, 1989) 187.

19. The same points may be made about Christy Desmet's *Reading Shakespeare's Characters: Rhetoric, Ethics, and Identity* (Amherst, Mass.: University of Massachusetts Press, 1992); Desmet dismisses the notion of self, innerness, and historical difference in the first page of her introduction, pursuing instead a de Mannean- and Burkean-inspired reading

of the reader's identification with character (see also p. 27). This different perspective apart, Desmet's book has many of the same concerns as this thesis, and her discussions of those concerns are valuable.

20. George T. Wright, '*Hamlet* and Hendiadys', *PMLA* 96 (1981), 168–93.

21. Georgio Melchiori, 'The Rhetoric of Character Construction: *Othello*', *SS* 34 (1981), 61–72; Patricia Parker, *Literary Fat Ladies: Rhetoric, Gender, Property* (London and New York: Methuen, 1987), 120. Donald K. Hedrick argues that such figure-spotting is a pointless game at which one cannot lose: '"It is No Novelty for a Prince to be a Prince": An Enantiomorphous Hamlet', *SQ*, 35 (1984), 62–76.

22. Rhodes, *The Power of Eloquence*, 40.

23. Walter J. Ong, *Rhetoric, Romance, and Technology: Studies in the Interaction of Expression and Culture* (Ithaca, NY: Cornell University Press, 1971), 2.

24. Desiderius Erasmus, *De Copia*, trans. Betty I. Knott, 3rd edn. (1534) in *Collected Works*, 86 vols. (Toronto: University of Toronto Press, 1974–1993), xxiv. 296.

25. For an argument that our conceptual system is itself metaphorical in nature, and so that metaphor is central to understanding (and an understanding of culture), see George Lakoff and Mark Johnson, *Metaphors We Live By* (Chicago: University of Chicago Press, 1980).

26. Marcus Fabius Quintilian, *Institutio Oratoria*, trans. H. E. Butler, 4 vols. (London: William Heinemann, 1920), i. 315 (Bk. II, ch. xv, 35).

27. Ong, *Rhetoric, Romance and Technology*, 14.

28. Ibid.

29. This passage is the same in both the A- and B-text; it is cited from the A-text of David Bevington's and Eric Rasmussen's edition.

30. For another example of the desire for dissolution, see Beatrice Joanna's request—at the end of Thomas Middleton's and William Rowley's *The Changeling* (1622)—that her defining life-blood be mingled in 'the common sewere' and so be taken 'from distinction' (5.3.153). This is cited from N. W. Bawcutt's edition.

31. *Certain Sermons or Homilies (1547) and A Homily against Disobedience and Wilful Rebellion (1570): A Critical Edition*, ed. Ronald B. Bond (Toronto: University of Toronto Press, 1987), 174.

32. It may also be related to the theory of humours.

33. See *OED*, 'limn' *v.*, senses 1, 3, and 5. The *OED* also credits Shakespeare with the first use of 'water-colour' in *The First Part of Henry the Fourth*: 'And neuer yet did Insurrection want / Such water-colours, to impaint his cause' (5.1.79–80).

34. Nicholas Hilliard, *A Treatise Concerning the Arte of Limning*, ed. R. K. R. Thornton and T. G. S. Cain (Northumberland: Mid Northumberland Arts Group, 1981; unpub. previously, wr. 1589–1603). Roy Strong argues that the attempt to capture the personality of the sitter is a humanist ideal, first brought to England by Hans Holbein the Younger. See Roy Strong, *Holbein: The Complete Paintings* (London: Granada, 1980), 6. Hilliard took Holbein as his example; Holbein's was the 'manner of limning I haue euer imitated & hold it for the best'. See Hilliard, 69.

35. Thornton and Cain argue that the shape of the frame was particularly important to Hilliard, who exploited the tension between the frame's formal pattern and the realism of the portrait within. See Hilliard, *Treatise*, 63.

36. Juan Luis Vives, 'A Fable About Man', trans. Nancy Lekeith, in *The Renaissance Philosophy of Man*, ed. Ernst Cassirer, Paul Oskar Kristeller, and John Herman Randall, Jr. (Chicago: University of Chicago Press, 1948), 389.

37. Giovanni Pico Della Mirandola, 'Oration on the Dignity of Man', trans. Elizabeth Livermore Forbes, in Cassirer *et al.*, *The Renaissance Philosophy*, 224.

38. For a succinct overview of the anti-theatrical form of this darker tradition as it has descended from Plato's writings, see Desmet, *Reading Shakespeare's Characters*, 17–24.

39. A. Bartlett Giamatti, 'Proteus Unbound: Some Versions of the Sea God in the Renaissance', in *Exile and Change in Renaissance Literature* (New Haven: Yale University Press, 1984), 115–50 (118).

40. Greene, 'The Flexibility of the Self', 260.

41. See the introduction and ch. 2 of Lawrence Danson, *Tragic Alphabet: Shakespeare's Drama of Language* (New Haven and London: Yale University Press, 1974). For a related argument see also John Paterson, 'The Word in *Hamlet*', *SQ* 2 (1951), 47–56.

42. Inga-Stina Ewbank, '*Hamlet* and the Power of Words', *SS* 30 (1977), 85–102 (88). See for a related discussion of language's expressive abilities within Shakespeare, Anne Barton, 'Shakespeare and the Limits of Language', *SS* 21 (1974), 19–30.

43. The following account of the role and importance of commonplace books is based upon a paper, entitled 'Commonplace Books', given by Dr Ann Moss to the British Section of the International Society of the History of Rhetoric on 6 Mar. 1993. Quotations are given from a printed copy of this. See also Ann Moss, *Printed Commonplace-Books and the Structuring of Renaissance Thought* (Oxford: Clarendon Press, 1996).

44. Moss quotes Erasmus' description of this process: 'After you have prepared yourself a sufficient number of headings and have arranged them in whatever order you prefer, and have next subdivided them one by one into their appropriate sections and have labelled these sections with commonplaces, ... then whatever you come across in any author, particularly if it is especially striking, you will be able to note it down immediately in its appropriate place, ... This will ensure both that what you read will stay fixed more firmly in your mind, and that you will learn to make use of the riches you have acquired by reading ... Finally, whenever occasion demands, you will have ready to hand a supply of material for spoken and written composition, because you will have, as it were, a well-organized set of pigeon-holes from which you may extract what you want' (p. 13). Moss argued that 'exactly the same prescriptions are enunciated by paedagogic theorists throughout the sixteenth century' (p. 2).

45. Ibid. 19.

46. Alan Fisher, 'Shakespeare's Last Humanist', in *Renaissance and Reformation*, 26:1 (1990) 37–47. Fisher sees Polonius as 'representative of a whole manner of thinking of which the play is aware and which it examines critically', which manner of thinking Fisher labels humanist. 'Humanist', I would argue, is here a misleading term, for Fisher is referring to the impact of rhetoric within humanist educational techniques and ideals. Fisher also treats the mind as a commonplace book, though he goes on to make assumptions as to the authority of the subject within such a way of thinking that the arguments advanced in this thesis reject.

47. Ann Moss notes how 'Every new text, every new discovery, every new observation, it seems, could be dismembered, fitted into the corpus of received wisdom, and rendered harmless by assimilation among the "endoxa" of universally sanctioned probabilities supported by dialectical argumentation' (p. 21).

48. Samuel Johnson, from his notes to his edition of Shakespeare, in *Samuel Johnson on Shakespeare*, ed. H. R. Woudhuysen (Harmondsworth: Penguin, 1989), 239.

49. Ong, *Rhetoric, Romance and Technology*, 20.

# Character Profile

Perhaps the most complex, cunning, and commanding character written into existence, Hamlet not only defies definition but is more apt to define us, his readers. Any attempt at summarizing such a large and bountiful character will necessarily miss the mark, and may only hope to provide a rudimentary sketch of what proves to be a character unlimited.

## ACT I

Following an ominous beginning in which the ghost of King Hamlet has appeared before the sentinels, our first introduction to Hamlet's melancholic and brooding disposition occurs with the King and Queen at court. After granting Laertes leave to travel to France, King Claudius turns his attention to the young Prince, asking why it is "that the clouds still hang on you" to which the brooding and accusing Hamlet responds punningly, "Not so my lord. I am too much in the sun." His mother, Queen Gertrude, further advises her son to shed his melancholy thoughts and thereby adopt a happier visage and a more politic demeanor by accepting the death of his father, the now-deceased King Hamlet, as an aspect of the human condition. Seeing the Prince in an unabating melancholic state, the Queen questions why he is taking the King's death so personally. Hamlet's responds that all appearances are but the "trappings and suits of woe." And King Claudius, listening to this exchange between Gertrude and Hamlet, resorts to an attack on Hamlet's masculinity and royal heritage. "'Tis unmanly grief. / It shows a will most incorrect to heaven, / A heart unfortified, a mind impatient."

Following this verbal assault, Hamlet delivers his first soliloquy. While contemplating a way out of his unbearable misery, Hamlet considers whether suicide is an option and debates with himself the nature of the human condition. Hamlet, enraged at his mother's weakness and infidelity to the memory of her loving husband, gives us his first indication that he has lost faith in all women. "Frailty, thy name is woman."

As the scene shifts to a conversation between Laertes and his sister Ophelia, we receive another interpretation of Hamlet's character as it relates to his royal status. Laertes speaks privately to his sister, Ophelia, and advises her not to take Prince Hamlet's amorous advances too seriously, for Hamlet is royalty and the burden of that royalty rests with the body politic, "whereof he is the head." Meanwhile, their father, Polonius warns Ophelia against appearances and reminds her of Hamlet's royal restrictions.

When the scene reverts back to Hamlet, in conversation with his trusted friend, Horatio, Hamlet is seen to be absolutely determined to respond to the Ghost's beckoning for a private audience. This resolution is manifested in SCENE V as Hamlet listens to the spirit of his dead father and learns how he was murdered by his brother, King Claudius. The Ghost commands Hamlet to take revenge against this heinous crime, stating his belief that Prince Hamlet is equal to the task. "I find thee apt, / And duller shouldst thou be than the fat weed / That roots itself in ease on Lethe warf, / Wouldst thou not stir in this."

## ACT II

SCENE I reverts back to the court with a conversation between Ophelia and Polonius, in which Ophelia describes Hamlet's deranged appearance and demeanor: "Lord Hamlet with his doublet all unbraced, / No hat upon his head, his stockings fouled, / Ungartered and down-gyvéd to his ankle, / Pale as his shirt, his knees knocking each other, / And with a look so piteous in purport / As if had been looséd out of hell." Polonius erroneously attributes Hamlet's state to overwhelming love.

As SCENE II opens, the King and Queen have commissioned Rosencrantz and Guildenstern to discover the cause of Hamlet's inexplicable behavior, which Claudius describes as "Hamlet's transformation," "Sith nor th'exterior nor the inward man / Resembles that it was." As they embark on the King's commission, Polonius once again protests that he has discovered the true cause of Hamlet's "lunacy." While Claudius wants to believe Polonius' diagnosis, Gertrude is able to articulate the truth, attributing Hamlet's behavior to "[h]is father's death and our o'erhasty marriage." Polonius soon returns and reads a letter from Hamlet to Ophelia in order to prove his theory that Hamlet is mad "with hot love on the wing."

At Polonius' suggestion, the King and Queen's agree to hide behind an arras, in order to observe Hamlet's behavior towards Ophelia. Hamlet first enters, reading a book and appearing completely mad, correctly labeling Polonius "a fishmongerer" and advising him: "for yourself, sir, shall grow old as I am, if like a crab you could go backward." In an aside, Polonius admits to himself that this display of madness notwithstanding, Hamlet may in fact be in control. Polonius recognizes a "method" to Hamlet's "madness" and that madness indeed has a special access to truth: "How pregnant sometimes his replies are! a happiness that often madness hits on, which reason and sanity could not so prosperously be delivered of."

Upon their entrance, Hamlet begins an inquiry as to the true motive behind Rosencrantz's and Guildenstern's visit. Through a series of probing questions and witty repartee, Hamlet accuses Fortune of being the "strumpet" who has sent these same two friends to prison, i.e. Denmark. And his distrust of women, which is increasing, is likewise equated with being in Denmark. "O God, I could be bounded in a nutshell and count myself a king of infinite space, were it not that I have bad dreams." When he finally gets his two companions to admit that they were sent to discover the cause of his insanity, Hamlet gives them a true description of his state of mind but does not outwardly appear to fully understand himself. "I have of late—but wherefore I know not—lost all mirth, forgone all custom of exercises; and indeed it goes so heavily with my disposition ... Man delights not me, nor woman either neither...." However, Rosencrantz and Guildenstern have brought with them a company of boy actors whom they passed on the way. And, no sooner does Hamlet greet these young players than we begin to see that Hamlet recognizes himself as a fellow actor. A little further on, Hamlet displays his full theatrical skills as a consummate playwright and director, instructing the players to perform *The Murder of Gonzago*, asking them to memorize some dozen or so lines of his own composition which he will insert into the play. As Rosencrantz and Guildenstern leave, Hamlet delivers another soliloquy, in which he begins with self-reproach "O, what a rogue and peasant slave I am? ... / Prompted to my revenge by heaven and hell, / Must like a whore unpack my heart with words," but concludes with an absolute determination to prove Claudius' culpability. "The play's the thing / Wherein I'll catch the conscience of the King."

## ACT III

SCENE I opens with Claudius questioning the returning Rosencrantz and Guildenstern, as to whether they have discovered the cause of Hamlet's "turbulence and dangerous lunacy," to which they respond that he professes himself to be "distracted." Yet, a serious question arises as to whether Prince

Hamlet may in fact be manipulating everyone into believing him insane. Guildenstern echoes Polonius' previous observation that there is a method to this madness, implying once again that Hamlet may very well be in full control of his emotions. "Nor do we find him forward to be sounded / But with a crafty madness keeps aloof." In the meantime, Polonius suggests, and Claudius agrees, that the two should hide and observe Hamlet and Ophelia, to determine whether it be "the affliction of love or no."

When Hamlet enters, delivering yet another brilliant soliloquy, he reveals an inner torment and struggle with his inability to avenge his father's murder. "To be or not to be, that is the question: / Whether 'tis nobler in the mind to suffer / The slings and arrows of outrageous fortune, / Or to take arms against a sea of troubles, ... To die, to sleep—No more; and by a sleep to say we end / The heartache, and the thousand natural shocks / That flesh is heir to." At the end of this soliloquy, turning to Ophelia, Hamlet's anger against women resurfaces. He states that although he did love her once because of her beauty, he now believes that same beauty to be another aspect of dissembling womanhood and wants to banish her from his thoughts. "Get thee to a nunnery. Why wouldst thou be a breeder of sinners?" An astounded Ophelia responds, "O, what a noble mid is here o'erthrown!" Immediately following this declaration, King Claudius enters, with Polonius, stating that Hamlet's condition is not that of love, and demanding that he be sent speedily to England to avoid his danger to the state. "Madness in great ones must not unwatched go."

As SCENE III opens, Hamlet is meeting with the actors, with very specific stage directions. We are given a very rational and resolute Prince who is in full control of his faculties. "Speak the speech, I pray you, as I pronounced it to you, trippingly on the tongue, ... Be not too tame neither, but let your own discretion by your tutor.... hold as 'twere the mirror up to nature ... and the very age and body of the time his form and pressure." As further affirmation of his self-command, Hamlet responds to his earlier quandary. "Give me that man / That is not passion's slave, and I will wear him / In my heart's core, ay, in my heart of heart."

Following the successful performance of his dumb show, Hamlet discusses Claudius's distress with Rosencrantz and Guildenstern. Hamlet shrewdly states that he cannot help the King, "for for me to put him to his purgation would perhaps plunge him into more choler." But his companions cannot understand this puzzlingly response because they do not truly understand Hamlet's dissembling nature. "Good my lord, put your discourse into some frame, and start not so wildly from my affair." Indeed, Hamlet is in complete control playing on the emotions of his interlocutors. To Rosencrantz his response is that he cannot "[m]ake you a wholesome answer;

my wit's diseased" and to Guildenstern, whom he has just challenged by presenting him with a recorder to play on, he declares that he cannot be manipulated: "[c]all me what instrument you will, though you can fret me, you cannot play upon me." As SCENE II concludes, Hamlet is now alone and preparing to speak with his mother. In this he will do the Ghost's bidding, careful not to cause her physical harm. "Let me be cruel, not unnatural; / I will speak daggers to her, but use none. / My tongue and soul in this be hypocrites."

In SCENE IV, as Hamlet is on his way to speak with the Queen, his thoughts return to his father and he again debates with himself about the appropriate time and circumstances to perform the long-awaited revenge upon the now-terrified Claudius. "Up, sword, and know thou a more horrid hent. / When he is drunk asleep, or in his rage, / Or in th' incestuous pleasure of his bed, / ... That has no relish of salvation in't–." When Hamlet finally confronts his mother, he tells her directly that he will make her look at herself in a mirror, "[w]here you may see the inmost part of you." Though briefly interrupted when he kills the indignant Polonius with his sword, Hamlet quickly returns to the far more important purpose of showing his mother the full extent of her sins. While he declares Claudius to be "[a] king of shreds and patches," the Ghost enters, invisible to Gertrude who believes Hamlet to be completely mad. "Alas, how is't with you, / That you do bend your eye on vacancy, / And with th'incorporal air do hold discourse? Forth at your eyes your spirits wildly peep, / ... Your bedded hair like life in excrements / Start up and stand an end. / ... Whereon do you look?" Hamlet responds that he is perfectly rational and in control and, further, challenges the Queen to test that rationality. "It is not madness / That I have uttered. Bring me to the test, / And I the matter will re-word, which madness / Would gambol from." Dragging Polonius' body into an adjoining room, Hamlet calmly bids his mother goodnight and declares that he must now depart for England.

## ACT IV

SCENE I opens with a very distressed Gertrude telling Claudius of the noble Polonius's murder by a deranged Hamlet. "Mad as the sea and wind when both contend / Which is the mightier. In his lawless fit, / ... cries 'A rat, a rat!' / And in this brainish apprehension kills / The unseen good old man." To which Claudius responds that Hamlet's "liberty is full of threats to all." However, as Claudius observes in SCENE III, Hamlet is beloved by his subjects and cannot be so easily disposed of. "How dangerous is it that this man goes loose! / Yet must we not put the strong law on him. / He's loved of the distracted multitude." Meanwhile, when Claudius questions Hamlet as to the whereabouts of Polonius, Hamlet, in full command of his incisive wit, responds that the old "fishmongerer" has been justly disposed of. "Not where he eats, but where 'a is eaten. / A certain convocation of politic worms are e'en at him." SCENE IV opens with yet another one of Hamlet's soliloquies, in which he debates the cause and consequences of his delay in achieving the revenge upon Claudius. "How all occasions do inform against me, / And spur my dull revenge! ... Rightly to be great / Is not to stir without great argument, / But greatly to find a quarrel in a straw / When honor's at the stake."

In speaking with Laertes, SCENE VII, Claudius discloses that Hamlet has murdered his father Polonius and again reminds Laertes that he could not take action against the young Prince whose spellbinding charm has won the hearts of the people. Nevertheless, he miscalculates Hamlet's character, believing the Prince to be careless and incapable of planning a preconceived course of action. Meanwhile, Claudius likewise misjudges Hamlet, plotting with Laertes to seek his revenge on the Prince. "He, being remiss, / Most generous, and free from all contriving, / Will not peruse the foils, so that with ease ... you may choose / A sword unbated, and in a pass of practice / Requite him for your father."

## ACT V

As Hamlet tells Horatio of his experiences at sea, he appears resolute and triumphant in his ability to outwit Claudius and thus save his own life, despite seemingly insurmountable circumstances. After stealing Claudius' letter to the King of England from Rosencrantz and Guildenstern, Hamlet replaces it with a forged letter, sealed with his father's signet, thereby ordering their immediate execution. Hamlet also makes perfectly clear that he harbors no anxiety about his actions. "Why, many, they did make love to this employment. / They are not near my conscience; their defeat / Does by their own insinuation grow." Nevertheless, Hamlet is doomed to defeat by Claudius' conspiracy to kill the Prince by means of Laertes' poisoned rapier. In his final moments, after learning of the plot from Laertes, Hamlet stabs Claudius with the poisoned blade and then forces him to drink the dregs of the poisoned wine. In so doing, Hamlet finally consummates his long anticipated revenge and is now ready to leave the stage. In his final moments, Hamlet remains the consummate actor and director that he has consistently been from Act I as he dictates the terms of his departure to Horatio. "If thou didst ever hold me in thy heart, / Absent thee from felicity awhile, / And in this harsh world draw thy breath in pain, / To tell my story."

# Contributors

HAROLD BLOOM is Sterling Professor of the Humanities at Yale University and Henry W. and Albert A. Berg Professor of English at the New York University Graduate School. He is the author of over 20 books, including *Shelley's Mythmaking* (1959), *The Visionary Company* (1961), *Blake's Apocalypse* (1963), *Yeats* (1970), *A Map of Misreading* (1975), *Kabbalah and Criticism* (1975), *Agon: Toward a Theory of Revisionism* (1982), *The American Religion* (1992), *The Western Canon* (1994), and *Omens of Millennium: The Gnosis of Angels, Dreams, and Resurrection* (1996). *The Anxiety of Influence* (1973) sets forth Professor Bloom's provocative theory of the literary relationships between the great writers and their predecessors. His most recent books include *Shakespeare: The Invention of the Human* (1998), a 1998 National Book Award finalist, *How to Read and Why* (2000), *Genius: A Mosaic of One Hundred Exemplary Creative Minds* (2002), and *Hamlet: Poem Unlimited* (2003). In 1999, Professor Bloom received the prestigious American Academy of Arts and Letters Gold Medal for Criticism, and in 2002 he received the Catalonia International Prize.

WILLIAM HAZLITT was an English essayist and literary critic of the Romantic period. Among his own best works are *Characters of Shakespeare's Plays* (1817–18), *Lectures on the English Poets* (1818–19) and *The Spirit of the Age* (1825).

A.C. BRADLEY was a pre-eminent Shakespearean scholar of the last 18th and early 19th centuries. Bradley held professorships of modern literature at the University of Liverpool, of English language and literature at the University of Glasgow and of poetry at Oxford University, best known for his book *Shakespearean Tragedy* (1904). Bradley also published *Oxford Lectures on Poetry* (1909), which includes an essay on Shakespeare's *Antony and Cleopatra*, and *A Miscellany* (1929), in which a well-known commentary on Tennyson's *In Memoriam* appears.

HAROLD C. GODDARD was Professor of English at Swarthmore College and the University of Chicago. He is the author of *Studies in New England Transcendentalism* (1908) and *The Meaning of Shakespeare* (1951).

RICHARD A. LANHAM  is Professor of English at the University of California, Los Angeles. He is the author of *Literacy and the Survival of Humanism* (1983); *The Electronic Word: Democracy, Technology, and the Arts* (1993); and *Tristram Shandy: The Games of Pleasure* (1973).

WILLIAM EMPSON was a pre-eminent English scholar and poet and held professorships at Cambridge University and the University of Sheffield. His *Seven Types of Ambiguity* (1930), a study of the meanings of poetry, is a classic of modern literary criticism. It was followed by *Some Versions of Pastoral* (1935) and *The Structure of Complex Words* (1951). In *Milton's God* (1961) Empson engaged in a vehement attack on Puritanism. His poetry *Poems* (1935) and *The Gathering Storm* (1940) was noted for its wit and metaphysical conceits. A collected edition of his poems appeared in 1955. William Empson was knighted in 1979.

Long considered one of Canada's literary treasures, for over fifty years NORTHROP FRYE served as a dedicated educator at the University of Toronto where he was a Professor of English. Among his many publication he is perhaps best known for the seminal work *Anatomy of Criticism* (1957).

YVES BONNEFOY has held the Chair of Comparative Studies in Poetics at the Collège de France, Paris. He is the author of *Remarques sur le regard: Picasso Giacometti Morandi* (2002) and editor of *The Lure and the Truth of Painting: Selected Essays on Art* (1995).

JULIA LUPTON is Associate Professor of Comparative Literature and Director, Humanities Out There (Renaissance literature, literature and psychology) at Yale University. She is co-author (with Kenneth Reinhard) of *After Oedipus: Shakespeare in Psychoanalysis* (1993) and *Afterlives of the Saints: Hagiography, Typology, and Renaissance Literature* (1996).

BERT O. STATES is Professor Emeritus of Dramatic Arts at the University of California, Santa Barbara. He is the author of *The Rhetoric of Dreams*. Cornell University Press (1988); *Dreaming and Storytelling* (1993) and *The Pleasure of the Play* (1994).

ANTHONY LOW is Professor of English at New York University. He is the author of *The Reinvention of Love: Poetry, Politics, and Culture from Sidney to Milton* (1993) and *The Georgic Revolution* (1985).

JOHN LEE is a Lecturer in English at the University of Bristol. He is the author of *Shakespeare's* Hamlet *and the Controversies of Self* (2000).

# Bibliography

Ackerman, Alan L., Jr. "Visualizing Hamlet's Ghost: The Spirit of Modern Subjectivity." *Theatre Journal* 53, no. 1 (March 2001r): 119–44.

Adelman, Janet. *Suffocating Mothers: Fantasies of Maternal Origin in Shakespeare's Plays, "Hamlet" to "The Tempest."* New York: Routledge, Chapman and Hall, 1992.

Alexander, Nigel. *Poison, Play, and Duel: A Study in "Hamlet."* Lincoln: University of Nebraska Press, 1971.

Barber, C.L. and Richard P. Wheeler. *The Whole Journey: Shakespeare's Power of Development.* Berkeley and Los Angeles: University of California Press, 1986.

Berry, Ralph. "*Hamlet's* Doubles." *Shakespeare Quarterly* 32 (Summer 1986): 204–12.

Berkoff, Steven. *I Am Hamlet.* New York: Grove Weidenfeld, 1990.

Blight, John. "Shakespearean Character Study to 1800." *Shakespeare Survey* 37 (1984): 141–53.

Bolt, Sydney. *William Shakespeare, Hamlet.* London: Penguin, 1990.

Booth, Stephen. "On the Value of *Hamlet.*" In *Reinterpretations of Elizabethan Drama*, Edited by Norman Rabkin. New York and London: Columbia University Press, (1969): 137–76.

Bloom, Harold. *Shakespeare: The Invention of the Human.* New York: Riverhead Books, 1998.

———. Hamlet: *Poem Unlimited.* New York: Riverhead Books, 2003.

Bradley, A.C. *Shakespearean Tragedy.* 2d ed. London: Macmillan; New York: St. Martin's Press, 1952.

Bulman, James C. *The Heroic Idiom of Shakespearean Tragedy*. Newark: University of Delaware Press, 1985.

Calderwood, James. L. *To Be and Not to Be: Negation and Metadrama in "Hamlet."* New York: Columbia University Press, 1983.

Cantor, Paul A. *Shakespeare, Hamlet*. Cambridge: Cambridge University Press, 1989.

Cassirer, Ernst, Paul Oskar Kristeller and John Herman Randall, Jr., editors. *The Renaissance Philosophy of Man*. Chicago: University of Chicago Press, 1948.

Cavell, Stanley. "The Avoidance of Love." In *Must We Mean What We Say?* Cambridge: Cambridge University Press, 1976.

———. "Hamlet's Burden of Proof." In *Disowning Knowledge in Six Plays of Shakespeare*. Cambridge and New York: Cambridge University Press (1991): 179–91.

Charney, Maurice. *Style in "Hamlet."* Princeton: Princeton University Press, 1969.

———. *Hamlet's Fictions*. New York: Routledge, Chapman and Hall, 1988.

Clemen, Wolfgang. *The Development of Shakespeare's Imagery*. 2d ed. London: Methuen, 1977.

Conklin, Paul S. *A History of "Hamlet" Criticism 1601–1821*. New York: Humanities Press, 1968.

Cruttwell, Patrick. "The Morality of Hamlet—'Sweet Prince' or 'Arrant Knave'?" *Stratford-Upon-Avon Studies* 5 (1963): 110–28.

Dane, Gabrielle. "Reading Ophelia's Madness." *Exemplaria* 10, no. 2 (1998): 405–23.

Desmet, Christy. *Reading Shakespeare's Characters: Rhetoric, Ethics, and Identity*. Amherst: University of Massachusetts Press, 1992.

Dietrich, Julia. *'Hamlet' in the 1960s: An Annotated Bibliography*. New York: Garland Press, 1992.

Eissler, Kurt R. *Discourse on Hamlet and "Hamlet": A Psychoanalytic Inquiry*. New York: International Universities Press, 1971.

Empson, William. "When Hamlet Was New." *Sewanee Review* 61 (Winter and Spring 1953): 15–42, 185–205.

———. "Hamlet." In *Essays on Shakespeare*, edited by David B. Pirie. Cambridge and New York: 1986.

Erickson, Peter. 1985. *Patriarchal Structures in Shakespeare's Drama*. Berkeley and Los Angeles: University of California Press, 1985.

Felperin, Howard. *Shakespearean Representation*. Princeton: Princeton University Press, 1977.

Fergusson, Francis. *The Idea of a Theater*. Princeton: Princeton University Press, 1949.

Foakes, R A *Hamlet versus Lear: Cultural Politics and Shakespeare's Art.* Cambridge: Cambridge University Press, 1993.

Frye, Northrop. *Fools of Time: Studies in Shakespearean Tragedy.* Toronto: University of Toronto Press, 1967.

Goldberg, Jonathan. "Hamlet's Hand." *Shakespeare Quarterly* 39 (1988): 307–27.

Granville-Barker, Harley. *Prefaces to Shakespeare.* vol. 1. Princeton: Princeton University Press, 1947.

Grazia, Margreta de. "Hamlet Before its Time." Modern Language Quarterly 62, no. 4 (2001 Dec): 355–75.

Hallett, Charles A. and Elaine 5. *The Revenger's Madness: A Study of Revenge Tragedy Motifs.* Lincoln: University of Nebraska Press, 1980.

Hobson, Alan. *Full Circle: Shakespeare and Moral Development.* London: Chatto & Windus, 1972.

Holland, Norman. *Psychoanalysis and Shakespeare.* New York: McGraw-Hill, 1966.

Holloway, John. *The Story of the Night: Studies in Shakespeare's Major Tragedies.* London: Routledge & Kegan Paul, 1961.

Honigmann, E.A.J. *Shakespeare: Seven Tragedies: The Dramatist's Manipulation of Response.* London: Macmillan Press, 1976.

Hussey, S.S. *The Literary Language of Shakespeare.* 2d ed. London and New York: Longman, 1992.

Jackson, James L. 1990. "'They Catch One Another's Rapiers': The Exchange of Weapons in *Hamlet.*" *Shakespeare Quarterly* 41 (1990): 281–98.

Jenkins, Harold. *Hamlet and Ophelia.* Oxford: Oxford University Press, 1964.

Jones, Ernest. *Hamlet and Oedipus.* London: Gollancz, 1949.

Jones, Emrys. *Scenic Form in Shakespeare.* Oxford: Clarendon Press, 1971.

Kahn, Coppélia. *Man's Estate: Masculine Identity in Shakespeare.* Berkeley and Los Angeles: University of California Press, 1981.

Kermode, Frank. *Shakespeare, Spenser, Donne.* London: Routledge & Kegan Paul, 1971.

Kitto, H.D.F. *Form and Meaning in Drama.* London: Methuen, 1956; New York: Barnes and Noble, 1960.

Knight, G. Wilson. *The Wheel of Fire: Interpretations of Shakespeare's Tragedy.* 4th ed. London and New York: Routledge, 2001.

———. Shakespeare's *Dramatic Challenge: On the Rise of Shakespeare's Tragic Heroes.* London: Croom Helm; New York: Barnes & Noble, 1977.

Knights, L. C. *Some Shakespearean Themes and An Approach to "Hamlet."* Stanford: Stanford University Press, 1966.

————. *Hamlet and Other Shakespearean Essays*. Cambridge: Cambridge University Press, 1979.

Kott, Jan. "Hamlet and Orestes." Translated by Boleslaw Taborski. *PMLA* 82 (1967): 303–13.

Kottman, Paul A. "Sharing Vision, Interrupting Speech: Hamlet's Spectacular Community." *Shakespeare Studies* 36 (1998): 29–57.

Lacan, Jacques. "Desire and the Interpretation of Desire in *Hamlet*." Translated by James Hulbert. *Yale French Studies* 55–56 (1977): 11–52.

Landau, Aaron. "Let Me Not Burst in Ignorance': Skepticism and Anxiety in *Hamlet*." *English Studies* 82, no. 3 (June 2001): 218–30.

Levin, Harry. *The Question of "Hamlet."* London and New York: Oxford University Press, 1970.

Levin, Richard. *New Readings vs. Old Plays: Recent Trends in the Reinterpretation of English Renaissance Drama*. Chicago: University of Chicago Press, 1979.

Levy, Eric P. "Universal versus Particular: Hamlet and the Madness in Reason." *Exemplaria* 14, no. 1 (2002 Spring): 99–125.

————. "The Problematic Relation between Reason and Emotion in *Hamlet*." *Renascence* 53, no. 2 (2001): 83–95.

————. "'Things Standing Thus Unknown': The Epistemology of Ignorance in *Hamlet*." *Studies in Philology* 97, no. 2 (2000): 192–209.

————. "'What Should We Do?': The Predicament of Practical Reason in *Hamlet*." *Renaissance and Reformation* 23, no. 4 (Autumn 1999): 45–62.

Low, Anthony. "Hamlet and the Ghost of Purgatory: Intimations of Killing the Father." *English Literary Renaissance* 29, no. 3 (Autumn 1999): 443–67.

Mack, Maynard. "The World of Hamlet." *Yale Review* 41 (1952): 502–23.

————, Jr. *Killing the King: Three Studies in Shakespeare's Tragic Structure*. New Haven: Yale University Press, 1973.

Mangan, Michael. *A Preface to Shakespeare's Tragedies*. London: Longman, 1991.

Margolies, David. *Monsters of the Deep: Social Dissolution in Shakespeare's Tragedies*. Manchester, UK: Manchester University Press, 1992.

Maus, Katharine Eisaman. *Inwardness and Theater in the English Renaissance*. Chicago: University of Chicago Press, 1995.

McGee, Arthur. *The Elizabethan Hamlet*. New Haven: Yale University Press, 1987.

Muir, Kenneth. *Shakespeare's Tragic Sequence*. New York: Barnes & Noble, 1979.

Nardo, Anna K. "Hamlet, 'A Man to Double Business Bound.'" *Shakespeare Quarterly* 34 (1983): 191–99.

Novo, Ruth. *Tragic Form in Shakespeare*. Princeton: Princeton University Press, 1972.

Newell, Axel. *The Soliloquies in* Hamlet: *The Structural Design*. Rutherford, NJ: Fairleigh Dickinson University Press, 1991.

Prosner, Matthew N. *The Heroic Image in Five Shakespearean Tragedies*. Princeton: Princeton University Press, 1965.

Prosser, Eleanor. *Hamlet and Revenge*. 2d ed. Stanford, Calif.: Stanford University Press, 1971.

Ratcliffe, Stephen. "'Who's There?': Elsinore and Elsewhere." *Modern Language Studies* 29, no. 2 (Fall 1999 Fall): 153–73.

———. "What Doesn't Happen in *Hamlet*: The Queen's Speech." *Exemplaria* 10, no. 1 (Spring 1998): 123–44.

Robinson, D.W. "A Medievalist Looks at Hamlet." In Robinson's *Essays in Medieval Culture*. Princeton: Princeton University Press (1980): 312–31.

Rose, Jacqueline. "Hamlet—the Mona Lisa of Literature." *Critical Quarterly* 28 (Spring–Summer 1986): 35–49.

Rosen, William. *Shakespeare and the Craft of Tragedy*. Cambridge, MA: Harvard University Press, 1960.

Russell, John. *Hamlet and Narcissus*. London: Associated University Presses, 1995.

Ryan, Kiernan. *Shakespeare*. Atlantic Highlands, NJ: Humanities Press, 1989.

Sewell, Arthur. *Character and Society in Shakespeare*. Oxford: Clarendon Press, 1951.

Schlueter, June and James P. Lusardi. "The Camera in Gertrude's Closet." In *Shakespeare and The Triple Play: From Study to Stage to Classroom*. Edited by Sidney Homan. Lewisburg, PA: Bucknell University Press (1988): 150–74.

Shoaf, R. Allen. "Hamlet: Like Mother, Like Son." *Journal x* 4, no. 1 (1999): 71–90.

Sibony, Daniel. "Hamlet: A Writing-Effect." *Yale French Studies* 55–56 (1978): 53–93.

Skura, Meredith Anne. *The Literary Use of the Psychoanalytic Process*. New Haven: Yale University Press, 1981.

Smidt, Kristian. *Unconformities in Shakespeare's Tragedies*. New York: St. Martin's Press, 1990.

Smith, Molly. *The Darker World Within: Evil in the Tragedies of Shakespeare and His Successors*. Newark: University of Delaware Press, 1991.

Spurgeon, Caroline. *Shakespeare's Imagery and What It Tells Us*. Cambridge: Cambridge University Press, 1935.

States, Bert O. *Hamlet and the Concept of Character*. Baltimore, MD: Johns Hopkins University Press, 1992.

Stockholder, Kay. *Dream Works: Lovers and Families in Shakespeare's Plays.* Toronto: University of Toronto Press, 1987.

Sypher, Wylie. *The Ethic of Time: Structures of Experience in Shakespeare.* New York: Seabury Press, 1976.

Waldock, A.J.A. *"Hamlet": A Study in Critical Method.* Cambridge: Cambridge University Press, 1931.

Weitz, Morris. Hamlet *and the Philosophy of Literary Criticism.* Chicago: University of Chicago Press, 1964.

Werstine, Paul. "The Textual Mastery of *Hamlet.*" *Shakespeare Quarterly* 39 (1988): 1–26.

Wilks, John S. *The Idea of Conscience in Renaissance Tragedy.* London: Routledge, 1990.

Wilson, John Dover. *What Happens in "Hamlet."* 3d ed. Cambridge: Cambridge University Press, 1951.

Wilson, Harold S. *On the Design of Shakespearean Tragedy.* Toronto: University of Toronto Press, 1957.

Williamson, C. C. H. *Readings on the Character of Hamlet: 1661–1947.* London: Allen & Unwin, 1950.

Wofford, Susanne L., editor. *Case Studies in Contemporary Criticism: 'Hamlet.'* New York: St. Martin's Press, 1994.

Wright, George T. "*Hamlet* and Hendiadys." *PMLA* 96 (1981): 168–93.

Zamir, Tzachi. "Doing Nothing." *Mosaic* 35, no. 3 (Sept. 2002): 167–82.

# Acknowledgments

"Hamlet" by William Hazlit. From *The Collected Works of William Hazlitt*, eds. A.R. Waller and Arnold Glover. © 1902 by McClure, Phillips & Co. Reprinted by permission.

"Hamlet" by A. C. Bradley. From *Shakespearean Tragedy: Lectures on* Hamlet, Othello, King Lear, Macbeth 2 ed. © 1905 by MacMillan. Reprinted by permission.

"Hamlet" by Harold C. Goddard. From *The Meaning of Shakespeare.* © 1951 by The University of Chicago. Reprinted by permission.

"Hamlet: Superposed Plays" by Richard A. Lanham. © 1976 by Richard A. Lanham. Reprinted from Richard A. Lanham, *The Motives of Eloquence*, Yale University Press, 1976, by permission of Rhetorica, Inc.

"Hamlet" by William Empson" From *Essays on Shakespeare* ed. David B. Pirie. © 1986 by William Empson. Reprinted by permission.

"Hamlet" by Northrop Frye. From *Northrop Frye on Shakespeare.* © 1986 by Northrop Frye. Reprinted by permission.

"Readiness, Ripeness: Hamlet, Lear" by Yves Bonnefoy. From *New Literary History* 17, no. 3 (Spring 1986). © 1986 by Yves Bonnefoy. Reprinted by permission.

"Truant Dispositions: Hamlet and Machiavelli" by Julia Lupton. From *The Journal of Medieval and Renaissance Studies* 17, no. 1 (Spring 1987). © 1987 by Duke University Press. Reprinted by permission.

"The Melancholy Dane" by Bert O. States. From *Hamlet and the Concept of Character*. © 1992 by The Johns Hopkins University Press. Reprinted with permission of the Johns Hopkins University press.

"Hamlet and the Ghost of Purgatory: Intimations of Killing the Father" by Anthony Low. From *English Literary Renaissance* 29, no. 3 (Autumn 1999). © 1999 by *English Literary Renaissance*. Reprinted by permission of the editors.

"A King of Infinite Space" by John Lee. From *Shakespeare's* Hamlet *and the Controversies of Self*. © 2000 by Oxford University Press. Reprinted by permission of Oxford University Press.

# Index